# DISCOVERING THE MYSTERIES

# *of* Ancient America

*Lost History and Legends,*
*Unearthed and Explored*

# DISCOVERING THE MYSTERIES

# *of* Ancient America

## Lost History and Legends, Unearthed and Explored

*Edited by* FRANK JOSEPH

*With Contributions From*
Zecharia Sitchin, Wayne May, Andrew Collins,
David Hatcher Childress,
Laura Lee, *and Others*

NEW PAGE BOOKS
A DIVISION OF THE CAREER PRESS, INC.

DISCOVERING THE MYSTERIES OF ANCIENT AMERICA
EDITED BY GINA TALUCCI
TYPESET BY KATE HENCHES
Cover design by Lu Rossman/Digi Dog Design
Printed in the U.S.A.

To order this title, please call toll-free 1-800-CAREER-1 (NJ and Canada: 201-848-0310) to order using VISA or MasterCard, or for further information on books from Career Press.

The Career Press, Inc., 220 west Parkway, Unit 12
Pompton Plains, NJ 07444
**www.careerpress.com**
**www.newpagebooks.com**

## Library of Congress Cataloging-in-Publication Data

Discovering the mysteries of ancient America : lost history and legends, unearthed and explored / edited by Frank Joseph ; with contributions from Zechariah Sitchin ... [et al.].

    p.cm.

Includes bibliographical references and index.

ISBN 1-56414-842-4 (pbk.)

    1. Indians of North America—Transatlantic influences. 2. Indians of North America—Transpacific influences. 3. Indians of North America—Egyptian influences. 4. Civilization, Ancient. 5. North America—Antiquities. 1. Joseph, Frank. II. Sitchin, Zecharia.

E98.T73D57 2006
970.01--dc22

2005050473

# Contents

## CHAPTER 2:
## ANCIENT TECHNOLOGY
## 55

## CHAPTER 3: LOST RACES
## 89

# Introduction

 AMERICA B.C.:
BEFORE COLUMBUS
BY FRANK JOSEPH,
EDITOR, *ANCIENT AMERICAN*

*Ancient American* is a unique publication; since publisher Wayne May founded it in 1993, this popular science magazine has released more than 72 issues presenting unconventional conclusions backed up by often startling discoveries that question established theories about America's past. A free-forum, bi-monthly periodical, *Ancient American* features the research of university-trained professionals and avocational enthusiasts alike. Between them, a new vision of our continent, radically at odds with mainstream archaeology, is beginning to emerge.

# CHAPTER 1:

# Bucking the Archaeological Establishment

## C-14 TESTING PROVES AMERICA'S AGE

Zechariah Sitchin is internationally famous for his controversial books describing the origins of man and civilization. *The Lost Realms, Genesis Revisited*, and *Cosmic Code* are read in translated editions around the world, and he has appeared in numerous television documentaries dealing with alternative science.

Born in Russia, Mr. Sitchin was raised in Palestine, and he graduated from the University of London with a degree in economic history. He worked for years as a journalist and editor in Israel before settling in New York.

In an original article for the April, 2001 issue of *Ancient American*, Zechariah Sitchin showed that civilization on our continent is 15 centuries older than believed. This more profound antiquity places prehistoric America squarely within the contemporary rise of high culture in the Nile Valley and Mesopotamia, where Egyptian and Sumerian civilizations did indeed share some provocative similarities with ancient Mexico. He helped prove his findings by using the Carbon-14 testing method.

Could there have been an overseas' connection between the Nile Valley and the Valley of Mexico, even at the dawn of organized society, as Sitchin argues?

*Ancient ruins on a Mexican island explored by an American astronaut back-dated the origins of high culture in the Americas by 15 centuries.*

## AMERICA'S FIRST CIVILIZATION: OLDER THAN BELIEVED POSSIBLE BY ZECHARIAH SITCHIN

If an astronaut were to corroborate any aspect of my writings, I would have expected it to be in regard to the inter-planetary matters discussed by my various published works. Surprisingly, such a corroboration concerns, of all things, the Olmec of ancient Mexico. It is tucked away in a recently released book, *A Leap of Faith*, by Mercury 7's crew officer, Gordon Cooper. My own book, *The Lost Realms,* mentions a colossal stone head with unmistakably black African features, discovered in Veracruz, Mexico, during 1869. This is indicative of an advanced civilization preceding the Mayas and Aztecs.

They were arbitrarily named by archaeologists, "Olmec." The academically embarrassing enigma of who they were, how they had come across the ocean, and why, was compounded by the timing of these sophisticated culture-bearers in the New World. If the Olmec people represented the earliest or "Mother Civilization" of Mesoamerica, the day of their arrival was at first determined to be about 250 B.C. However, the most recent Carbon-14 testing places Olmec beginnings at 1500 B.C. I have argued for a date twice that old.

The Carbon-14 testing is a procedure invented in 1947 to determine the age of organic materials. Christopher Dunn, a manufacturing executive, explains, "C-14 is created when the reaction of cosmic rays with the ionosphere precipitates neutrons through the atmosphere. These neutrons react with Nitrogen 14, creating C-14. Upon creation, C-14 starts to decay, and originally it was determined to have a half-life of approximately 5,568 years. Organic material takes in C-14 at a constant rate, and, knowing what the level of C-14 in an object was before it died, scientists can measure the amount left in it and calculate its age. Apart from normal variations, C-14 stays at a constant level in the Earth's atmosphere."

My conclusion that an Olmec presence in the New World went back at least 5,000 years to 3000 B.C. was reached by many paths. The first was an attempt to identify the great god of Mesoamerica, the "Feathered Serpent," who promised to return on the first day of a 52-year cycle. He was known as Quetzalcoatl to the Aztecs and Kukulcan to the Mayas. In 1519 A.D., the Aztec Emperor, Moctezuma II (more commonly and erroneously remembered as Montezuma), mistakenly believed that the Spanish Conquistador, Hernan Cortez, was the returned man-god, because he arrived on the Atlantic shores of Mexico on the anticipated sacred date near Veracruz—the same place at which Quetzalcoatl was said to have landed.

In *The Lost Realms*, devoted to the prehistory of the Americas, I suggest that the arrival of the Olmec and the Feathered Serpent might be established with convincing precision. The key to unlocking the enigma is found in the Olmec calendar itself. In addition to a practical calendar of 365 days called, in Mayan, the *Haab*, the peoples of Mesoamerica employed a sacred calendar (the *Tzolkin*) of 260 days. It was said to consist of two wheels with meshing teeth that turned and returned to the same spot once every 52 years. That was the sacred numeral of the Winged Serpent deity, and also the holy numeral of a man-god known to the Egyptians as Thoth. He, like Quetzalcoatl, was the divine patron of science and the calendar, and had been exiled from Egypt circa 3100 B.C. I suggest, therefore, that this figure was not entirely legendary, but an actual culture-bearer who led a group of his followers to a new land, bringing the "Olmec" to Middle America.

In addition to the Haab and the Tzolkin, there was a third calendar in Mesoamerica used to inscribe dates on monuments. Called the "Long Count," it was not cyclical, as were the other two, but linear, counting consecutively the total number of days that had passed since the original counting began on a mysterious "Day One." By means of glyphs denoting days—one, 20, 360, 7,200, or even 154,000— and dots giving the number for each group-gylph, monuments indicated the days that passed, as though to say, "A total of so many days after Day One have passed when this monument was erected."

But what was that "Day One"? When did it occur, and what was its significance? It has been established beyond doubt that this Long Count version was the original Olmec calendar, and it is now generally agreed that Day One was equivalent to August 13, 3113 B.C. But what did that date signify to the Olmec? The only plausible answer must be the date of Quetzalcoatl's arrival on the Atlantic shores of Mexico, near present-day Veracruz.

Outside confirmation of this event at the time it occurred appears in Chapter 11 of Gordon Cooper's new book. "During my final years with NASA," he writes, "I became involved in a different kind of adventure: undersea treasure-hunting in Mexico." Accompanied by a *National Geographic* photographer, Cooper and his companions landed in a small plane on an island in the Gulf of Mexico. Local residents showed them some pyramid-shaped mounds, where they found pre-Columbian ruins, artifacts, and bones. Upon examination in Texas by chemical analysts, the artifacts were determined to be 5,000 years old.

"When we learned the age of the artifacts," Cooper writes, "we knew that what we'd found had nothing to do with 17th-century Spain. I contacted the Mexican government, and was connected to the head of the National Archaeology Department, Pablo Bush-Romero." Together with Mexican archaeologists, the two returned to the site. Cooper writes, "The age of the ruins was confirmed: 3000 B.C. Compared with other advanced civilizations, relatively little was known about this one called the Olmec. Engineers, farmers, artisans, and traders, the Olmec had a remarkable civilization. But it is still not known where they originated. Among the findings that intrigued me most were celestial navigation symbols and formulas that, when translated, turned out to be mathematical formulas still used for navigation. There were also accurate drawings of constellations, some of them not officially 'discovered' until the age of modern telescopes." This left me wondering, "Why have celestial navigation signs if they weren't navigating celestially?"

And Cooper asks, if "someone" had helped the Olmec with this knowledge, who were they?

An answer was found at Jalapa's outstanding museum of Olmec Civilization, in the Veracruz province of east-costal Mexico. Featured there is a wall panel showing the extent and dates of Mexico's various pre-Columbian cultures. On my first visit to this institution, I could hardly believe my eyes: The first and therefore earliest civilization, that of the Olmec, was shown as beginning circa 3000 B.C. I urged the members of my tour group to take photos of me pointing to the date. On a second visit to the museum, however, the column indicating the Olmecs' 4th Millennium beginnings had been removed. The official museum catalog, concerning Olmec Civilization, reverted to the previous, official 1500 B.C. date. But Gordon Cooper reports, as a professionally trained eye-witness, what he mistakenly learned from the chief Mexican archaeologist. Namely that the Olmec material dated to 3000 B.C., the same moment another great, and apparently related, civilization suddenly arose in the Nile Valley. Was Egypt's Thoth the Feathered Serpent of Mesoamerica? Their shared mission and time frame is far more than coincidental.

# KENNEWICK MAN

On the banks of Washington state's Kennewick River, the skeleton of a most unusual murder victim was found in 1991. Since their discovery, his remains have been hotly contested between scientists anxious to study them and Indian rights activists, supported by the U.S. Army Corps of Engineers, who are determined to re-bury the bones without further delay. The man to whom they belonged to 90 centuries ago was Caucasian, and therein lies the controversy. Until little more than 500 years ago, only the ancestors of Native Americans were believed to be the sole inhabitants of our continent. But this long-held assumption has been called into question by the mere existence of the anomalous stranger, because he was probably not alone. In the October, 2004 issue of *Ancient American*, James J. Daly highlighted some of the serious ramifications generated by this contentious find.

## KENNEWICK MAN: STILL POLITICALLY INCORRECT AFTER NINE THOUSAND YEARS
### BY JAMES J. DALY, SR., PH.D.

Media can influence public opinion and provide support for politicians in the form of established authority. If the "experts" have said it, then it must be true. In this light, it would be of interest to know how the controversy of the Kennewick Man has been presented in books, newspapers, and educational documentaries. This review covers three such presentations: *What It Means to be 98% Chimpanzee*, by Jonathan Marks, *The Journey of Man*, by Spencer Wells, and a documentary film, *The Real Eve*, narrated by actor Danny Glover. All three mediums have misrepresented the evidence regarding the discovery of a skeleton in North America that does not conform to the physical features of indigenous peoples or Native Americans.

There has been a great deal of reluctance by many in the soft sciences of anthropology, archeology, psychology, and sociology to accept this *prima facia* evidence of other peoples arriving in the New World before the paleo-Indians, because the findings do not agree with their preconceived sociopolitical ideologies. Some of these obstructive academics have been called radical scientists. The most important feature of radical scientists is that they support "good" science and oppose "bad" science. However, this support has nothing to do with the accuracy, precision, or repeatability of the science in question, but whether or not the science is "good" for the people. Their science is a wholly relative and subjective viewpoint and is much more sociopolitical than scientific. Facts are not important; intention is. They know better than you as to what you should know. The best way to understand their approach to science is to quote Jack Nicholson's famous line in the movie, *A Few Good Men*: "The truth? You can't handle the truth."

It was important to define the radical scientist viewpoint because it explains the position on Kennewick Man taken in the book written by Jonathan Marks, which is ostensibly about chimpanzees and humans. Marks is an associate professor at the University of North Carolina at Charlotte. In his book, Marks criticizes the molecular genetics that have been used to make the case that we are the same as apes. His view: Apes are not men and vice versa. But this critique is a smoke screen for other agendas in the book, including racism in science, genetic determinism, sociobiology, Human Genome Projects, and Kennewick Man. Marks discusses the ape/human business in and out of the first 50 pages of the book, after which, he adds something here and there about apes and humans.

However, his strategy is that if you criticize molecular results and techniques in ape/human comparisons, then you can further extend this critique to the genetic studies regarding the diversity of populations or subdivisions of mankind. A question arises as to the motive(s) for this book. It almost seems that the main reason that Marks wrote this book may be for the 19 pages covering Kennewick Man to support the Native American claim on the ancient remains. The ape business might have been somewhat new and different, but it is only covered in about one fourth of the book's contents. All of the anti-race material is old news and can be found elsewhere, and is included in other publications, including those by Marks. He admits that he received a National Science Foundation grant to help with the formation of the book.

From my own understanding of federal granting agencies, it is highly unusual that NSF would support the writing of a book that is only one person's opinion and without new research data. There is a suspicion here that some hidden hands were involved in helping to get this book out to create an "expert's" view to be used in future legal battles, or to persuade the public to be sympathetic to the claims of the Native Americans. A further indication is that it's badly written in places that makes it look like it was rushed into print without much editorial input. Critical, balanced argument is lacking. Topics such as human homosexuality drift in from nowhere.

But from a literary standpoint, the worst offense is the often puzzling metaphors and analogies that Marks sprinkles throughout his text. However, the chapter attacking the Great Apes Project and human rights for chimps is really worthwhile reading. It is highly entertaining and from an animal rights perspective, is very politically incorrect. Marks' approach to Kennewick Man can be summarized by one of his chapter's sub-titles: Give Back Kennewick Man. Marks also summarizes his findings by saying, "Kennewick Man has different significance for the two groups that want his remains, and his importance as a symbol to Native Americans, I would argue, out-weighs this importance to the scientists as a basis for thoughtless and irresponsible speculation. Kennewick Man lay at the crossroads of the sciences and the humanities. He represented a confrontation between the politics of identity and human rights, on the one hand, and an archaic and transgressive science on the other hand."

In other words, science should be subservient to personal feelings. Marks does not consider it important in his treatment of the Kennewick Man that the skeleton does not resemble that of Native Americans. Just give it back. It's the law. Something is being missed here. No one, not Marks, physical anthropologists, judges, or Native Americans, seems to realize that a case for human rights can be made for Kennewick Man, because it would be unjust to return his remains to the descendants of those who killed him.

One of Marks' favorite *ad hominems* is to call someone who doesn't agree with him a "pseudoscientist," but it is he who may be the real pseudoscientist. In one paragraph, he almost gloats at the failure of one scientist to extract usable DNA from the remains, as though this was a triumph of nondiscovery. Intact DNA is almost impossible to extract from ancient remains. That it was done in one case of a Neanderthal skeleton was remarkable. Marks' worst anti-intellectual comment, however, was that it was only a single skeleton, and single skeletons don't mean much. Marks was being disingenuous, or better yet, duplicitous. Finding a piece of skull, finger, tooth, humerus, or any part of ancient remains have often been hailed as monumental discoveries when unearthed in other parts of the world.

What Marks fails to say is that finding a complete 9,000-year-old skeleton is a remarkable piece of good luck. Then there is that inconvenient (for Marksists, anyway) Paleo-Indian spear point embedded in Kennewick Man's pelvis. Being slightly droll, Marks makes it clear that he disdains those scientists who claim that races or distinct human populations don't exist, and then do research to find differences that prove otherwise. This would describe Spencer Wells perfectly. Wells has been searching for genetic markers that can identify and separate various groups of humans. His excuse to avoid being called a "racist" is that the evolution and migrations of humans throughout unrecorded history can be traced through such markers, and such data is race neutral (as long as you don't call the differentiated groups "race"—Wells prefers the term "clans").

Wells, as has Marks, has become a collator and interpreter of other scientists' data by writing books and producing documentaries, such as the one that inspired this current book. In *The Journey of Man*, Wells has used the available genetic data to explain the journey of man. The genetic markers do tend to correlate with other evidence from anatomy, linguistics, and cultural artifacts. Wells is a molecular anthropologist, although he would probably more prefer the term molecular geneticist. He would appear to be straightforward in his presentations, depending more on scientific facts then emotional outbursts.

However, his background may still be somewhat suspect, because Wells was at Harvard, which is the epicenter of radical bioscience in the form of Lewontin, Gould, and Montague. Wells did work later with Cavalli–Sforza at Stanford, who pioneered the field of genetic markers in diverse human groups. Such research now has the appellation of being politically incorrect, which explains Jonathan Marks's crusty comment. One needs to have a somewhat sophisticated grasp of the field of genetic diversity to recognize that Wells is also somewhat of a radical scientist, although much more muted than Marks. Where Wells tips his hand is in the short (very short) discussion of the migrations into the New World by people other than Native Americans.

Wells covers the presumed first two waves into North America as indicated by genetic and corroborative linguistic evidence, the latter being from exhaustive studies by Joseph Greenberg. For Kennewick Man, however, he merely says, "Furthermore, because Siberians and Upper Paleolithic Europeans initially came from the same central Asian populations, they probably started out looking very similar to each other. Kennewick Man, as a likely descendant of the first migration from Siberia to the New World, may have retained his central Asian features—which could be interpreted as 'Caucasoid.' In fact, many early American skulls look more European than those of today's modern Native Americans, suggesting that their appearance has changed over time. The more Mongoloid, or East Asian, appearance of modern Native Americans may have originated in the second wave of migration, carrying M130 (a genetic marker) from East Asia."

A few caveats are in order here. First, the use of "probably," "likely," "may have," "could be," and "suggesting," means that the hypotheses presented are "just-so stories," which may or may not have long-term validity. Second, the emphasizing of "Caucasoid" indicates doubt about the physical description for Kennewick man. In the beginning of the same paragraph Wells says, "As for other migrations, from Europe or Australia, there is no compelling evidence." Unfortunately, if Kennewick Man had not been discovered, then any suggestion of "Caucasoids" being in the New World before Native Americans would have been even less than "compelling" to Wells. Also, because Europeans and central Asians were one and the same at that time, why not use a designation of "Euro-Asians?" Unless one is trying to avoid using the term *European* in any fashion. One has to wonder if Wells is of the "Anybody but Europeans" school. In any case, the real question is, who was in North America first: the Caucasoids or the Mongoloids?

A third caveat is that it must be understood that genetic markers differentiating diverse human groups are not easy to find. A good example relevant to this discussion can be found with breeds of dogs. Would anyone doubt that an Irish wolfhound is different from a Chihuahua, or a dachshund from a bulldog, a bloodhound from a Saint Bernard? Nevertheless, it was not until 2003 that researchers were able to find markers that would differentiate breeds of dogs, and then only for a few breeds. Molecular genetics, in terms of markers, is still in its infancy. However, new techniques will undoubtedly come forth in the future that will clarify and expand existing information. This is what the radical scientists are afraid of.

So, as suggested by Marks, get rid of the evidence before these new techniques become available. Lastly, the comment that Native Americans may have changed their features because Kennewick Man sounds positively Lamarckian (or superficial) and deserves more speculative discussion as to how this may have occurred than what Wells was willing to give us. In fairness, one does have to understand that Wells is speaking as a molecular geneticist, about genetic markers, and not as a physical or cultural anthropologist. But,  as do his colleagues, he will cherry-pick data from other fields, if and when it suits him.

The last media example is a documentary called *The Real Eve*, narrated by Danny Glover. In this presentation, the history of the evolution of mankind and its spread over the earth are well documented and there appears to be little favoritism here, allowing one to agree or disagree, depending upon your own perspective, except for Kennewick Man. Kennewick Man is covered and his differences from Native Americans are mentioned as his earlier arrival in the New World.

However, the graphic depiction of Kennewick Man's death in a dynamic chase with Kennewick Man fleeing Native Americans was misleading. The "Indians" were dressed as Plains Indians with war paint, buckskin clothes, and feathers in their hair. I wondered how the advisors to this production knew that this was how "Indians" dressed 9,000 ago. Now, this may seem to be a small item, but when the cameras caught up to Kennewick Man, laying injured in the grass, on his back, he was dressed in the same fashion, and his face was that of a Native American. It would have been very easy for the producers to show a differentiation. The skeletal remains of Kennewick Man are most closely related to the Ainu on the island of Hokkaido. The Japanese call them the "Hairy Ones." That distinguishes them from the less hirsute Japanese. Giving Kennewick Man a beard would have then identified him as being much different from his pursuers.

It was obvious that the people making this documentary didn't want to associate Native Americans with beating up on an unfortunate indigenous victim. Frankly, from the way the action was presented, I couldn't tell the players without a scorecard. Another oddity, for which I am awaiting an answer, is the spear-point. In the documentary, the spear was thrown at Kennewick Man. I have bow hunted and taught human anatomy. I find it difficult to believe that a thrown spear would have enough force to be embedded in the pelvic bone of the victim. A more reasonable scenario would be that his pursuers had caught up with him and stabbed him at close range, while he was lying down, hard enough to penetrate bone.

If my "just-so story" has merit, it means that he was viciously finished off, on the spot, and had other more lethal soft-tissue wounds that probably killed him in the end. Those wounds would not necessarily be evident from the skeletal remains.

These two books and a documentary run the gamut from "Be nice, get rid of Kennewick Man," to "We need more genetic data," to "Kennewick Man exists, but what's the real story?" Whatever the "experts" may conclude, the overall significance and importance of Kennewick Man can't be denied. His discovery has not only revised the picture of populations coming into America, but exposed the motives of radical scientists and other academic elites as being political and not scientific. It has now put doubt into the minds of many people about the trust that can be given to some of these so-called "experts" to make fair and unbiased observations.

Other claims about people entering the New World, before or after Kennewick Man, are now open to much more serious consideration than was previously given. Perhaps that is the best and final legacy of a 9,000-year-old Caucasoid, who might indeed have the last laugh in more ways than one.

## TABLETS: HOAX OR HISTORY?

During the first decades of the 19th century, early pioneers in what later became the State of Michigan were confronted by literally thousands of manmade mounds. Local Native Americans made no claim to the structures, claiming that they were raised by a previous people very long ago. When settlers dug into the ancient earthworks, they often found long, slate tablets covered with an unintelligible written language. These strange texts were often accompanied by crude, incised illustrations of scenes familiar only to the Christian farmers clearing their lands. Depicted on the tablets were biblical episodes, the most recognizable being Noah's Ark and the Flood.

When the last of the Michigan mounds were excavated around 1920, approximately 7,000 mystery tablets had been removed, some under controlled conditions, and attested by eye-witnesses swearing affidavits. Although the sheer magnitude of this state-wide discovery, made by literally hundreds of persons, most of them unknown to each other, argued convincingly on behalf of its prehistoric authenticity, the mostly terra-cotta, or baked-clay, artifacts were universally condemned as "fakes" by Victorian scientists. But their ill-considered verdict may have concealed the truth about the Michigan Tablets; namely, that they were religious documents and teaching aids made by Coptic Egyptians who fled the persecution of fellow Christians in the fifth century to find distant refuge in the Great Lakes region of the American Midwest.

The Copts were and still are members of a unique Christian sect, more gnostic than papal, whose church ceremonies are conducted in a liturgical language scholars believe is the closest surviving example of Egyptian as it was spoken in pharaonic times. At least some Coptic imagery has been found on the Michigan artifacts, underscoring a connection.

Writing in the February, 2000 issue, J. Golden Barton and *Ancient American* publisher Wayne May exposed the deliberate falsification of evidence that led to the suppression of American prehistory.

## THE MICHIGAN TABLETS:
## AN ARCHAEOLOGICAL SCANDAL
## BY J. GOLDEN BARTON & WAYNE MAY

In 1961, James Bird and Paul Roundy had been assigned by the Church of Jesus Christ of Latter Day Saints to South Bend, Indiana. While there, they met with Father Charles E. Sheedy at the University of Notre Dame. The two missionaries told him the story of Joseph

Smith and the inscribed gold plates from which they believed he transcribed the Book of Mormon. "I have some of Joseph Smith's type of writing here at Notre Dame," Father Sheedy interrupted. He showed the two surprised men to the attic of the nearby O'Shaughnessy Building. There they discovered three open boxes from which the Catholic priest removed several slate and copper tablets covered with hieroglyphics, pictographs, and inscriptions. Father Sheedy hoped someone might be able to authenticate or disprove the collection. Perhaps the Mormons with their "golden plate" theory would come to the rescue.

Bird and Roundy wrote a letter to researcher Milton R. Hunter of the First Council of the Seventy in Salt Lake City, Utah, but waited in vain for a reply. As it turned out, Hunter had misplaced the letter. When he finally found it several years later, he contacted Father Sheedy, requesting an interview. Sometime before, the priest had turned down a chance to expand his number of alleged artifacts, when Ellis Soper, of North Carolina, offered to donate similar items. Notre Dame was running out of storage room, so Father Sheedy was anxious to meet anyone who might take the questionable objects off his hands. He had even cooperated with Henrietta Mertz, a Chicago attorney and author, who wanted to write a book proving the artifact's authenticity.

After examining and studying his attic collection for six years, her efforts were stymied by publishers convinced the inscribed tablets were part of some 19th-century hoax. It was Father Sheedy's personal opinion that they were perhaps of ancient Greek or Egyptian origin. These bizarre objects were not credibly explained by the convoluted theories Mertz advocated of transatlantic fifth- century Christian cultists. Such wild ideas might compromise the priest's academic standing and even embarrass the Notre Dame authorities. Washing his hands of the whole affair, he presented the astounded Hunter with his entire collection. Since then, the strange tablets continue to fascinate antiquarians puzzled by the mysteries of pre-Columbian America.

*One of an estimated 7,000 inscribed tablets excavated from prehistoric earthworks across Michigan.*

These early investigators were long aware of our Continent's prehistory, which seemed to stretch back farther in time with each new discovery. As North America's forests were cleared, plows turned over the virgin soil, pioneers stumbled upon bizarre artifacts, vacant mines, and shafts— all testimony to some civilization that rose and fell long before modern Europeans arrived. As historian John Baldwin wrote, "An ancient and unknown people left remains of settled life, and of a certain degree of civilization, in the valleys of the Mississippi and its tributaries. We have no authentic name for them either as a nation or a race; therefore, they are called 'Mound Builders," this name having been suggested by an important class of their works."

He was seconded by Francis Carter and James Cheeseman: "The Mound Builders were thought of as white, cultured, and not the ancestors of the Native Americans....Whoever these ancient people were, they left behind some very puzzling remains. The number of earthworks, when considered with their size and the area of the country they cover, becomes evidence of a great achievement." In fact, the prehistoric mounds were so numerous that the total is unknown. In Ohio alone there were more than 10,000 such sites. Tens of thousands more once existed throughout Michigan, Illinois, Indiana, Wisconsin, and Missouri. Eighteenth, and early 19th-century antiquarians were virtually unanimous in their conviction that the remains of an ancient civilization of white people long ago spread across America from the gulf coast to Canada, from New England to the Pacific coast.

These "Mound Builders," as they were called, were believed to have been a highly developed race far superior to the Native Americans known to the first pilgrims. No other explanation for the profusion of evidence on behalf of some advanced, vanished culture seemed feasible. Indeed, the Indians themselves spoke of populations of white men predating their own arrival in parts of America. Yet today, very few archaeologists believe that the Mound Builders belonged to a lost, white race. What brought about this re-interpretation? According to historian John Baldwin, "It is rather interesting to consider the circumstances that led to the abandonment of this theory as a myth. The fact is that by 1890 the tide of opinion had shifted, and men of science denied that there had ever been a highly cultured white race in America's past. This very radical turn-about came as a result of the scientific leadership of one man, Mr. John Wesley Powell."

In 1879, when Congress created the Smithsonian Institution's Bureau of Ethology, Major Powell, a Civil War hero, received additional power and prestige as the Bureau's first director. He was disposed to think that the Mound Builders were the ancestors of the Native Americans, and presented his theory as dogma in the Bureau's first annual report, published in 1880. "The vestiges of art discovered do not excel in any respect the arts of the Indian tribes known to history," he declared. "There is, therefore, no reason for us to search for an extra-limited origin through lost tribes for the arts discovered in the mounds of North America."

So prestigious was the Smithsonian and its authoritative director that within a few years the scientific community had unilaterally adopted Powell's opinion, ignoring the vast amount of physical evidence previously accumulated. Scholars without significant new findings began to discredit and re-interpret the civilization of the Mound Builders in favor of Powell's theory. As one writer put it, "Evidence contrary to Powell's stated opinion was explained as fraudulent, as buried in the mounds intrusively, or simply re-interpreted to favor the new theory. From this time forward, anything that referred to the original, glorious Mound Builder theory was considered mythical. It was a very hostile academic environment for anyone who ventured to propose that there had ever been a highly civilized group of people in the New World."

Despite Powell's intractable stance against any form of cultural diffusion, stories such as those told of James O. Scotford continued to plague conventional scholars. And it explains why so many anomalous artifacts appeared around the turn of the 20th century, as the following case illustrates.

James Scotford was tired, having already set three quarters of a mile of fence and still had a few more hours before sunset. He drew the line taut in an effort to clear the mound between him and the last post, then grabbed at his auger and began to dig another hole at the center of an old Indian mound. He would have to hurry, as his companion had almost caught up in placing more poles. Scotford gave a groan, as the auger hit something hard. He pushed harder, but it didn't budge, then shouted to his companion to bring a spade. He hadn't expected a rock, because there were no stones in the area. He would have to dig around it. To his great surprise, the shovel uncovered a large earthen casket. The auger had broken its cover, but the larger portion was in tact. Scotford was wild with excitement, as he rode toward Edmore, Michigan, with the casket nestled in the bed of his wagon.

During the weeks and months that followed, the citizens of Edmore and those of surrounding communities opened up more than 500 mounds, all blanketed with dense vegetation. Large cedar trees and

*Ancient American* shows that, contrary to prevailing wisdom, the vast oceans were not impassable barriers to human beings in the deep past, but rather highways that carried them to America from many parts of the globe. *Ancient American* alone describes overseas' visitors centuries and even millennia before the arrival of Christopher Columbus. Time has worn, not erased, the impact made on our shores by ancient Egyptians, Minoans, Phoenicians, Greeks, Hebrews, and Romans. They were followed by Welsh rovers, Viking warriors, Irish missionaries, and even the Knights Templar. Sailors from the great kingdoms of West Africa braved mid-ocean crossings to leave their enduring mark on Mexico's oldest known civilization. Culture-bearers, merchants, explorers, and refugees came from Japan, China, India, and Java. Their influences still echo in the oral traditions of Native Americans themselves and are physically brought to light in numerous artifacts. Apparently, America was a meltingpot long before the Statue of Liberty was set up at Liberty Island.

*Discovering the Mysteries of Ancient America* is a selection of some of the best articles appearing in *Ancient American* magazine since its inception 12 years ago. Although the authors mostly emphasize the contributions of overseas visitors to our continent before Columbus, contrary views are included, allowing for a lively debate, as engaging as it is provocative. But this collection does not focus exclusively on cultural diffusion; Old World influences at work in the New World before 1492 are also prevalent. It also plunges into arguments about the official suppression of politically incorrect evidence; the paradigm-smashing discovery of a 9,000-year-old Caucasian skeleton in Washington state; physical evidence of a lost super-science; proof of a far deeper antiquity of mankind in the Americas going back a quarter-of-a-million years; late word on the sunken civilizations of Atlantis and Lemuria; and the giant beasts that challenged our ancestors with extinction. These controversies are not openly discussed in the polite society of Establishment archaeology.

The history presently being taught in our schools will not be the same history our children and grandchildren will learn. As such, *Discovering the Mysteries of Ancient America* represents the first chapter in the New History of our land.

oaks covered a few of the mounds. The searchers uncovered hundreds of different relics, including other ancient earthen caskets, tablets of clay, slate, sandstone, and copper. They were all beautifully carved with ancient biblical and historical scenes, writings, and symbols.

"So many citizens from the towns of Wyman and Edmore were eyewitnesses and involved in the excavating and recovery of the relics and the evidence," reported a local newspaper, "that doubts were never entertained for a moment as to the authenticity of the work. In one case, a casket was found under the roots of a tree which by its concentric circles was shown to be about 300 years old; and one of the roots of the tree had grown through the corner of the casket and was coiled up inside the box, but so decayed that it was broken with a touch."

Although farmers for years had been finding copper and slate artifacts while clearing and plowing new ground, the activities in Montcalm County exploded into excavations throughout Michigan. Perhaps no man helped to open more mounds in Michigan than Father James Savage, a priest of the Roman Catholic Church of the Most Holy Trinity, in Detroit, Michigan. He described the mounds as follows: "On these mounds you may find large and aged trees; oaks, pine, and other varieties. The decayed roots of pine and other trees that grew, thrived and died on these mounds. They contain another peculiarity. There is a strata of charcoal and ash in each mound. This strata often shows the basin-shaped contour of the interior of the mound when its possessor was laid away to rest. There does not appear, as a rule, sufficient charcoal and ashes for cremation, only enough for purification. In some mounds, however, there is heavy strata.

An associate of Father Savage stated, "these prehistoric mounds of Michigan contain caskets, lamps, bowls, pipes, and tablets of clay; battle-axes, knives, spears, daggers, and arrow-points, domestic utensils, saws, chisels, spades, and a variety of ornamental wearing apparel— all of chilled copper; stone tablets, medallions, metals, skinning knives, various implements with strange designs, the object of which we can not imagine. One remarkable feature of these mounds is that they contain no flint implements of any kind, nor have I seen any stone or copper beads; other ornamental wearing apparel is frequent. Many curious things were unearthed, such as caskets, tablets, amulets of slate stone, cups, vases, altars, lamps of burnt clay, and copper coins hammered out, rudely engraved with hieroglyphics. The caskets are of sun-dried clay, and are covered with picture writing and hieroglyphics. The caskets seem to be intended as receptacles for the tablets of record. They have close-fitting covers, which are cemented on with Assyrian-like cement, and various figures were molded on the top—an ancient sphinx, beasts, serpents, and human faces with head dresses or crowns."

For the next 20 years, Detroit was the center of interest for people seeking ancient relics. To give some order to such popular archaeology, Father Savage joined Daniel E. Soper, a former U.S. Secretary of State, and a respected businessman, to form a discovery team. Savage reported, "We have opened more than 500 of these mounds in the four counties in which we have worked—a territory exceeding 260 miles. We have diligently inquired regarding the locality of other finds and have so far located 16 counties in Michigan in which these specimens have been found. We are confident that we are only in the border area of the great prehistoric people."

Between 1858 and 1920, many thousands of mounds were excavated, but the vast majority were empty. According to Russell, "It must not be imagined that every mound opened has been a storehouse of objects of interest. On the contrary, the proportion of productive to non-productive mounds has not been greater than one to 10."

Nonetheless, many thousands of artifacts were indeed found, and, as time passed and descriptions of the relics appeared in many newspapers, people throughout the state reported finding similar relics. In Soper's own words, "I have personal knowledge of more than 3,000 articles that have been found and if they are fakes and were buried to be found, whoever buried them had been a very busy person, because they have been found throughout the state by hundreds of different people.

"The objects recovered from the mounds are of copper, sandstone, limestone, burned clay, and slate. The copper appears to be true mass-lake copper. Of the slates, the grayish black variety predominates, this being of the quality which outcrops near Baraga, in northern Michigan. The sandstone is of fine texture now quarried in Amhurst, Ohio. Red and green slate limestone appear, these being of an argillaceous character and having a good polish."

The research undertaken by Soper and Savage led them to believe that long before the ancestors of modern Native Americans arrived in North America, an alien people left their mark in the vast, prehistoric graveyard that covered the state of Michigan. Both men felt they had the evidence to prove their conclusions. But their ideas brought them ferocious criticism.

The so-called "men of letters" in America's contemporary scientific community condemned Soper and Savage as conspirators of an archaeological hoax. For every published report even mildly in favor of the two hapless investigators, some university-trained scholars would issue a charge of fraud. So unrelenting was the official campaign of academic hysteria that anyone even remotely associated with the Michigan artifacts distanced themselves from the bitter controversy. Eventually, any discussion of the artifacts' possible genuineness was no longer considered. And over the decades, the Michigan Tablets fell into almost complete oblivion.

Today, however, they are being re-examined in the new light of unprejudiced investigation. Many collections private and public are being photographed and cataloged for the first time. Their illustrated texts have been preserved for present and future researchers into the lost history of North America.

## HUMAN HISTORY'S NEW FACE

A discovery that should have rocked the scientific Establishment to its foundations and rewritten the story of human evolution was killed by mainstream scholars who had too much to lose by its disclosure. As it first appeared in the October, 1998 issue of *Ancient American*, here is the personal account of a university-trained professional whose career was terminated because she refused to be silenced.

## HUMANS IN AMERICA ONE-QUARTER OF A MILLION YEARS AGO BY DR. VIRGINIA STEEN-MCINTYRE

According to current established theory, humans entered the New World, our part of the globe, 12,000 years ago, at most. Modern man, or *Homo sapiens*, supposedly evolved only about 100,000 years ago. And that was somewhere in the Old World. This view is taught throughout America's educational system and propounded by most of our anthropologists. But a late 20th-century discovery seriously challenges this dominant paradigm. It was made about 70 miles southeast of Mexico City, approximately 2 miles south of Puebla, another much smaller city.

There, in a high mountain valley, lies the Valsequillo Reservoir, surrounded by three of Mexico's famous volcanoes: La Malinche, lztaccihuatl, and Popocatepetl. Exposed in the eroded bluffs along the reservoir's shoreline is a series of ancient sedimentary beds and volcanic ash layers. For more than a century, these beds have been famous with paleontologists for their rich variety of well-preserved bones from extinct animals from the last Ice Age, such as mammoth, mastodon, glyptodont, horse, camel, and saber-toothed cat. As first noted by the Mexican prehistorian Juan Armenta Camacho, man-made artifacts of flaked chert and flint are also eroding from these beds. A Puebla native, he stumbled across a large mammoth pelvis protruding from a stream bank in the nearby Alseseca arroyo, in June of 1933. Two years later, at the same place, he found the leg bone from another elephant-like creature with a flint spear point solidly driven into it.

Obviously, someone at one time had hunted that beast. Who was that hunter, and when did he live? For the next 30 years, Camacho tried to answer these questions by combing the bluffs around the reservoir, looking for more signs of early hunters. His search was well rewarded with the discovery of more than 100 partial skeletons of mastodons, mammoths, camels, ancient horses, and antelopes. To his experienced eye, many of the bones appeared to have been scratched by human-held blades. There were intentional cut-marks on some bones, while other splinters of bone seemed sharpened, smoothed, and made into tools. Bones were cracked to remove the marrow, a food delicacy for primitive hunters, even today. There were engraved bones, and some with drawings.

But leaders of the archaeological establishment in Mexico City ignored the evidence, declaring, without discussion, that the grooved and smashed bones were the results of nature, not man. At this time, foreign researchers began to take notice of Camacho's discoveries. Preliminary fieldwork under their direction turned up even more evidence of early hunters. With funding from the American Philosophical Society, Harvard University, the National Science Foundation, and others, the "Valsequillo Project" was born in 1962. Cynthia Irwin-Williams was the youngest archaeologist selected to work with Juan. She had attended Radcliffe and was finishing up her Ph.D. in anthropology at Harvard at the time. Later in the Project, she accepted a position on the anthropology staff at Eastern New Mexico University, in Portales, where she remained for several years.

During joint fieldwork, Juan and Cynthia discovered four sites where fossil bones and stone artifacts were found together *in situ*, that is, in the sediment layers, not lying loose on the ground surface. They were named El Horno, El Mirador, Tecacaxco, and Hueyatlaco (pronounced "way-at-la-co"). El Horno is the lowest, oldest location in the sedimentary section. It only is exposed when the waters of the reservoir are abnormally low. Hueyatlaco is the highest, youngest site. It is also the one with the thickest overlying sedimentary cover and one where several volcanic ash and pumice layers occur. Additional excavations at Hueyatlaco were carried out in 1964 and 1966. Many bones were found, along with stone tools. They were roughly of two types. Those in the older, lower layers were made of blades and flakes of flint with their edges retouched to make them sharp. Those from the upper layers were bifacially worked artifacts. That is, stone flakes were chipped off both faces of the tool. Both the upper and lower layers contained projectile-point spear heads, which showed that the hunters actually pursued game. They did not just cut up a dead carcass that they happened across.

Cynthia realized at once that she had something special here, not just a run-of-the-mill series of excavations, and she wisely called in reinforcements to help her. The University of Arizona's Paul S. Martin was an expert in fossil pollen, and Clayton Ray, a vertebrate paleontologist from the Smithsonian Institution, would study the fossil bones. Dwight Taylor of the U.S. Geological Survey examined the fossil mollusks—snail and clam shells, while Hal Malde, another USGS expert, mapped the regional and local geology. Thanks to Hal, I joined the project in 1966 as their tephrochronologist; in other words, someone trained in analyzing volcanic ash to determine the age or time-lime of a specific place or object.

The research was to be part of my Ph.D. dissertation at the University of Idaho. I began my work, scrutinizing one ash sample after another. Tens of them. Hundreds of them! No luck. No correlation. And Hueyatlaco had to be dated, because new evidence suggested the site could be 20,000 years old. This would have made it twice as old as the accepted earliest date for human existence in the New World. If confirmed, textbooks around the world would have to be revised. It would also make our careers, or such was our professional ambition at the time.

Gradually, evidence took the form of a single stone flake, probably used as a scraper, and definitely man-made. They were then associated with shells and bone in a high bank of sediment exposed at Barranca Caulapan, about 2 or 3 miles northeast of Hueyatlaco. Irwin-William herself spotted the tool. Shells were collected to obtain carbon-14 testing and bone for a uranium-series time frame. When a scientist quotes a number for a radiometric date, he or she is actually quoting the *mid-point* of a possible range for that date. Instead of saying, "The Carbon-14 date for a stone flake can range anywhere from 21,000 to 22,700 years," he/she says, "21,850+/-850 years." It is much shorter and quicker that way. We were shocked by the dates obtained from shell and bone found close to the stone artifact in the same sedimentary layer: 21,800+/-850 years by the Carbon-14 method; 22,000+/2,000 years and 20,000+/-1,500 years from the uranium-series.

The Caulapan tool was what Cynthia called a "non-diagnostic flake." It can be fitted in anywhere, from ancient to modern times. We were very lucky to have even that one, because it was associated with materials that *could* be dated. Things weren't all rosy. We may have been scientists, but we were also human. And the dark side of our humanity began to raise its ugly head—especially the raw emotions of jealously and fear. The first to feel the effects was Juan Armenta Camacho. The archaeological establishment in Mexico City could no longer ignore him and his research. But he was not "one of them," not a professional archaeologist. He did not have the right degrees. In fact, other than an honorary certification from the University of Puebla, he did not have any degree at all! And that made him a nobody in their view. Moreover, they were only indirectly involved in the work at Valsequillo, a project that was quickly growing in scope and importance. And they reacted negatively.

A branch of the federal government descended on Juan, confiscating all his fossils and artifacts, everything discovered during the Valsequillo Project, together with his bone collection at the University of Puebla's anthropology department and all his equipment. Everything was removed to Mexico City. He was forbidden by law to do any more fieldwork, ever. Shortly thereafter, Establishment archaeologists sank a complex series of excavations less than 100 feet south of Hueyatlaco, paralleling its trenches. But their diggings missed the artifact-bearing stream gravels, exposing only the fine-grained over-bank silts and clays. After much effort and expense, they found nothing. Juan could have told them that. Thirty years of fieldwork had shown him that it was only in the coarse-grained stream channel deposits that significant numbers of artifacts would be found.

Frustrated, the government-sponsored professionals claimed in print that all the artifacts at Hueyatlaco had been planted by workers. They accused the excavators of incompetence and hinted at darker things. It was a tense time for Juan, Cynthia, and the rest of us. After a year of trying, I still could not find a good match between the volcanic ash and pumice layers at the Hueyatlaco site, nor any layers in the dated sequence on La Malinche volcano, a sequence that went back more than 25,000 years. I did come across a possible correlation, with a dated ash layer on the flanks of Iztacchuatl volcano, tens of miles to the northwest.

But that dated layer was beyond the limits of the C-14 method and was older than 40,000 years, then a universally unacceptable time frame. Cynthia did not like that date at all. She was part of the eastern Archaeological Establishment, whose doyens would have a hard time accepting a 20,000-year old date, let alone one twice that age. They mocked and ignored anyone claiming such advanced antiquity for the first Americans, as did Cynthia herself. Officialdom then was an unforgiving bunch. But along with the bone from Caulapan, she had sent away butchered skeletal remains from Hueyatlaco and from the older El Horno site for dating.

Barney Szabo, a USGS geochemist, wanted to test them all using Uranium-series dating. Then, in the mid-1960s, the dates came back. The one for Caulapan brought her joy, because the results of the test agreed with the site's Carbon-14 date, around 22,000 Years Before Present. But the time frame for a fragment of the butchered camel pelvis from the upper artifact layers at Hueyatiaco were more than 10 times older than she wanted: 180,000 years and 245,000+/-40,000 years. Dates for a tooth from a butchered mastodon at El Horno were even older: 154,000 years by one method and 280,000 years by the other. "Poor Barney," we thought. "His new method only works some of the time."

Gradually, however, my thinking changed. What if Barney was right after all? If his dates were indeed correct, I'd never find a match between the volcanic layers at Hueyatlaco and those on La Malinche volcano. The matching layers would be too deeply buried in the flanks of the mountain, covered by a quarter million years of younger material. There was also other geologic evidence that the site was old. When one takes into account the bluff behind the excavations, the artifact-bearing layers at Hueyatlaco were buried by more than 30 feet of younger material. And that sediment pile was probably much thicker at one time than at present, because a great deal of erosion had occurred. In fact, the nearby river had cut down through at least 150 feet of sediment to form the modern river valley, now flooded, and by the waters of the reservoir.

The stack of sediments in the bluff additionally contained several buried soils. These had formed at the ground surface for perhaps hundreds or thousands of years. Then they were buried by a mudflow or volcanic deposit of some kind. The sediments themselves were highly weathered, with crystals and glass fragments partly turned to clay. This suggests they had been exposed to the elements for a very long time. If the site was an "unthinkable" 250,000 years old, could it be dated by other radiometric means besides the uranium-series? Perhaps we could borrow the methods and techniques used to date ancient archaeological sites in Africa dated using volcanic ash layers. In essence, that's what we did.

*Virginia Steen-McIntyre found physical proof of human existence in the Americas dating back to 250,000 years ago.*

Our colleague Ronald Fryxell, Hall Malde, and I returned to Hueyatlaco in 1973 for more excavation and sampling. There had always been a nagging question: Did the tool-bearing sediment layers there pass beneath the bluff sediments, or were they cut into the bluff? If the former, then the tools were older than the bluff sediments, because they lay beneath them. We could then use the volcanic ash and pumice layer there to date them. In fact, the volcanic units would be slightly younger. If the latter, all we could say is that the artifacts were younger than the dated volcanic units. How much younger, it would be impossible to tell.

We excavated a trench at right angles to those at Hueyatlaco, through the bluff of sediment, connecting with excavations dug by the Mexican archaeologists. There in the new trench walls was all the proof we needed. The artifact-bearing beds did indeed pass beneath, and thus were older than the sediments in the bluff. We could now use the volcanic ash and pumice layers exposed in the bluff to help date the site. We used tiny zircon crystals from two of the volcanic units exposed in the bluff, the

Hueyatlaco ash, and the Tetela brown mud pumice. The method is called fission-track dating. It relies on the fact that zircons contain minute traces of radioactive materials. When they fission, or disintegrate, they leave behind tiny trails of damage within the crystal which, after chemical preparation, can be seen with a microscope. By knowing how much radioactive materials are present, the rate this material breaks down, and how much of the material has fissured, a rough age estimate can be made.

Chuck Naeser, a geochemist at the U.S. Geological Survey, did the work for us, but we did not ask him for precise dates at this stage. All we wanted to know was if his dates for the volcanic layers would be closer to Cynthia's 20,000-year estimate or Barney's quarter-million-year uranium-series conclusion. Chuck's dates, even with a large plus-or-minus value, were far older than the dates Irwin-Williams would accept, and much closer to those of Barney Szabo. They ran as follows: for the Tetela brown mud pumice, 600,000+/-340,000 years; for the Hueyatlaco ash, 370,000+/200,000 years. We were thunderstruck. Here was physical proof that men and women already able to make tools had established themselves in the Americas not only millennia before the first Ice Age settlers were supposed to have arrived, but prior to the advent of modern humans.

We now had several lines of geologic evidence, including four radiometric dates, all indicating that the artifacts at Hueyatlaco, the youngest of four sites excavated in the Valsequillo area, were in the neighborhood of a quarter-million years old. Incredible or not, as far as I was concerned, it was an open-and-shut case. How naive I was! Irwin-Williams was against us going public with these extremely revolutionary dates from the beginning. Because, according to her, they were "impossible." She wanted time to prepare her side of the story and for us to publish jointly. That was fine, except that she had finished the Mexican excavations seven years before and hadn't begun a detailed site report. It could be years before she was ready for a joint publication.

We decided on a press conference to announce our date findings and their geologic evidence. Fryxell and Malde were not as comfortable with the oldest time parameters as was I. They had worked with archaeologists before and knew that our data would mean that some very famous names in the field would have to eat crow. And archaeologists have never been famous for their small egos! We nonetheless called a news conference at a geologic meeting in Dallas, during the fall of 1973. The story of our discovery was picked up by the wire services and broadcast around the world. I received a lot of good-natured ribbing from fellow scientists on the long plane ride to New Zealand, where I would make a presentation describing our efforts. Several colleagues had read about Hueyatlaco in the papers the day before. My New Zealand presentations were very well attended. Things were looking good, both for our work in Mexico and my career as an internationally recognized scientist. None of us realized at the time that our enterprise had already peaked. Everything was downhill from here for the next 20 years.

In early 1974, Hal Malde, Ronald Fryxell, and I began to write up our research at Hueyatlaco for publication. It was to be a preliminary report; a more detailed description would come later, after Cynthia had published her site excavations. Then, tragedy. Ronald was killed in a car crash on a lonely road in the middle of the night. Not only had we lost a good friend and valued colleague, but the most charismatic personality of our trio. Fryx had been the media's darling. Whether he was explaining the importance of soil samples or battling for an important archaeological site against the encroaching water of a reservoir, he had their ear and their columns. Hal and I finished the manuscript, then submitted it to the editor of a volume of scientific papers presented at a regional meeting of anthropologists, who I lectured on Hueyatlaco.

We knew that no anthropological journal would print our report over Cynthia's objections, so the only chance we had to get our proof in something published was this symposium volume. That was in 1975. We waited for the volume to be published. And waited. From 1976 to 1979, letters to the editor inquiring about the delay went unanswered. Calls were never returned. Meanwhile, Cynthia, who by now had ceased all communication with us, was busy getting out "her side of the story," while ours still went unread. The quarter-million year time-frame at which we so painstakingly arrived was discounted as a matter of course. All geologic evidence was ignored. Only the 22,000-year-old date at Caulapan was mentioned, and that's what began to appear in the literature.

The site was mentioned briefly in a 1979 *National Geographic* article on early man, but the only date mentioned was an "estimated" 22,000 years. The following year, Juan Armenta Camacho finally found the funds to publish something on his 30 years of work in the Valsequillo region and slipped in our dates on a surreptitiously added page. Even so, he wrote that he believed they represented the true age for his finds. Unfortunately, his monograph was published privately, with only a 1,000-copy press run. And even though it is printed in Spanish, it has been ignored by the Archaeological Establishment, both in the United States and in Mexico. By now, the Hueyatlaco dates were beginning to adversely effect my career. In 1973, we had made a startling statement about 250,000-year-old hunters in Mexico. But nothing further appeared in print. Were we wrong? Were the dates wrong? Where was the evidence? Was it only my imagination, or did my geology colleagues begin to look at me askance? My correspondence both national and international dropped off. I was suddenly caught by a long-neglected nepotism rule in the government bureau where my husband, Dave, and I worked, and I was suddenly out of a job. After much searching, I was able to get on as an adjunct professor in anthropology at a state university. No pay, but at least I belonged somewhere. At least for a while.

Finally, in early 1980, it became clear that our paper on Hueyatlaco would never see the light of day in that symposium volume. Editor #1 had passed it on to Editor #2, who had in turn passed it on to #3, and #3, apparently, decided to drop the whole thing. The manuscript was returned. So here it was, five years later, back to square one, as far as getting our old dates for the site into print. About that time, I was contacted by the editor of a new science magazine for the general public. It was to be called *Science 80* (in 1980), *Science 81* in 1981, and so on. He seemed very interested in Hueyatlaco and wanted to publish our report. Hoping once again, I sent the manuscript off to him, now a little shopworn and yellowed around the edges, and waited. It was the same thing all over again. Letters unanswered and calls not returned. Eventually, I caught him in the office. Seems that the manuscript had fallen behind his file cabinet and been misplaced. It was returned. I was almost in despair.

Then a lucky thought. I contacted a prestigious geological journal, *Quaternary Research*. Steve, the editor, knew me personally, and if anyone would give me and the manuscript a fair shake, he would. Sure enough, he responded as a true scientist. As long as we had good evidence to back up our claims, he didn't care how controversial our findings were. He sent the submission out for peer review, and it was approved, accepted, and published as the first article of their 1981 volume.

But it was too late. That 22,000-year-old date for the Valsequillo sites was set in concrete. I sent out a news release through the publicity office of the university where I was affiliated. The news editor thought it was one of the most exciting pieces she'd worked on. But no one picked it up; not the wire services; not the Denver metro papers; not the editors or columnists who, over the years, had specifically asked me to let them know when the paper was published. That included the editors of *Science 81, Science News, The Washington Post, The New York Times,* and *The Valley Voice* in Visalia, California. I even sent a copy of the news release to *The National Inquirer!* Nothing. The Chairman of the Anthropology Department forbade it from appearing in the faculty newsletter.

Needless to add, when my contract with the university came up for renewal, it was dropped. So, there I was at the end of 1981: no job, tarnished reputation, stone-walled, discouraged, crushed emotionally. I pretty much turned my back on science and went in other directions. From 1987 to 1994, I cared for elderly relatives and became a professional flower gardener. During this time, Hal Malde retired from his government job and took up a second vocation: taking exquisite photographs for *Nature Conservancy*. Juan Armenta Camacho died of a painful kidney disease. Cynthia Irwin-Williams has also since passed away after a long struggle with failing health.

In 1993, *Forbidden Archaeology*, by Michael Cremo and Richard Thompson, was released and soon after received favorable attention in some alternative media circles. It and the condensed version, *Hidden History of the Human Race*, have a nice section on Hueyatlaco, the dates, and our problems (entirely academic) with them. Publicity from *Forbidden Archaeology* resulted in a short appearance on a syndicated television show, *Sightings*, in 1995. It was seen by videographers making a documentary on controversial archaeological sites; I was flown down to Mexico for location shots and an interview. Their program, *Mysterious Origins of Man*, was shown on NBC the following year to the violent disapproval of Establishment scholars.

Today, human hunting sites in the 200,000-to-400,000-year range are popping up all over the place: Germany, England, and Siberia are dated using the same methods we used at Hueyatlaco. But such sites in the New World are ignored. My recent letters to *Science News, Science,* and *Nature* concerning these old New World sites were never published. That stone wall is as high as ever. But there is hope. We are trying for some more dates with the view of more excavation this fall (1997). The Valsequillo area is big, and many bones found there are well preserved. Somewhere in that pile of sediments and volcanic ash should lie the skeletal remains of the men who hunted and killed the mighty Ice Age beasts of a quarter-million years ago. Let's go find them!

# NEW EVIDENCE OF EARLY MAN

Marc Roland is a student at Brighton Hill College, in Kent, Wyoming, where he is studying for a Ph.D. in anthropology. His report of new evidence for early man in America demonstrates how rapidly the science of human origins is changing in favor of not only a far greater antiquity for the first settlers of our continent, but their surprising sea-faring capabilities in the deep past.

## NO MORE CLOVIS MOSES
## BY MARC ROLAND

Since its foundation in 1993, the writers of *Ancient American* magazine have argued that the first human visitors to this continent arrived from overseas, tens of thousands of years ago. Our conclusion was consistently ridiculed or dismissed by Establishment archaeologists, whereas their version of the past was almost universally embraced by educators and television commentators as indisputable dogma. They insist that post-glacial man crossed a land-bridge from Mongolia into Alaska no earlier than 13,500 Years Before Present.

However, a major discovery to the contrary, made two years ago by university-trained experts and independently validated earlier this summer, confirms a human presence in America some 40,000 years old. The find is additionally important because it proves that men were on the move around the world much earlier than main-stream scholars would have us believe. Moreover, it pointedly implies that the 40,000-year-old residents originated in someplace other than Mongolia.

The origins of the newly found evidence coincide with the Upper Paleolithic, or Late Stone Age, when modern men appeared for the first time in Europe and began painting cave art on the subterranean surfaces of Lascaux in southwestern France, and Altamira in northern Spain. Meanwhile, they mined red ochre at a place called Lion Cave, in Africa's Swaziland, and manufactured the earliest flaked stone tools, mostly of chert, in Southeast Asia. Australia simultaneously experienced its first human settlements, proving that even during this remote era, men were able to navigate stretches of the open sea. Clearly, some universal impetus inspired them to populate the world. But until now, conventional archaeologists were certain America was not part of this global event. On July 5, 2005, British scientists announced that literally hundreds of human footprints, approximately one-third of them children, found in Central Mexico during 2003, have been conclusively dated to the very dawn of modern man. Silvia Gonzalez, a geo-archaeologist at Liverpool's John Moores University, in England, co-discovered the impressions in an abandoned quarry near the city of Puebla, 60 miles southeast of Mexico City. They are perfectly preserved as trace fossils in ash laid down by a nearby volcano, known as Cerro Toluquilla, during the ancient past. The footprints were made on the shoreline of a long-vanished lake. Contemporary sedimentary shells and sand grains baked into the ash were dated using optically stimulated luminescence. Researchers at the University of Oxford, in England, also used argon-argon, uranium-series, and electron spin resonance techniques to date the layers. According to team member Tom Higham, "The footprints are clearly older than 38,000 years." He and his colleagues additionally employed laser scans and rapid prototyping equipment to create highly accurate, three-dimensional copies, accurate to a fraction of a millimeter.

Although the footprints remain in place where they were found, photographs and descriptions of their discovery were featured at an exhibition of the Royal Society's Summer Exhibition, in London. Their co-discoverer, Matthew Bennett, of Bournemouth University, believes the impressions were made by colonizers who arrived in the Valsequillo Basin by sea, sailing down the Pacific coast of North America.

Long before the Puebla footprints were found, *Ancient American* investigators wrote of Brazil's Pedra Furada site, which pre-dated mainstream notions of the Continent's earliest human settlers by some 16,000 years. Ongoing discoveries such as these are replacing outdated paradigms, while validating the very premise of our magazine. Its writers have presented readers with abundant, neglected, and sometimes suppressed material to show that many of the first inhabitants arrived from overseas as skillful sea-farers, sometimes thousands of years before the earliest time lines drawn by conventional scholars. For more than 70 years, these guardians of academic doctrine have clung to their conviction that distinctive stone projectiles found in large numbers near the New Mexican town of Clovis were made by the first Siberian Americans, despite accumulating evidence from around the country pointing to the existence of much earlier inhabitants from Europe.

One of the authorities long accused of promoting the Bering Land-Bridge fable was the famous Smithsonian Institution, in Washington, D.C. In view of this venerable organization's reputed hostility to archaeological heresy, an article in the November, 2004, issue of its *Smithsonian* magazine came as a pleasant surprise. In "America's First Immigrants," author Evan Hadingham writes in words similar to those found in back-issues of *Ancient American* that the first human arrivals in America more likely made their way into our continent, not across some hypothetical land-bridge, but by sea routes from Asia and even Europe. He cites the latest scientific evidence to show that the ice-free corridor could not have exited until at least 12,000 years ago, too late to allow the earliest visitors access to Alaska from Siberia.

Hadingham, senior science editor of the Public Broadcasting System's popular Nova series, cites the discoveries of archaeologist Thomas Dillehay, who found evidence for a settled human population in Monte Verde, Chile. The residents lived in a log structure and used herbal medicines as early as 1,000 years before Clovis. It took Dillehay 20 years to overcome the opposition of his professional colleagues, but separate testing vindicated his claims in 1997. Hadingham describes an even earlier find, the Meadowcroft site, dated to a remarkable 17,500 Years Before Present. Its location in Pennsylvania means either that human settlers first arrived in North America long anterior to that date, if they walked all the way from Siberia, or, they came by sailing vessels across the North Atlantic—a far more credible alternative, given the unlikelihood of any passable land-bridge.

Older still is Virginia's Cactus Hill site, where stone blades have been confirmed by independent dating techniques to 19,000 years ago. Hadingham wonders if those deeply ancient Pennslyvanians and Virginians could have been Ice Age Europeans responsible for the Solutrean Culture. They were master painters, whose vivid murals may still be seen in the French caves of Cosquer and Cougnac. Lending credence to the possibility of their impact on our Continent, the Solutreans invented the *atl-atl*, or spear-thrower, a weapon highly characteristic of Native American tribes from Alaska to Patagonia. Still more importantly, Solutrean spear-heads are virtually identical to Clovis points. Hadingham cites Bruce Bradley, a prehistoric stone tool specialist at Britain's University of Exeter, that a connection must have existed between the two, very similar types. The Smithsonian's own Clovis expert at the Institution's Department of Anthropology, Dennis Stanford, went himself to Siberia, where he found that older or contemporary spear-heads bore no resemblance to Clovis points. Stanford concluded that the Siberian hunters who supposedly walked into northern Alaska were not armed with Clovis technology. Perhaps most convincing of all, Hadingham reports on mitochondrial DNA testing undertaken on living Native Americans by Dennis Wallace, a geneticist at the University of California at Irvine. From these subjects, he and his colleagues were able to identify five distinct lineages, which demonstrated four or more separate waves of migration into North America long before 20,000 years ago. Hadingham cites Mercyhurst College author, James Adovasio, in his book, *The First Americans*, to the effect that conventional scholars, despite the contradictions of new discoveries, continue to depict the parting of the Bering Sea ice sheet similar to the parting of the Red Sea by some "Clovis Moses" leading his deeply prehistoric people into a new world.

Clearly, the days of that long-discredited portrayal are numbered, if mainstream magazines such as *The Smithsonian* are finally discussing the facts *Ancient American* has been publishing since 1993. Though we heartily congratulate Mr. Hadingham on the appearance of his enlightening article, we may be permitted to allow ourselves a friendly "we told you so!"

# CHAPTER 2:

# Ancient Technology

## EGYPTIAN INFLUENCE ON AMERICA

Laura Lee is an award-wining producer and host of a nationally syndicated radio talk-program, "The Laura Lee Show," since 1990. During the course of hundreds of broadcasts, she has introduced leading authorities on alternative history and technology to millions of listeners from coast to coast, including some of the authors featured in this collection. A world traveler to many of our planet's most remote corners, Ms. Lee returned to her home in Washington state in 1997 from a trip to Egypt, where she found intriguing comparisons with the monumental stonework of pre-Columbian Peru. Her report appeared in *Ancient American's* March/April, 1997 issue and has since been regarded as something of a "classic" by collectors of back issues of the magazine.

*Modern construction engineers would find duplicating the massive walls of Peru's Sacsayhuman a daunting challenge. Yet, similarly massive public building projects were undertaken on the other side of the world in Ancient Egypt.*

## SUPER SCIENCE FROM PHARAONIC EGYPT TO PRE-SPANISH PERU
## BY LAURA LEE

I found much to marvel at during a recent trip to Egypt. Mostly, I was in awe of the ancient stonework, such as the huge blocks in the Great Pyramid, and how they could have been put into place with such a high degree of engineering precision millennia before the Industrial Age. But I was also enchanted by an aspect of ancient stonemasonry that gets little press, yet offers tangible clues to another mystery.

Cairo Museum's "Old Kingdom" rooms are full of vases, bowls, large lidded boxes, and statues carved from schist, diorite, granite, and obsidian. These artifacts defy simple answers to the question:

"How did ancient sculptors carve in hard, igneous rock with such exactitude?" Surely, not with clumsy pounding balls and primitive cooper and stone tools, as explained by most Egyptologists. After our tour, my husband, Paul, and I spent a full day in the museum, where we could leisurely examine the wonders inside. To our eyes, the oldest artifacts had an austere, "modern" look, with their clean lines and perfect proportions that make New Kingdom items seem baroque by comparison. The big stone boxes wore marks in corners where two curved lines came together, for example, that I could only guess were made by machine tools.

I was especially puzzled by life-size diorite and granite statues with satin-smooth surfaces and precisely, delicately carved features. A few crooked rows of crudely carved, rough-edged hieroglyphs had been chipped on the base of several statues. Now, this is more the look you get with chisels on hard stone. I imagined those hieroglyphs to be the equivalent of graffiti on a fine work of art, a later addition to an heirloom antique. Two very different techniques on the same artifact implies two different dates. And why use a lesser technique, unless the first, superior technique had been lost? When the standards are inadequate, new theories arise. So, I went looking for them.

I find great benefit in crossing disciplines. Following the trail of evidence to see where it leads often requires stepping outside the constraints of the preconceived notions of a particular field. I went looking, not among Egyptologists or archaeologists, but to those who would know about rocks and tools. I found two independent researchers, a geologist and a machine tool manufacturer, to learn what the stone artifacts could tell us, and what the marks left behind by precision machine tools looked like. Both were recent guests on "The Laura Lee Show," the weekly, nationally syndicated radio interview/talk show that I host. Here is their story. Ivan Watkins is a Professor of Geology, Department of Earth Sciences, at St. Cloud University, in St. Cloud, Minnesota. He is investigating the finished surface of Inca stone masonry.

Watkins says the surface of stone at the microscopic level indicates how it was, or wasn't worked. "And you can rule out the standard issue explanations when it comes to ancient Inca stonemasonry, which is very similar to that of Egypt," he says. Watkins explains that soft rock is easy to cut; granite and the other hard, igneous rocks are difficult. Granite contains 15 percent to 30 percent quartz crystals, and a few other minerals of varying degrees of hardness, which is important to know when viewing the signature marks left in stone under the microscope. The methods that are supposed to have been used by the ancients, such as pounding, hammering, grinding, polishing with abrasives, and wedging, just don't match up with what Watkins sees under the microscope. What he sees, in the case of hammering, is rock wanting to break along pre-existing planes of weakness.

When river sand, which is mostly quartz, is used to grind and polish rock with quartz, the softer minerals in the rock are sanded out, while the quartz crystals, little affected, are left standing above the rest of the minerals on the surface. In the case of wedging rock, Watkins finds the absence of low-angle fractures, and no ability to control the cracking of the rock. On a surface worked with pounding stones, all the minerals are unevenly fractured. All of which is incompatible with what Watkins sees with Inca stonemasonry. What he does see on some Inca stones are slick surfaces at Machu Picchu and Ollantaytambo, and the Rodadero at Sacsayhuman, still used as a slide by children. Similar to a ceramic glaze, heat can melt quartz fragments into a glaze that fills in irregularities, creating a smooth surface. In an effort to discover just how such surfaces could have been obtained by ancient cultures, Watkins went looking for modern technology that produces a similar signature.

He found an important clue in the work of geologist David Lindroth, at the U.S. Bureau of Mines, Twin Cities' Research Center, in Minnesota. Lindroth was using 100 watts of light energy focused to a circle of 2 millimeters to cut through any rock in a process called "thermal disaggregation." The cuts were only two millimeters deep, but repeated passes can cut through rock of any size, he reports. Quartzite fragments cut quite easily with this process, whereas basalt melts. And he concludes, Inca stone surfaces are similar to those that have been thermally disaggregated. What about a process that could cut stone, produce this signature, and used an energy source available to the Inca? Watkins found another clue in the bracelet worn by a modern-day priest in Cuzco, the old Inca capital. In the yearly Festival of the Sun, fire must be given by the hand of the Sun. The ceremony requires lighting wisps of cotton on fire by using the Sun's rays, which are concentrated with a highly polished, concave indentation on a large, gold bracelet. The bracelet is similar to those worn by ancient Inca.

Then Watkins noticed large, parabolic golden bowls in a Peruvian museum. "These bowls were not meant to sit on a table holding fruit," he observed. "They'd roll around the table. They must have been used for something else. They are just the right shape and material for catching the Sun's rays and focusing them into a beam of light." Sunlight strong enough to cut stone? Watkins suggests ancient Inca stonemasons heated and cut stone by using a series of very large, golden parabolic reflectors to concentrate and focus solar energy. He points to the Conquistadors' own records mentioning an Inca dish of gold so large it spanned the length of two men.

It was later cut up for poker chips before it was melted into ingots and carried back to Spain. Interestingly, large, granite bedrock posts at Machu Picchu may have originally served as supports for such a mirror. Peru, as does Egypt, gets strong sunlight all year round, and gold is most reflective when alloyed with silver, a metallurgical process used by both Incas and Pharaonic Egyptians. Some pyramidians, or capstones, found in Dynastic Egypt were made of electrum, an 80/20 ratio of gold to silver. Watkins's research led him to develop a solar-powered device for cutting and polishing stone, for which he received a patent, application Number 4611857.

Someone able to connect Watkins' invention with its ancient precursor is a man who reads the signature of precision machine tools, even when he sees them in places that just "can't be," according to mainstream Egyptologists. And read them he did, from core drills more efficient than our diamond bits today, to space-age precision planning, to intersecting lathe marks. Chris Dunn, presently in senior management at Danville Metal Stamping, in Danville, Illinois, has spent much of his career working with machinery for jet-engine components and nonconventional manufacturing methods, such as laser processing and electrical discharge machining. He also brings a fresh perspective to viewing an ancient artifact, describing himself as "unencumbered with dates and histories and chronologies." Two visits to Egypt for personal inspections of selected artifacts had him asking, "How was this created? How, precisely, is this engineered? What tools were used to make this?"

The tools on display were used for creating many ancient artifacts. His theory on this is: "They are simply physically incapable of reproducing those artifacts today. So, why should I believe that they could do so thousands of years ago?" Logical enough. And it does not deter him that ancient tools capable of reproducing these artifacts have not been unearthed. "The tools haven't yet been found," he said, "but that shouldn't stop us from deducing what they were by the marks they left on the artifacts." What marks? According to Dunn's investigation, the marks of sophisticated sawing, drilling, lathe, and milling practices and a standard of even, level, flat surface planes impossible to achieve by hand. For example, there's the diorite bowl in the Cairo Museum that appears to have been cut on a lathe. Dunn points out the simple stone bowl has a "sharp cusp, where two spherical, concave radii intersected. This indicates the radii were cut on two separate axes of rotation. Cutting stone on a turning lathe is a pretty sophisticated use of a wheel."

And how to explain the spherical stone drill cores, the piece removed when a round hole is cut? Dunn points out that ancient drill cores fascinated famed British archaeologist, Sir Flinders Petrie, who first established, by examining the cores and the holes left behind in the stone, that a tubular drill was used, the same as used today. Dunn found in "Pyramids and Temples of Giza," published in 1883, that Petrie had calculated the rate of descent of this ancient tubular drill by measuring the distance between the spiral grooves it left behind on the core, as one-tenth of an inch per revolution. Which means, according to Dunn, that these ancient drills cut through solid granite with a feed-rate 500 times greater than today's diamond drills.

"I presented Petrie's astonishing calculations to other craftsmen," said Dunn, "asking them to determine what possible method could create that same feed-rate, and the other characteristics we see in ancient drill cores, such as the hole and core tapering into the stone, and grooves cut deeper in quartz than in feldspar. Most gave up. Only one figured it out, and he independently came up with the same method I did." What method was that? "Ultrasonics." How do we use sound today to cut through rock? Dunn explains, "Modern ultrasonic drills use very high frequency vibration sound traveling through a medium. It induces a tool to oscillate, or reciprocate back and forth about 19,000 to 25,000 hertz in a rapid grinding process. A paste or slurry stimulates the cutting action." Today's ultrasonic machine bits are used for the precision machining of odd-shaped holes in hard, brittle materials. It is significant that ultrasonic drills cut through quartz more easily than through feldspar or granite.

"Ultra sound gets the quartz in the granite vibrating in sympathy," says Dunn, "and therefore cuts more easily." Then there's the so-called "sarcophagus" in the King's Chamber of the Great Pyramid. Why assume it was meant to hold corpses, when no human remains, mummified or otherwise, were ever found there? Was it instead a chamber of initiation? Or did it have something to do with the biblical Ark of the Covenant, because the Ark's outside dimensions are said to be a perfect it to the sarcophagus's inside dimensions? In any case, Dunn points out the end piece of this granite box. "The side facing north bears saw marks that are very similar to saw marks on modern granite surface plates. According to Dunn, surface plates are precision-ground, flat blocks that serve as a reference plane when measuring other flat planes in the manufacturing process. Granite is used because it's stable and extremely hard. Metal surface plates can swell. Granite surface plates don't."

And this is why he finds it intriguing that the big, black granite boxes on the Serapeum, at Sakkara, were only roughed out when first brought into underground chambers with quite different atmospheric conditions than the dry, outside air. Once inside the chambers, after the stone had a chance to adapt to the atmosphere, it was finished. This helped the granite retain its precise dimensions. And "Space Age precision" is how Dunn describes the level surface of the inside of the Great Pyramid's sarcophagus, or granite box, and those of the Serapeum. He brought along a portable instrument which measures the accuracy of a level surface, and shone a flashlight behind a straight edge held against the smooth sides. No light escaped between the straight edge and the granite to indicate slight imperfections.

"Of course, to really measure it," Dunn said, "I'd like to bring in laser surface scanning equipment. But from my brief measurements, I'd say it was so even, so level, it would be impossible to achieve that by hand." Still, why was such precision needed? It's an open question as to exactly what the ancient builders were doing with these artifacts. Unfortunately, the dynastic stonemasons were not giving away any secrets, or writing them down. Judging from the Freemasons, architects, and builders, they were a secretive lot. This does not deter Dunn, however.

"The interpretation and understanding of a civilization's level of technology cannot hinge on the preservation of a written record for every technique that they developed," he says. But what about the preservation of an artifact? In this case, these were precision tools. What was their function, and what were they made of? Copper is just not tough enough for this kind of work. "Ferrous metal tools would have rusted away by now," Dunn observes. Petrie, who was the leading Egyptologist of his day, also determined that saws 9 feet in length were used by the ancient Egyptians and noticed that, during construction of the Great Pyramid's sarcophagus, the drill had wandered away from its course, leaving a scallop cut a little deeper in the corner. Yet, today's Egyptologists never seem to mention such curiosities. When a theory cannot adequately explain the evidence, let's throw out the theories, not the evidence!

# 100-Year-Old Artifact Still Unidentified

Two man-made objects were encrusted in rock long before human evolution supposedly began. Although both were found more than 150 years ago, archaeologists are still unable to explain their geological context. Were the artifacts somehow enveloped in a natural process that still eludes scientists? Or could at least one of them—as incredible as it seems—have actually been used when dinosaurs roamed the Earth? These intriguing questions were raised in *Ancient American*'s February, 2001 issue.

## The Bell and Hammer: Two "Impossible" Finds by Dennis Ballard

In its June, 1851 issue *Scientific American* carried an item about a metallic vessel that had been blasted out of an "immense mass of rock" when workmen were excavating on Meeting House Hill, in Dorchester, Massachusetts.

"On putting the two parts together, it formed a bell-shaped vessel, 4 1/2 inches high, 6 1/2 inches at the base, 2 1/2 inches at the top, and about an eighth of an inch in thickness. The color resembles zinc, or a composition metal, in which there is a considerable portion of silver. On the sides there are six figures of a flower, or bouquet, beautifully inlaid with pure silver, and around the lower part of the vessel a vine or wreath, inlaid also with silver. The chasing, carving, and inlaying are exquisitely done by the art of some cunning workman. This curious and unknown vessel was blown out of the solid pudding stone, 15 feet below the surface.

Dr. J. V. C. Smith, who has recently traveled in the East...and examined hundreds of curious domestic utensils, has never seen anything resembling this. There is no doubt that this curiosity was blown out of the rock."

*The discovery of man-made objects in settings that pre-date current understanding of human origins defies scientific explanation.*

Recently, the present owner of this curious artifact wrote to the well-known investigator of anomalies, Brad Steiger, and informed him that the vessel is still unidentified after more than 100 years. Although he wrote at some length about the bell-like object in his 1971 book, *Atlantis Rising,* Steiger could offer nothing new on it. According to Milton Swanson of Maine, "It had been given to Harvard College, but because of its mysterious origin they relegated it to a closet. The building supervisor finally brought it home to Medford, Massachusetts." Mr. Swanson sold it to me just before passing away in his eighties. Through the years I have had so-called experts look at it, and no one ever came up with an answer. Its age and use are just unexplainable. It is almost black, but the metal appears to be composed of brass with zinc, iron, and lead. The inlay is pure silver, and the application of lacquer was necessary to protect it. Perhaps it is a burial ash container of some kind.

I hoped to learn something more definite at the Museum of Fine Arts in Boston, which operates a state-of-the-art analysis laboratory built in cooperation with M.I.T. Its examiners ran the object through a thorough battery of tests for two years, which failed to confirm its origin. Privately, however, geologists dated the bell's rock matrix to approximately one million Years Before Present. None of them, of course, would dare go on record with their conclusion for fear of ridicule, despite the evidence of acid testing to determine credible time-parameters. The very suggestion of a man-made object dating so long ago is anathema to most scientists.

A far older artificial item was embedded in Cretaceous rock. It was found by Max Hahn near London, Texas, in June 1934. Tests verified the hammer head is of metal, with an iron purity that resists erosion, and which would be difficult to duplicate, even today. The metal in the hammer seems to be similar to the metal in the axe of *Oetzi,* the 5,000-year-old remains of the so-called "ice man" recovered 10,000 feet high in the Alps, three years ago. The same is true of the hammer broken out of Cretaceous stone. Chemical analysis demonstrated that the find is all that is claimed for it: a man-made object of relatively recent times, but encased by stone that is roughly 70 million years old.

The hammer is unquestionably man-made, and it had to be in existence before it could be encased by the Cretaceous stone matrix. But clearly, it cannot be, because modern man (*Homo sapiens*) has only existed for the last 100,000 years. Until the lingering paradox of the bell and hammer has been resolved, these two objects represent the most challenging mystery of their kind. They represent the idea that both came to be encrusted through natural processes still to be discovered by science, or the prehistory of the human race is radically different than the current theories explain it.

# BERMUDA TRIANGLE REVEALS ANCIENT ROOTS

An area of ocean east of Florida is infamous for the unexplained disappearance of airplanes and sea-going vessels. Through its reality is still hotly debated, the so-called "zone of death" may have been familiar to the pre-Columbian inhabitants of our continent, many centuries ago. Renowned for his ability to translate mathematical languages encoded in ancient structures, Carl Munck applied his insightful expertise in *Ancient American*'s June, 2001 issue to reveal the ancient roots of a very contemporary phenomenon.

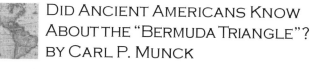 ## DID ANCIENT AMERICANS KNOW ABOUT THE "BERMUDA TRIANGLE"? BY CARL P. MUNCK

Authorities have been so perplexed by the hundreds of ships and air-craft losses in the Bermuda Triangle, and unable to find answers, that they have thrown their hands up in despair. We cannot just turn off the traffic in the region. Not only is it bad business, but tourism might go bust.

We have all heard the term, *wind sheer*, a definite hazard to aviation. But suppose there is something called "electromagnetic sheer," which is just as deadly if one enters it at the wrong angle and at the wrong moment in time? Is such a phenomenon real? Amazingly, the prehistoric inhabitants of North America appear to have known about that perilous area of ocean we call "the Bermuda Triangle," and left monumental hazard signs which still exist.

For example, why does the mile-long panther effigy in Florida's Everglades, at the western tip of the Triangle, walk so carefully on its heading of 36 degrees? The effigy can be recognized from the air, resembling the shape or outline of a large cat. What is he, largest of all the cats, trying to warn us about? Second in size to the Panther Mound is the five-thousand-foot-long "Device" effigy at Portsmouth, Kentucky, with its 12-foot-high and 40-foot-wide walls. Interestingly, this rifle-like effigy points southwestward at an azimuth of 216 degrees, or just the opposite of the Panther's 36-degree heading.

Almost midway between Kentucky's "Device" and Florida's Panther is Georgia's Rock Eagle effigy. It is one of a handful of aboriginal North American monuments that were rendered in stone. Does it really represent the eagle which was so revered by the Indians? If so, its anatomy is all wrong. An eagle's wings are large, and its body is small. This effigy more resembles a turkey. As is the Panther Mounds, Rock Eagle's azimuth is 36 degrees. Why the consistency? The slow-stepping Panther is made of earth—soft, as a cat should be. But why a rock bird? Birds are not hard. Could this be another warning, as if one flies at high speed on an unseen heading of 36 degrees in this part of the world, he might slam into something unseen? The cat, a land creature, should not walk in this direction, nor should anything that flies. There is a certain sense to it.

Next, we go east, off Florida, to a point well within the eastern edge of the Bermuda Triangle. Here we find the Shark Mound of East Bimini Island, 57 miles from Miami, in the Bahamas. Interestingly, 216 degrees is the direction toward which this 500-foot-long shark effigy "swims." What does this obvious symbol of danger tell us? "If you travel into this zone on a heading of 216 degrees, I'll have you for lunch!" Perhaps in confirmation of this interpretation, when an R.A.F. Lancaster bomber that had been converted into transport known as the Star Ariel disappeared south of Bermuda on January 17, 1949 during a flight to Jamaica, its last heading was known to have been 216 degress.

❧❧❧❧❧

## CALENDAR STONE

The so-called "Calendar Stone" is perhaps the most famous pre-Columbian artifact in the world. But few persons awed by its alluring complexity suspect the advanced astronomy that went into its creation. Did the Native Americans really design it, or was this scientific marvel an heirloom from another, much older civilization? And what does it predict for the world in 2012? These are some of the great disc's enigmas explored in the March/April, 1994 issue of *Ancient American*.

*Restored to its original colors, this re-creation shows how the Aztec "Calendar Stone" appeared to the 15th century residents of imperial capital, Tenochtitlan.*

 THE AZTEC "VESSEL OF TIME"
BY FRANK JOSEPH

One of the greatest discoveries in American archaeology was made by sewer workers. In front of the large cathedral of the Plaza Mayor, labor crews broke up the pavement to get at Mexico City's dilapidated drainage system. By the time they worked their way almost parallel to the front of the viceroy's palace, their picks suddenly struck an unusually hard object just two feet below street level. Clearing away the debris of centuries, they revealed a huge, circular stone decorated with mysterious carvings. A major engineering effort over the next several weeks finally pried the 24-ton disk from its grave, from whence it was transported to lean against the cathedral's eastern wall.

Dusted off and cleaned, the 12-foot-tall monolith could be examined for the first time. Observers beheld a hypnotic puzzle of innumerable, enigmatic figures, similar to the frozen images of a dream. All anyone could deduce from the immense artifact was that it had been sculpted from a single, 3-foot-thick piece of gray-black basalt; faint traces of paint implied the entire face of the object was brightly colored at one time. It belonged to the Aztec Empire, destroyed by the Spanish Conquistadors in the early 16th century. Fearing it might come to be regarded as an idol for recalcitrant pagans, the Catholic priests urged their Native American congregations to demonstrate true Christian piety by desecrating the old heathens' "sacrificial altar."

Despite superficial damage incurred since its discovery, the Aztec Calendar Stone, as it has come to be known, is housed today in relatively pristine condition at Mexico City's renowned Museum of Archaeology and Anthropology. In the more than 300 years after it was found, the great disk has gained recognition as the outstanding symbol of Aztec Civilization. Zelia Nuttall, the early 20th century's leading archaeologist in Mesoamerican research, valued the Stone as "the most precious and remarkable monument ever unearthed on the American Continent, and one of the most admirable and perfect achievements of the human intellect." Her high regard for the find, echoed since for four generations of investigators, resulted from the abundance of extraordinary information they deciphered from the monolith.

Today, it is one of the most universally recognized images in the world, its reproduction adorning everything from T-shirts and album covers to tourist agencies and restaurants. Despite its international recognition, few people understand its layered, cryptic meanings. To most, it is no less puzzling, however aesthetically dazzling, than it was to the sewer workers who found it in 1790. The Stone is far more than a "calendar" or an archaeological curiosity. It is an exceptional work of scientific genius simultaneously extending backward and forward in time. And although the origins of the high-level technology that produced it are shrouded in speculation, the disk's physical creation is mostly understood. The 50,000-pound slab was hewn from quarries in the mountains near the floating gardens of Xochimilco, south of today's Mexico City. Then it was somehow transported 30 miles to the main square of the Aztec imperial capital, Tenochtitlan, and hauled more than half way up the steep steps of the Great Pyramid to a broad landing, where carving began in 1479 A.D., during the reign of Emperor Axayacatl.

Two years later, the painted work was complete, and set up a special, throne-like cradle to face out over the city. There the stone stood for the next 40 years. After Hernan Cortez landed at Vera Cruz with his small army and conquered Mexico in 1519, the Spanish aggressively set about demolishing Tenochtitlan. While the soldiers confiscated all the gold, silver and gems they were able to lay their hands on, the clergy were intent on ecclesiastical matters. Anything they could not smash to pieces, they buried.

In a frenzy of religious zeal, they dislodged the Calendar Stone from its stand and sent it careening down the broad staircase, at the foot of which it crashed, chipped but otherwise intact. Standing righteously over the deposed "altar," they ordered their enslaved native parishioners to "bury with the stone the memory of the abominable acts perpetrated on it." After its resurrection nearly three centuries later, the fateful disk has achieved a world-wide interest it never attracted during the four decades it perched on the steps of Tenochtitlan Great Pyramid.

But what does it mean? What is the significance of its curious, sometimes nightmarish imagery? Is it possible to read or decipher its messages? Happily, the Calendar Stone has given up many, perhaps most, but not all of its secrets to the investigators who found themselves challenged by its mystery. Their findings are scattered over several different books. In all their literature, however, there are no references to some decisively important aspects of the Aztec Stone that should seem apparent.

For example, as noted by the Spanish invaders, the broad masses of the Aztec people were beardless. Only some members of the royal elite, such as Emperor Moctezuma II himself, could grow thin patches of facial hair, implying a genetic distinction between the ruling minority and the ruled majority. This distinction is important in any examination of the Calendar Stone, because, at its very bottom, a pair of stylized serpents confront each other with open jaws, from which protrude two human heads. The man on the right sports a mustache and goatee, but his companion on the left is fully bearded. These characters were used in temple-art to portray Tezcatlipocha ("Jaguar") and Quetzalcoatl ("Feathered Serpent"), respectively, the Sacred Twins. Here they represent the Sacred Duality, a sacred concept pervading the universe: light and darkness, hot and cold, hard and soft, good and evil, pleasure and pain, and so on.

Quetzalcoatl was the famous founding father of Mesoamerican Civilization, the culture-bearer of science and art from across the Atlantic Ocean, whose foreign, that is, Old World, origins are underscored on the disk by his full beard. The Feathered Serpent's appearance on the monolith suggests that its technology was among the gifts he brought from his homeland over the sea. Indeed, the Aztecs did not invent the Calendar Stone. All they did was supplant the names of their own gods for those they copied from the Mayas, whose end preceded the Aztecs by 400 years. Nor were the Mayas responsible for its invention. They obtained it from their predecessors, the Olmecs. Yet, even among these earliest known Mesoamericans, the same calendar shows no sign of having been evolved by them, because the Olmecs were using it in a fully developed form from the earliest days of their society, beginning around 1500 B.C. Alfonso Caso, Mexico's leading archaeologist, wrote, "This calendar's development is without doubt very old, and it must have been the creation of a people who attained a high degree of culture prior to that of all the peoples with whose culture we are now familiar."

If the calendar shows no sign of evolution in Mesoamerica, then comparisons with similar systems overseas lead us foremost to prehistoric Britain. Here, on the Salisbury Plain, stands the country's most famous megalithic relic: Stonehenge. Seen from directly overhead, its essential resemblance to the Calendar Stone is remarkable. And stripped of its Aztec mythological images, that resemblance grows considerably. Both Stonehenge and the Calendar Stone comprise concentric circles, in which the numbers five and six reoccur as the leading numerological symbols for the site and the artifact. And both were astronomical almanacs, or celestial computers, to determine the positions of various heavenly bodies and the recurrence of particular sky phenomena, especially solar eclipses and lunar phases. Could the same science that made Stonehenge possible also have been responsible for the Mesoamerican Calendar, which suddenly appears fully developed in the 16th century B.C.?

At that time, Stonehenge was approaching the zenith of its use and final building episode. This is not to argue that the inventors of Mesoamerica's calendar were ancient Britons. More likely, both they and the Olmecs were recipients of an astral technology from some intermediary civilization, as implied in a comparison of relative dates between the megalithic site and the megalithic artifact: Stonehenge's earliest building stage occurred around 3000 B.C.; the present epoch of the Mesoamerican Calendar opened on August 12, 3113 B.C. The Aztecs claimed that their calendar came into use after their ancestors arrived in Mexico from the deluge that destroyed their homeland, a volcanic island in the Atlantic Ocean they remembered as Aztlan.

Although comparisons with "legendary" Atlantis are beyond the scope of this article, they are unavoidable, as they must have seemed to Alexander von Humbolt, Germany's great explorer-scientist of the early 19th century. He devoted 100 pages of his *Atlas Pittoresco* to the Aztec Calendar Stone, and, according to Peter Tompkins, author of *Mysteries of Mexican Pyramids*, "concluded that the peoples of the two continents might have developed their astronomical ideas from a common source. He found evidence for a common origin of the cultures of the two continents, including systems of both the solar and lunar zodiacs, with many similar animals allotted and even similar sounds of some of the astrological terms." The Aztec constellation, *Colotl Ixayac*, the "Scorpion," is the same constellation, also known as "Scorpio," in the European Old World.

A third point never discussed elsewhere, at least so far as this writer has been able to determine, is that the Aztec Calendar Stone appears to be only an artistic copy, the hugely oversized representation of an original machine, or, more precisely, some portable instrument, probably no larger than 2 or 3 feet across, for the computation of significant astronomical data. The sculpture, no doubt a faithfully accurate reproduction, however much larger than the original device, plainly shows five or six disks within its shallow bowl superimposed on one another like stacked plates. These were meant to turn either clockwise or counterclockwise independently of each other, aligning with certain points around the calendar to obtain desired coordinates. Its real identity as an apparatus seems underscored by the notches and gears that comprise its outer circles. Certainly, its overall impression, when all its various parts are highlighted separately, is that of a working instrument. Perhaps there was more than one, and the Tenochtitlan Calendar Stone was meant to memorialize astronomical calculators owned by every high priest. In any case, no such device has yet been found to prove that ancient Mexico's monumental sculpture was the artistic facsimile of an ancient computer, although the monolith itself suggests as much.

More certain is the symbolic meaning of the Aztec Calendar Stone, reading it from the center outward. At its hub is the ghastly visage of the sun-god, Tonatiuh. A flaming fire-pot over his forehead or Third Eye, his tongue lolls for bloody sacrifice, fire blazes from his ears and nostrils, and his talons (in circles on either side of his face) grip human hearts, because he was symbolized by the eagle. He is not alone in this bloody business. Queztalcoatl and Tezcatlipocha, the Sacred Twins mentioned earlier, are likewise depicted with human hearts dangling from their clenched teeth. Here is the real mystery, not only of the Calendar Stone, but of the Aztec people themselves: How could such a race, which achieved great heights in all the arts of civilization, delight in the most horrific religious practices? The Stone embodies this awful contradiction, but it does not explain it.

Yet, Tonatiuh was among the most popular gods in the Aztec pantheon, because he made human redemption possible when, at the beginning of the world, he threw himself into a fire. Rising from his own immolation, he takes the souls of persons who died heroic deaths into heaven. All others descend into nine levels of hell before vanishing forever like mist. Acceptably heroic deaths included falling in battle for men and expiring during childbirth for women. Voluntarily sacrificing their hearts to the flint knife, represented by his greedy tongue, guaranteed paradise for both sexes. Tonatiuh himself contains a secret that conceals his and perhaps the entire calendar's real identity and origins. His ferocious expression is the mirror image of a classical facial exercise in Hatha Yoga, known as "The Lion," which is Sanskrit for "union" or "yoking." Yoga is an ancient spiritual discipline of physical and mental procedures still used to achieve an inner meditation so profound that its practitioners believe they become one with the universal soul of Creation.

The yogic Lion exercise calls for the extension of the tongue to its limits, the tensing of all facial muscles, widening of the eyes, and stretching of the fingers to resemble lion's claws, the same posture expressed at the center of the Aztec Calendar Stone. This particular exercise signifies the relief of a tense period, an ending or completion, just as 4-*Olin* marks the end of a tension-filled epoch, our present Fifth Sun. The yogic Lion and the Aztec face on the disk are both physically and symbolically identical. Yet, the origins of Yoga are lost in the depths of prehistory, its images traced back to the Indus Valley Civilization of the early fourth millennium B.C. Yoga was and still is the dominant spiritual discipline of Asia, particularly identified with ancient India generally and the Buddha specifically.

Previous issues of *Ancient American* featured several articles by various investigators, who competently established the presence of Hindu and other Asian visitors in the Americas during prehistoric times. Their influence among native society was profound and undeniable, apparently extending to a central position in the Aztec conception of ritual time. Given the extremely important spiritual influence at work behind the Calendar's true nature and in its subtle, unrecognized esoteric significance, the Stone is as much a monument to Aztec art as it is to foreigners from Asia. They were probably ancient Hindus, who taught the mythical code of Yoga to the high priests of Tenochtitlan.

Though the Calendar Stone's earliest origins may have begun with the lost city of Atlantis-Aztlan, the additional appearance of this vital theme from the Far East may be crucial to unlocking the Calendar Stone's hidden meanings. In other words, if its images are seen as yoga symbols, then the disk may suddenly reveal an incredibly ancient spiritual outlook that once dominated Aztec Civilization and continues to be practiced by millions of people around the world. Surrounding Tonatiuh are four circles, which define his calendrical name, 4-*Olin*, or 4-Earthquake. He stands for the present epoch in historical time, known as the Fifth Sun, each "sun" representing a separate era.

The Aztecs believed that four worldwide catastrophes took place in the past. Each cataclysm marked the end of a time-period, or Sun, in human history and the beginning of the next. Those that preceded 4-*Olin*, our time, are hieroglyphically pictured in a quartet of boxes on all sides of Tonatiuh, beginning in order of their latest occurrence with the bottom-right square. In it is 4-*Atl*, or 4-Water. The picture here shows an overturned bucket dumping out a deluge of water in the form of the goddess of storms on an already half-sunken pyramid. She was Chalchiuhtlicue, "Our Lady of the Turquoise Skirt," a name that colorfully suggests her identification with swirling or stormy water. Indeed, she was often represented in religious art as seated upon a throne surrounded by whirlpools of drowning people. It was her disaster that ended a former age of civilized greatness and ushered a new one in Mexico, with the arrival of survivors, the ancestors of the Aztecs.

If all of this sounds strangely similar to the destruction of Atlantis, beginning with the obvious 4-*Atl*, the impression deepens when we learn that, on her feast day, Chalchiuhtlicue was honored by the priests, who collected reeds and ceremoniously placed them around her temple to signify her identification with Aztlan, the island home of the Aztec's forefathers. The ritual name for Aztlan (literally, "Place-in-the-Water") was "Field of Reeds," a metaphor for "great wisdom" or literacy, because reeds were used as writing utensils. Coincidentally, on the other side of the world, the Ancient Egyptians wrote in the "Book of the Dead," a guide for souls to the next world, that their ancestors came from a great island in the Distant West, called Sekhet-aaru, or "Place of Reeds." The reed-pen had the same symbolic significance for learning in Egypt.

The Sun that preceded 4-*Atl* appears bottom-left of Tonatiuh. Known as 4-*Quihuitl*, or "Fire from Heaven," it depicts another up-turned bucket, this time dumping flames on a pyramid. It appears that 4-*Quihuitl* signified some large-scale meteor fall that devastated pre-Atlantean civilization. Upper-left, 4-*Ehecatl*, or "Windstorm," is an eagle breathing at a pyramid, as a dragonfly scoots away. The first and earliest Sun is upper-right, 4-*Ocelotl*, or "Jaguar," in which early humans and a race of giants were destroyed by wild animals. This box is unique, because it is the only square that does not feature a pyramid, implying that 4-*Ocelotl* took place before man attained civilization.

The next ring surrounding this central section of the Suns, or ages, contains the 20 day-signs of the Aztec month. Their original names, translations, and aspects begin top-right, going around to complete the circle: *Xochitl* (Flower, Life), *Tecpatl* (Flint, Violence); it also stood for the concept of zero and, as mentioned above, Tonatiuh's horrid tongue. As though to emphasize an Asian-American connection sited earlier, the Hindus and early Mesoamericans were the only ancient people who used zero in their computations.

Continuing around the ring of day signs is *Olin* (Earthquake, Limitations), *Cozcaquauhtli* (Vulture, Disease), *Cuauhtli* (Eagle, Time), *Ocelotl* (Jaguar, Transformation), *Acatl* (Cane, Emptiness), *Quihuitl* (Fire from Heaven, Judgement), *Ozornatli* (Monkey, Baser Instincts), *Itzcuintli* (Dog, Loyalty), *Malinalli* (Grass, Peace), *Atl* (Water, Life-Death), *Tochtli* (Rabbit, Sensitivity), *Mazatl* (Deer, Harmony), *Miquiztli* (Skull, Death), *Coatl* (Serpent, Change), *Cuetzpallin* (Lizard, Dreams), *Calli* (House, Preserver), *Ehecatl* (Windstorm, Travel), and *Cipactli* (Alligator, Earth).

Each month had its own ceremonies, which ranged from requests to Tlaloc, the rain-god, *Altcualcaco*, or "Wants Water," and the spring celebration, *Tlaxochimaco*'s "Birth of Flowers," to military parades of the *Ochpaniz*, "Month of Brooms," and the *Atemoztli* "Fall of Waters" music festival, culminating in the *Izcalli* mass-sacrifice of tens of thousands of victims. These holidays are included here for their insight into Aztec society. As someone once said, "Show me how a people celebrate, and I will tell you what they are."

With the exception of the Sacred Twins at the bottom of the Calendar Stone, the remaining four rings depict no mythically symbolic themes, but are given over entirely to mathematical notation. Even the smallest details, to the lone dot and a single diagonal line, signify arithmetical values. For example, the squares at the outer perimeter contain representations of the manguey plant, whose leaves and stem each add up to a *Xiuhmolpili*, a unit of 365 days. The 10 dots around each manguey represent a decade. There are 20 such squares on the Stone, in addition to two other squares surrounded on three sides by 16 dots, for an additional six years. Here, we have a repetition of the sacred numerals five and six mentioned earlier, and cited by Plato in his account of Atlantis, the *Kritias*, as the holy numbers used for the construction of religious objects and structures.

The Calendar Stone's eight pointers, or indicators, were each mounted on different rings of the instrument after which the great, sculpted object was modeled. As a ring was turned to a different position, its arrow pointed to the desired computation. The four larger indicators, raised over the four lesser pointers, are the Major and Minor Cardinal Directions, respectively. They also stand for the eight divisions of the Aztec day, from sunrise to sunset in eight intervals of three hour duration each. The Aztec year was begun and divided by solstices, equinoxes, and days of the zenith, celestial events all accurately computed by the Calendar Stone.

Its innermost arrow, atop the ring encircling Tonatiuh, indicates the day when the sun stands at its highest point directly over Mexico City, which, considering the Stone's original position on the steps of Tenochtitlan's Great Pyramid, is entirely appropriate. At that time, it held small obelisks known as *gnomens* around its edge. They threw shadows over different details of the sculpted face, pointing to the days when solstices, equinoxes, and zeniths would occur. They also recorded the annual rotation of the circumpolar star groups, and the apparent course of the sun each year. Clearly, the monolith represents a surprisingly high level of astronomical computer science.

The real name of the Calendar Stone was *Cuauhtlixicalli* (literally, the "House of the Eagle," the "Eagle Bowl," or, closest to the real meaning of its name, "The Vessel of Time"). It was not a calendar in a restricted, modern sense, but a complex, sophisticated almanac for divination. For it was not Tonatiuh that the Aztecs really worshiped, but the greater power he symbolized: time, as signified by the eagle and the sun, monarchs of the sky. To the Aztecs, the God of Time seemed to be a fitting supreme deity, because he brought everything into existence. It was said that he destroyed everything, and brought everything into being again as a cycle of creation, new forms, destruction, and recreation.

As described, the Aztecs believed that the world had been successively destroyed four times before by overwhelming cataclysms that obliterated society and virtually exterminated all mankind. After years of misery and hardship, the survivors were always able to rebuild, eventually flourishing as before in civilized greatness, but only so long as they obeyed the will of heaven. When again they grew corrupt, the gods sent them another holocaust, and whoever was spared had to start the slow ascent back to civilization all over.

It was of the utmost importance, therefore, that society be run strictly within the observable laws of Nature, as perceived in the time tables of the heavens, the regular movements of celestial bodies, and revealed each day to the 150,000 inhabitants of Tenochtitlan by the great disk gleaming from the steps of the Great Pyramid. As Peter Tompkins writes of Zelia Nuttall, she saw the Stone as "a calendar designed to control the actions of all the human beings of the state, bringing their communal life into accord with the periodic movements of the heavenly bodies." The Aztecs' awe of the cycles of time absolutely dominated their lives, because they believed that moral law and cosmic law did not influence each other, but rather, were one and the same.

A similar situation would result if the U.S. legal system were substituted by the rules governing astrology, rules rigidly enforced on the population as federal laws. A person's fate was socially set by his horoscope, and the day-sign under which he or she was born, determined everything in a person's life, including the profession taken in adulthood, even an infant's name. Each day had its own deity, whose glyph was a stylized portrait of its functions and character.

La Malinche, Cortez's native mistress, was a Spanish mispronunciation of her real name, *Ce Malinalli*, "One-Grass," of the Aztec Calender. Even the Aztecs' most popular national pastime was laid out in a cross-version of their calender. Patolli, a board game in which players gambled heavily as testimony to their faith in the gods, was made up of 52 squares to reproduce the 52-year cycle of the Eagle Bowl. Marriages were contracted, travels undertaken, rituals enacted, wars declared, treaties enacted, buildings erected, business deals concluded, sexual activity allowed or forbidden—in fact, virtually every movement was regulated by the Vessel of Time.

It was a device perfected with more than 30 centuries of use, involving the best brains of at least four Mesoamerican cultures: the Olmec, Maya, Zapotec, and Aztec. Millennia of painstakingly recorded celestial observations and so much high-level science went into the *Cuauhtlixicalli* for so long that modern investigators are still finding surprises in its challenging complexity. As an astronomical alarm clock for alerting humanity to impending doom, the great and terrible disk seems to have worked only too well. It predicted for Emperor Moctezuma the disastrous return of the Feathered Serpent, on Reed-One, or the Christian year 1519—precisely when Cortez first set foot in Mexico.

At the very top of the Stone perches a glyph comprising a square, in which a manguey plant is surrounded on three sides by 13 dots, each representing the 13 "heavens," which made up one "Sun," or time period. This glyph is, in fact, known as "Reed-Thirteen" and signifies the end of a "World," or major epoch. In this case, the year 1479 A.D.—exactly 13 years before Columbus landed on the Atlantic shores of Mexico, marking the beginning of the end of the Aztec world.

Reed-Thirteen's prediction of, or coincidence with (depending on one's point of view), the Spaniards' devastating arrival calls into question why the Calendar Stone came to be made when it was. It is an eminently valid question, in light of the Aztecs' obsession to do the right thing at the right time, all the time. Certainly, something as momentous as the creation of the colossal and intricately carved

monolith was not undertaken arbitrarily by a people fanatically dedicated to timely procedures. Construction on the great disk began in
1479, the same year of the fateful glyph. Indeed, Reed-Thirteen not
only occupies the top position of the Stone; it is pointed to on both
sides by arrow heads and beneath by the uppermost indicator, as
though all the elements of the Calendar were culminating in this
particular sign.

It is the outstanding and supreme date of the whole object, and
suggests that the Stone was made just then, because the astrologer-
priests determined that 1479 to 1492 would simultaneously encap-
sulate the year of its creation and the year of their society's downfall.
It was primarily to foreshadow this doom that the disk was constructed
when it was and set up to hang over the inhabitants of Tenochtitlan.
To them, it was a monstrous clock, winding down the last years of
the Aztec Empire and reminding them to prepare for the inevitable
end of their world. Hence, all the graphic references around the
horrid face of Tonatiuh, the personification of time in its utterly
destructive aspect.

Certainly, the most disconcerting message of the Calendar Stone
for our time is its prediction of 4-*Olin*, the Fifth Sun—the fifth world-
wide destruction yet to come. The Aztecs believed that so long as man
lived in harmony with the predictable rhythms of the universe, he
could indefinitely postpone that destruction. But if he fell into sin
once more; if he preferred greed and selfishness to the laws of Nature,
the "World" would be destroyed just as surely as those which preceded
his. This Fifth Sun, in which our present time occupies the final years,
is set to end through the power of 4-*Olin*, or "Earthquake."

This does not mean that seismic activity alone will be the agency
of our destruction. Rather, "Earthquake" is a poetic or ritually descriptive
title, meaning that the next cataclysm will be a rebellion of the whole

Earth against mankind. In other words, an ecological catastrophe. That the Aztecs or their scientific predecessors so many centuries ago could have envisioned such a planet-wide disaster for our environmentally self-destructive age lends an eerie credence to the ominous Calendar Stone. It developed, as mentioned above, from previous time-keeping systems. In fact, the Aztec stone disk seems hardly more than a physical expression of the much earlier Maya version, which specified that the present age, or Fifth Sun, will come to an end on an early 21st century Winter Solstice. A modern computer simulation, known as "Voyager," reveals that on the morning of 21 December 2012, when the Sun is one degree above the horizon at the equator (73 degrees West), the ecliptic will intersect with the galactic ecliptic to place the Sun at the very center, in the "cross-hairs" between the solar path and that of our galaxy. The ecliptic is a line the Sun follows across the sky.

Though the ability of Maya astronomers predicting this cosmic event more than two millennia ago with such pin-point accuracy seems remarkable, it is nothing compared to the real significance of their prediction. From our Earth-bound perspective, the Sun moves into the ecliptic cross-hairs only once every 26,000 years. Astronomers refer to this moment as the Precession of the Great Year of the Equinox. But late advances in astrophysics tend to confirm that this great Precession is entirely subjective and theoretical—meaningless—because observations extending out into space beyond 18,000 light-years disintegrate. In that case, 2012's Winter Solstice sunrise takes place only once in the whole history of the universe! More amazing still, modern scientists did not even discover the whereabouts of the galactic center until 1963. How could the ancient Maya have known its exact location? And why did they choose this cosmically unique event as the date to terminate their calendar?

According to the Aztec astronomer-priests, our Fifth Sun, which began 5,106 years ago, is supposed to come to an end between December 21st and Christmas Eve, 2012. Or will it be the eve of something else?

## NIEBRA DISC PROVES EVIDENCE OF PRE-COLUMBUS EXPLORERS

Critics arguing that sailors before the time of Christopher Columbus lacked a navigational instrument needed to find their way across the Atlantic Ocean were challenged when such a piece of ancient maritime technology was found at the turn of the 20th century. Its discovery was preceded 100 years earlier by a similar, though more complex, apparatus dredged up in a Greek fisherman's net off the coast of Antikythera, in the Aegean Sea. "It was like finding a turbo-jet engine in Tutankhamun's tomb," exclaimed an astounded archaeologist 60 years later, when the object's identity was finally understood. These two, sophisticated instruments are physical proof that ancient man did indeed possess the scientific means to cross the oceans of the world. Their very existence suggests they must have been used for that purpose during the deep past, as described in the February, 2004 issue of *Ancient American*.

*The Niebra Disc was considered high technology in the Ancient World.*

## GERMANY'S BRONZE AGE DISC: A TRANSATLANTIC DEVICE? BY DR. R.M. DE JONGE & J.S. WAKEFIELD

In 1999, a bronze disc was looted from a prehistoric grave in the neighborhood of Sachsen-Anhalt, in the Harz Mountains of Germany. Three years later, the curious object was recovered and has since begun to throw new light on connections between the Old and New Worlds during the deep past.

With a diameter of 32 centimeters and weighing 2 kilograms, the strange, metal disc is unlike anything previously found in Europe. It is partially covered with pieces of gold-plate, though in some places gold-plating is missing. The 3,000-year-old grave from which it was taken is located within a circular-shaped wall system 200 to 350 meters up Mount Mittelberg, in Niebra, close to a tributary of the Weser River, 250 kilometers from the North Sea coast. The bronze disc contains a relatively high quantity of arsenic, and the gold is contaminated with other substances. But these contaminants and strong corrosion of the surface, together with its context in the grave in which it was found, date the object to circa 1600 B.C.

On the front side of the Niebra Disc, as it has come to be called, appears a large solar image with some damage to its gold plating, and the representation of a crescent quarter moon. Either side originally featured strips of gold-plating, now missing from one side. The celestial images might signify the eastern and western horizons, usually conceived of as land or mountains in ancient pictographs. A cup or bowl-shaped object at the bottom (4) possibly perhaps symbolizes the Milky Way, while a group of seven stars (22) is most likely meant to be the Pleiades. There are 23 other stars on the Disc, making for a total of 30 stellar images. The stars to the left of the crescent lunar image appear to represent the planets Jupiter (13)

and Venus (12). Interestingly, the relative position of (11) corresponds to a super nova (a stellar explosion) documented by
Chinese astronomers around 1600 B.C., just when the Niebra Disc
was made.

Its surface also suggests a human face or head. What seems to
be a complete "eye" is beside a crescent, or half-closed eye. Below
them, there is a smiling mouth. At the sides might be hair, ears, or
ear-spools. Contemporary petroglyphs sometimes depicted sun-faces,
apparently representing a solar deity, and in Egyptian temple art,
the sun-god was usually depicted rising from the eastern horizon,
with the Moon in the west, the direction of the land. Each day, Ra
traversed the sky from horizon to horizon, and each evening he sailed
in his celestial ship to the other side of the world. His vessel was
sometimes shown as an upside-down boat in the sky, or an upright
sun-boat on water. Similarly, there may be no conventionally
understood "up" or "down" on the Niebra Disc, because it might
have been intended as a three-dimensional instrument, including the
four Cardinal Directions, plus a vertical, skyward dimension.

Its Pleiadian constellation and 23 other stars correspond to the
latitude of the Tropic of Cancer, at 23 degrees north. The latitude
was said to be holy by followers of solar religions around the world,
because at noon on midsummer day the Sun is directly overhead at
this latitude, having moved up from the south. After holding this
latitude for a couple of days, the Sun begins a slow movement back
toward the south. Most European megaliths incorporate this sacred
position, underscoring the conclusion of archaeo-astronomers that
the Paleolithic structures, such as Britain's Stonehenge, were deliberately oriented to significant celestial phenomena. The Niebra
Disc's separate stars also corresponded to the latitude of the southern
Egyptian empire at 23 degrees north, the geographical mid-point
of Ra's religious cult.

The Disc's 30 stars coincide with the latitude of the Nile Delta, the center of the northern Egyptian kingdom, at 30 degrees North. The group of seven stars may also represent the same degrees of latitude of Egypt from 23 degrees north to 30 degrees north. In the hierarchy of deities immediately beneath Ra, the god of resurrection, Ausar (known as Osiris in Greece and to the rest of the outside world), and the sky-god, Horus (originally Hr) correspond to the pair of "eyes" on the "face" of the Niebra Disc, which, consequently, represents the spherical Earth, and especially the North Atlantic Ocean. Its "mouth" is Ra's sun-boat, sailing toward the west. Details of the crossing may be encoded in the placement of the stars on the face of the disc.

Let us assume that the "boat" is upright on the ocean, with the moon near the eastern horizon, and the Sun moving toward the west. Usually, in megalithic petroglyphs, the center of the eastern horizon is the Straits of Gibraltar, on the coast of the Old World. The Tropic of Cancer leaves the continent of Africa at 23 degrees North, synonymous for the disc's 23 stars. This is the historic place they wanted to cross the ocean in honor of the sun-god, Ra.

In the bowl, or "boat" image on the Niebra Disc are three stars (1, 2, 3) which correspond to the three island groups of the Cape Verde Islands, off the West African coast. Below the centers of the Sun and the Moon are 15 stars, the latitude of the most southern Cape Verde Islands (15 degrees north), and the sailing direction from there, 15 degrees west south west, to South America, as well as Cape Gracias-a-Dios, the east Cape of Honduras, also at 15 degrees north. The 15th star touches the western horizon, where the culture of Central America begins. The Disc's 30 stars comprise the correct length of the Southern Crossing, 30dl (distance lines), or 30 degrees, equal to 3,333 kilometers.

On the left side of the Sun is another star (15), the position of which is associated with Maya ceremonial centers along the North

Coast of Honduras, Belize, and Guatemala at 16 degrees north. Above them are two more stars (17, 18) at the center of Olmec Civilization near the southern basin of the Gulf of Campeche at 18 degrees north. Above these, are two more stars (19, 20), bordering the northern border of the Olmec world at 20 degrees north. The center of the western horizon (formerly in gold on the Niebra Disc) corresponds to the southern coast of the Gulf of Campeche and is clearly situated on the artifact west south west of the center on the eastern horizon. It thus agrees with latitudes for Gibraltar at 36 degrees north, confirming the discovery of America before the 1600 B.C. date for the Niebra Disc).

At its top appears the 21st star (21) corresponding to the northeast Cape of Yucatan at 21 degrees north. The 22nd star gives the latitude of southwest Cuba at 22 degrees north. If the group of seven stars did, in fact, signify the Constellation of the Pleiades, their appearance in the sky may have coincided the end of the sailing season each late autumn. They likewise join two more adjacent stars (22, 23) to form the Azore Islands. The moon on the Disc then corresponds to Madeira. If we count two more stars behind the eastern horizon of the gold object (15, 16), their total number would be 32, encoding the latitude of Bermuda at 32 degrees North.

Through the use of encoded latitudes such as these, the Niebra Disc reveals itself as an ancient astrolabe. It was a navigational instrument that enabled Bronze Age sea-farers to complete their transatlantic voyages to and from America millennia before this device was re-invented in the High Middle Ages. The discovery of this singular artifact shows that pre-Classical sailors were, in fact, aided by a maritime technology sufficiently advanced to allow successful round-trip expeditions between the Old and New Worlds many centuries before Columbus.

# CHAPTER 3:

## Lost Races

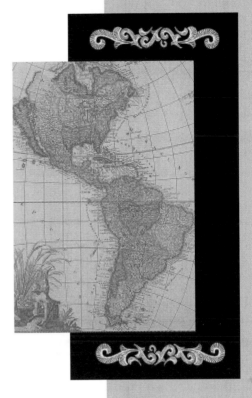

## MYSTERIOUS CITY IN CUBAN WATERS

The best-selling books of British author Andrew Collins have won him a worldwide following for his bold inquiries into the ancient past. *Gods of Eden, From the Ashes of Angels,* and *Tutankhamun, the Exodus Conspiracy* have each achieved best seller status in Europe and the United States.

But it was *Gateway to Atlantis* that proved remarkably prescient. Its original argument that the lost civilization had been located on the island of Cuba was provided powerful physical evidence four years after its release, when sonar images of a sunken city began to appear off the shores of Havana.

In July, 2001, Collins not only laid out his Cuban Atlantis theory for *Ancient American* readers, but offered them among the most credible, engaging descriptions of the underwater mystery found anywhere.

## WAS ATLANTIS IN CUBA?
## BY ANDREW COLLINS

A "lost city" that could turn out to be the fabled capital of Atlantis has been located by a Canadian scientific research team. In a press release dated Havana, 14 May 2001, Reuters of London informed the world that Russian-born ocean engineer Paulina Zelitsky, president of Canadian-based company Advanced Digital Communications, had detected "a sunken city" in deep waters off the west coast of Cuba, the largest island of the Caribbean.

Satellite-integrated ocean bottom positioning systems, echo-sounders, and high-precision side-scan double-frequency sonar have detected the presence of what are being described as shapes that "resemble pyramids, roads, and buildings." Their regularity seems consistent with the idea that they represent an "urban development" composed of "symmetrical architecture." Reuters reported that the deep-sea city is located on a huge land plateau lying in around 2,200 feet (700 meters) of water.

Furthermore, in Paulina's opinion, the complex belongs to "the pre-classic period" of Central American history, and was populated by "an advanced civilization similar to the early Teotihuacán culture of Yucatán. It is stunning," she said during an interview with the Reuters representative at her office at Tarara, east of Havana. "What we see in our high-resolution sonar images are limitless, rolling, white sand plains and, in the middle of this beautiful white sand, there are clear, man-made, large-size architectural designs. It looks similar to flying over an urban development in a plane, and seeing highways, tunnels, and buildings. We don't know what it is, and we don't have the videotaped evidence of this yet, but we do not believe that nature is capable of producing planned symmetrical architecture, unless it is a miracle," she added.

Paulina is cautious about what lies beneath the glistening blue waters of the Yucatán Channel, admitting only that she is "excited but reluctant to speculate until a joint investigation with the Cuban Academy of Sciences and the National Geographic Society takes place early this summer."

The discoveries were made last summer during deep-sea surveys made by Paulina and a trained scientific research team aboard the Cuban research vessel, *Ulises*. Sonar images revealed "an extensive series of structures" over a several-mile area in darker and lighter shades. The site is close to the edge of an underwater geological feature known as the Cuban Shelf. It falls off sharply in a series of shelves dropping down to several thousand meters. The anomalous target area sits on one of these shelves. The mass of rectilinear features are said to be located in the proximity of an "extinct volcano, geological faults, and a river bed." This last fact alone shows that the land shelf, which rises to a height of around 40 meters, was once above water.

"Whenever you find a volcano, there is often a settlement associated with it," Paul Weinzweig, Paulina's husband and a director of ADC, observed. "I don't know the exact relationship, but it is in the same vicinity as the volcano, the fault lines, and the river. They're quite close to one another." On the matter of whether the sonar imagery really does show "pyramids, roads, and buildings," Paul stated, "We had been looking at the images for some months. We keep a picture on the wall showing pyramids in the Yucatán, and let's just say they kept reminding us of these structures. They really do look like an urban development." As to whether the light and dark areas of the sonar imagery appear to be three-dimensional features or not, he answered, "There's a lot of symmetry, apart from actual shapes, and some suggestion of structure. Some American geologists have looked at them and said that the darker shadings are suggestive of metal roofing."

In order to explore the site more closely, ADC are currently planning to send down remote robot video cameras and a one-man submersible. *Ancient American* readers may look forward to further news of these discoveries in coming months.

Interestingly, ADC's intentions had never been to search for sunken cities. Their scientific operation to survey the deep waters off the Cuban coastline forms part of a joint venture set-up between the Canadian company and the Cuban government, in particular its state partner, Geomar. One of the most important goals was to find billions of dollars of bullion and lost treasure disgorged from sunken ships from the time of the Spanish Conquest. As Paul said, "Cuba has the richest galleon cemetery in the world."

Over the past five centuries, it is estimated that hundreds, if not thousands, of vessels must have been lost in Cuban waters because of poor navigation, piracy on the high seas, and the violent Caribbean storms that plague the region on a frighteningly regular basis. Visa Gold, a Toronto-based low-tech company that operates out of Havana's Marina Hemingway, already claims to have found some 7,000 objects from sunken vessels including jewelry, diamonds, and pistols. They are believed to be artifacts from the brigantine *Palemon*, lost off Cuba's northern coast in 1839. Visa Gold's next target is the *Atocha y San Jose*, another old Spanish vessel. It sank in Havana Bay during January 1642, after fleeing storms at sea.

Renewed interest in treasure salving among Cuban coastal waters comes after Fidel Castro's government recognized its own lack of oceanographic technology to conduct scientific operations of this nature. Its divers, who are considered some of the best in the world, have been diving off Cuba's coast, treasure hunting for decades. Yet, Cuba lacks expertise and technology for deep-sea science. That is why its government leaders invited ADC to take up the challenge. Their 80 meter oceanographic research vessel is equipped with high-tech instrumentation and a trained scientific team to survey the sea bottom up to a depth of several thousand meters.

It was their skilled sonar software analysts who detected the reported underwater remains in the Yucatán Channel.

"These projects are very important in helping us rescue things from history, which contribute to our national patrimony," said Eddy Fernandez, vice president of Geomar. "As you know, we have financing problems. This is a very expensive activity. They give us technology and financing. We provide historical and ocean expertise."

The implications of ADC's discoveries off Cuba's western coastline are far-reaching and quite extraordinary. An online pole was conducted by the NBC home news service, MSNBC, of the 1,827 persons who had voted by May 26, 2001, no less than 73 percent believed that the find "could be something big: Next stop, Atlantis." In fact, NBC executives are considering the possibility that the sunken city could be linked with Plato's account of the lost city. This is good news for me, as my book *Gateway to Atlantis*, published in 2000, concluded that the most likely location of Plato's sunken empire was Cuba, the first time that Castro's island had ever been proposed in this respect.

I pointed out that evidence contained in Plato's works, the *Timaeus* and *Kritias*, hinted strongly that his view of Atlantis was based on stories and rumors reaching the ancient world via Phoenicians and Carthaginians, who were crossing the Atlantic prior to his age. Moreover, Plato's description of Atlantis' great plain, said to have been three 3,000 by 2,000 stadia (552 by 368 kilometers) in size, matches Cuba's great western plain.

Before the rapid rise in sea level following the end of the last Ice Age, this stretched southward across the Bay of Batabanó to the mysterious "Isle of Youth" and was originally 540 by 160 kilometers in size. Although I speculated in the book (since published in the U.S., Italy, Holland, Germany, and Portugal) that the Atlantean city might await discovery beneath the shallow waters of the Bay of Batabanó, word that a sunken city may now have been detected in the Yucatán Channel, between Cuba and the Yucatán Peninsula, is exciting news. Incidentally, the ADC has plans to explore the Bay of Batabanó during the next year, so it should be interesting to see what, if anything, they find there.

In September 1972, American oceanic explorer J. Manson Valentine was flying over the Bahamas in a light aircraft with his associate, Jim Richardson. He noticed a mass of rectilinear and curvilinear features in shallow waters on the southwestern edge of the former Bahamian landmass, now the Great Bahamas Bank. Valentine referred to this mass of possible archaeological features as "the mother lode" of all archaeological discoveries. They face out across the Old Bahamas Channel, like some kind of ancient port serving the Cuban mainland.

As early as the 1950s, light-aircraft pilots reported seeing what they described as underwater "stonework" that was "well within Cuban waters." Similar sightings north of Cuba of an alleged "submerged building complex covering over 10 acres" might even have convinced the Cuban government that a veritable city awaited discovery in its vigorously defended waters. There are, for instance, unconfirmed reports that this "building complex" was explored with the assistance of Soviet submarines based in Cuba during the 1960s. Strange then, that these recent discoveries of a sunken city in Cuban waters are being conducted by a Russian-born Canadian oceanographer.

Among those who felt they had glimpsed the remains of a lost citadel in Cuban waters was Leicester Hemingway, brother of writer Ernest Hemingway. During a flight into the country, Leicester noticed, beyond its northern coast, "an expanse of stone ruins, several acres in area and apparently white, as if they were marble." The exact location of these underwater features remains unclear. Only time will tell whether the discoveries made by Paulina Zelitsky and ADC do constitute firm evidence of Plato's Atlantis. For if they do, then it will fix, once and for all, its geographical location in the Bahamas and Caribbean, and not anywhere else in the world. However, the location of a lost city on a huge land plateau lying at a depth of around 600 to 700 meters poses new problems for the Atlantis debate.

Plato wrote that his Atlantic empire was destroyed by "earthquakes and floods" in "one terrible day and night" post-8570 B.C. in the *Timaeus*, and around 9421 B.C. in the *Kritias*. This time frame corresponds with the cessation of the last Ice Age, when we know that sea levels began to rise fairly rapidly, as ice fields which had covered vast areas of North America and Europe for tens of thousands of years began to disappear.

In *Gateway to Atlantis*, I proposed that the mechanism behind Atlantis's destruction was a comet impact, which devastated the eastern Atlantic coast of America, causing about half-a-million elliptical craters, known today as the Carolina Bays, sometime around 8500 B.C. (+/-500 years). Fragments of the comet falling in the Western Atlantic basin, north of the Bahamas, would have created tsunami tidal waves perhaps hundreds of meters high. These would have drowned, temporarily at least, large parts of the Bahamas and the Caribbean, as well as many low-lying regions of the eastern United States. Myths and legends told by the indigenous peoples of the Bahamian and Caribbean archipelagos, when the Spanish first reached the New World, spoke of such a cataclysm. They said that the waters suddenly rushed in and drowned the great landmass, breaking it up into the individual islands seen today.

Although a fragmentation of the former land masses of the Bahamas and Caribbean in the manner indicated could not have been caused by tsunamis alone, the gradual rise in the sea level that followed this cataclysmic event would have drowned, more permanently this time, all low-lying regions, creating the archipelagos we see today. Yet, in the thousands of years which it took for the ice fields to melt in full, the sea level rose only 300 meters; some estimates place it as much as 400 meters. If the "city" does lie in 600 to 700 meters of water, we will need to propose a suitable geological mechanism in order to justify its submergence to this depth, post 9000 B.C. Either that, or we will have to define a geological time frame in which the land plateau, with its volcano, fault lines, and river, was above sea level.

Paulina's statement that the "city" might belong to "the pre-classic period" of Mesoamerican history, and was populated "by an advanced civilization similar to the early Teotihuacán culture of Yucatán," is very difficult to equate with the discovery. The Teotihuacán Culture, which thrived in Central Mexico from around 400 B.C. until around 500 A.D., remains an enigma to archaeologists. Its origin is unclear. What we do know is that legends once told by the Totonac peoples of eastern Mexico spoke of the founders of its sacred city of Teotihuacán, with its mighty Pyramids of the Sun and Moon, as having arrived on the Gulf coast from an island homeland that lay beyond the sea. Here was to be found Chicomoztoc, or "Seven Caves," where it was said that the first humans emerged out of the darkness at the beginning of time.

For many reasons, not least of all the appearance of sea-shells of a purely Caribbean nature carved on the walls of the Temple of Quetzalcoatl at Teotihuacán, the Teotihuacános saw their ancestral homeland as connected in some way with the Caribbean. Moreover, in *Gateway to Atlantis*, I identified the original "Seven Caves" complex as the Punta del Esté caves on Cuba's "Isle of Youth," one of which, Cueva Number 1, has been described as a veritable "Sistine Chapel" of the prehistoric world. Many thousands of years ago, unknown artists adorned its walls and ceilings with abstract petroglyphs of a blatantly celestial nature.

Even so, any sunken city lying off the northern coast of Cuba, in 600 to 700 meters of water, must antedate the Teotihuacán Culture by many thousands of years. Curiously, Pauline Zelitsky visited Ceuva Number 1 at the Punta del Esté complex during the summer of 2000, shortly before she made her dramatic discovery of the underwater "city." There is something magical about this place. It assaults the senses and inspires thoughts regarding the origins of Cuba's indigenous peoples, and their apparent knowledge of the cataclysm which devastated the region so many thousands of years ago.

If Paulina Zelitsky and her oceanographic colleagues are right in their belief that "pyramids, roads, and buildings" do indeed lie off Cuba's western coastline, then it is clear that the prehistory of the Caribbean, and its influence on the rise of Mesoamerican Civilization, will have to be revised dramatically. Moreover, it could well be that at long last the mystery of Atlantis, mankind's greatest historical enigma, is about to unfold in a most spectacular fashion.

# ANCIENT GRAVEYARD

Archaeology's best-kept secret was the mining of some half-billion pounds of copper from North America's Upper Great Lakes Region more than 3,000 years ago. To find out who achieved this gigantic enterprise and what became of them, *Ancient American* publisher Wayne May visited their final resting place and filed this report in the October, 2000 issue.

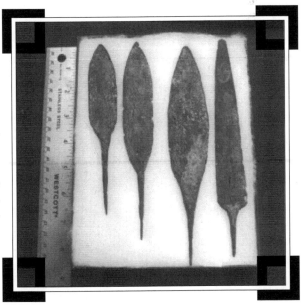

*Well-made copper spear-heads from Michigan's Upper Peninsula date from the third millennium B.C. The specimen on the far right is very Bronze Age European in appearance.*

America's Oldest Cemetery: The Copper Miners' Graveyard by Wayne May

In the summer of 1952, a 13-year-old boy from Oconto, Wisconsin, was exploring an abandoned gravel pit on the western outskirts of the city, when he uncovered a cache of human bones. Donald Baldwin's accidental discovery would lead to one of the most significant archaeological investigations ever undertaken in the state. It would grow to involve not only the Milwaukee Public Museum, but the University of Chicago, the Natural History Museum of Chicago, and the Wisconsin Historical Society.

Excavations were conducted jointly by the Oconto County Historical Society and the Wisconsin Archaeological Survey. Young Baldwin's find and subsequent discoveries at Oconto established the area as one of monumental archaeological importance. Carbon-14 dating revealed human habitation there in excess of 7,500 years ago. The remains of at least 45 individuals and a virtual treasure trove of copper, bone, and stone artifacts were the oldest (at least at that time) cultural materials found east of the Mississippi River.

The site contained the oldest known cemetery in North America. Artifacts and burials provided powerful new evidence about the antiquity, complexity, and diffusion of ancient North America's Copper Culture. Yet, in the end, everything learned and gained from the discovery would be soon after packed away and virtually forgotten. But the Copper Culture tradition grew to represent one of the most controversial interpretations of North American prehistory. Currently at Wisconsin State Park and open to visitors, the archeological precinct is located some 150 yards from the Oconto River, and approximately 3 miles from where it flows into Green Bay.

The site lies in a Pleistocene glacial till plain overlain with a 1.5-foot layer of sand and 0.5-foot layer of humus. Area surrounding the site was once a fairly level one, but gravel mining operations during the 1920s removed a substantial amount of the soil and substrata, destroying most of the site. Investigators estimate it originally may have contained as many as 200 burials. Both grave and cremation pits were found, but no mounds associated with them exist. Pit outlines were generally round for cremation and elliptical or rectangle for graves. In cross-section, they were basin-shaped. The incineration and burial areas were separated from each other by 1 to 5 feet. In two instances, the burials intruded into prior or adjacent graves.

Eight cremation pits were found altogether. They were generally 2 to 4 feet in diameter, 1 foot deep, and often did not penetrate into the gravel layer. Each cremation pit contained the remains of at least one individual. The presence of charcoal, blackened stones, and other evidence of fire on the sides and bottoms of the pits suggests that cremation took place within the pits. Split bones, skull fragments, and the general chaotic position of the bones indicated the dead may have been dismembered, or given scaffold or tree-burials before cremation. Altogether, 21 grave pits were uncovered during excavations.

A total of 33 men, women, and children were recorded. One of the pits was empty, 11 contained a single individual, seven were occupied by two persons each, and one held three human remains. Five individuals were interred in a single pit. Graves were dug into the gravel stratum (glacial till), while the burials were laid in and covered with sand. These pits were discernible by their gravel outline when seen from above. The entombed individuals had been interred in several positions varying from prone to partially flexed (in the ancient Egyptian manner). A number of graves contained bundle burials, implying they died elsewhere and were reburied at the Oconto site. Artifacts discovered at the site are perhaps the most telling evidence of the Copper Culture. They show that the Oconto site inhabitants used a deep knowledge of metallurgy, and established a strong economy based on extensive trade.

Travel, too, would have played an integral part in their commerce, and is demonstrated by the many copper artifacts found up and down the Mississippi River Valley. In all, 26 copper artifacts were discovered at Oconto, including 10 awls ranging in length from 2 to 4 inches, four crescents, three clasps, two spatulas, a spiral-shaped piece of metal, a fishhook, rivet, bracelet, and a number of projectile points. Several items were found in conjunction with fiber and birch remains preserved by contact with the copper. Except for the awls, all the artifacts were found in graves or cremation pits.

In addition to these copper relics, a number of other revealing artifacts were discovered. For example, a whistle made of bone and two lumps of hematite were found near the base of a child's skull in the grave of an infant. The simple instrument was a polished bone about 6 inches long and three-quarters of an inch in diameter. It had a rectangular hole in the center, two smaller holes on the sides, and several rows of short lines cut into the top and bottom sides, apparently for decoration. At first, investigators thought the work had been carved from a deer tibia. Later, Robert Blake, at the Natural History Museum of Chicago, determined it was made from the humerus of a trumpeter swan.

The bone whistle is similar to instruments of the same type found in Kentucky at Indian Knoll, and in the Carlson Annis Mound (where it was discovered at the base of a human skull, just as the Oconto whistle had been). In addition, the whistle also resembles a similar specimen from the Oklahoma Fourche Maline culture. Artifacts such as the whistle were recovered in all stages of burial including cremations. Most had been interred with children and infants, not adults. These and other items suggest possible trade contacts, or perhaps even the culture's travel habits. In a single burial, the portions of two unworked shells were recovered.

One shell was a portion of a freshwater clam (*Unio ellipsis*), whose nearest present source was the Mississippi River. A second shell formed the portion of a large "lightning shell," a marine snail

(*Fulgar perversus*) with distribution along the Atlantic coast from North Carolina to Florida. The presence of this second shell implies contact with a region more than a thousand miles from Wisconsin. Dating of the Oconto site materials was conducted by Dr. W. F. Libby, a physicist at the University of Chicago. He subjected 56 grams of charcoal gathered from one of the cremation burials, to Carbon-14 analysis. Results stunned investigators when the dates came back indicating that the site had been occupied in 3646 B.C. (+/-400 years).

In an effort to disprove this officially unacceptable date, conventional scholars removed and tested additional samples of charcoal. To their astonishment and chagrin, this second battery of tests produced a date even more remote in time, to 5556 B.C. (+/-400 years)! Subsequently, the Oconto site had to be officially dated around 7,510 years old; that is some 2,000 years before the earliest known beginnings of civilization in the Nile Valley and Mesopotamia. In 1952, these dates made Oconto the oldest cultural find east of the Mississippi River, the first date for prehistoric man in Wisconsin, and the earliest date for human remains in all of northeastern North America. The discrepancy of 1,910 years between the two tests was later explained as a result of the first sample having been contaminated by materials bearing younger carbon.

The significance of the Oconto discoveries would overshadow and further validate another find of Copper Culture materials made seven years earlier in southeastern Wisconsin. This site, near Osceola in Grant County, was disclosed in 1945, when the waters of the Mississippi exposed a similar cemetery. As with the Oconto site, this burial ground had been disturbed prior to discovery, and only a small portion of the graves could be excavated using careful archaeological methods. But this site was estimated to have contained more than 500 burials. The two locations shared many commonalities, including copper artifacts and chipped or ground stone implements found in the burials. Osceola interments, however, were predominantly single or multiple bundle burials, with no evidence of the cremation of articulated bodies.

The Osceola discovery also showcased a variety of artifacts including copper beads, awls, clasps, and projectile points. Other items found at the site, but not directly associated with the burials, included clumps of red ocher, clay wads, and cubes of galena. In addition to the Copper Culture artifacts, three categories of chipped stone were represented in an abundance of chert projectile points. This differs significantly from Oconto, where the predominant projectile points were copper. As years passed since the Oconto discovery, artifacts from the 1952 excavation were packed away in the dark recesses of the Milwaukee Public Museum, their significance apparently all but forgotten.

Yet, the Oconto site lives on because of the concerted efforts of a group of concerned citizens who staff the Oconto County Historical Society Museum. Each summer the archaeological area itself is open to the public, and a variety of knowledgeable local historians are on hand to describe the discovery to visitors who otherwise would nothing about it.

## Alaska's Mummy People

Even archaeologists usually do not consider Alaska when thinking of American prehistory. Yet, one of our continent's foremost enigmas is found in the Far North. The elusive identity of a technological advanced people and their ultimate fate were questions tackled only in the June, 2001 issue of *Ancient American*.

## THE CAUCASIAN MUMMY PEOPLE OF ALASKA BY F.S. PETTYJOHN

Alaska's "Mummy People" belonged to a prehistoric ethnic group inhabiting the Aleutian Islands from 7,000 years ago until historic times. There were still a few members of this mysterious race surviving in the westernmost Alaskan Islands when the Russians arrived in 1741. The Aleuts, who inhabit Alaska at the present time, are a mixture of the Eskimo, who began an island-to-island conquest 1,000 years ago, and this distinctly different "Mummy People." The Eskimo, who overran the entire Catherine Archipelago from the Alaskan mainland, intermarried with the original inhabitants and inherited much of their physical characteristics, as well as their culture, to become the historic Aleut, very few of whom still exist.

The origin of the long-dead Mummy People is unknown. Few archaeologists have studied their remains. However, some scientists remark on the resemblance of this vanished people to the ancient Ainu, a Caucasoid race that occupied the Japanese Islands from Neolithic times until driven out by the Mongoloid Japanese. As were the Mummy People, the Ainu were long-skulled, used wooden armor, helmets, broad swords, and pikes. They lived in subterranean dwellings. They hunted in the sea for subsistence, practiced mummification of the dead, were medium-sized, muscular men wearing beards and mustaches, and (again, as with the Mummy People of Alaska) there were only a few left alive on the Northern Kurile Islands when the Russians arrived there in the mid-18th century.

The ancient Aleuts were known as the *Ta-iagu-muit*, meaning "younger brother," by the Eskimo. Each village had a chief called the *Toukoo* or *To-en*, as a common-consent chief. He was mainly an arbitrator whose edicts were enforced by the people. Top in authority was a Council of Elders; second came the Shaman. In time of war, the chief assumed full dictatorship under common consent and held full power until peace was re-established.

*Skulls of Alaska's Mummy
People often have red hair.*

Savage warfare was waged against Eskimos of the Bristol Bay area, the Kodiak Island, and people of the Alaska Peninsula. They never attacked Cook Inlet, Kenai, or Chugachmuits. Slaves were taken and belonged to the taker for life. They could be given away as gifts or as payment in a trade. Body armor, wrist guards, helmets, masks, and body-shields protected them in combat. The shields were made from wood and bone slats held together with sinew, and covered with rawhide. These were called *kuyake*. Armed with daggers, lances, pikes, and broad swords, many of which were made of crude iron, individual warriors were formidable. Their portable breastworks were used principally during an attack and served to cover warriors who were launching spears, stones, arrows, and darts with throwing-sticks, and by hand with deadly two-stone bolos from behind their fortress-like shields.

The first Russian ships arriving on Kodiak Island were driven away by armed men using these huge shields, which were proof even against cannon fire. The natives openly attacked, driving the Russians off the beaches under a rain of stones thrown from catapults, spears, darts, and lances. The Russians retreated, but suffered extensive losses of ships and men.

The Aleuts used a decimal system that could tabulate up to 100,000 and used a 12-month calendar. They manufactured a white parchment that has endured through the ages. They made fishing nets, harpoon lines, and bidarka ropes from the core of seaweed, and wove baskets and sleeping mats from the roots of tall grass. Geese were domesticated by catching them during the molting season and then clipping their wings; thus, a yearly supply was assured. They had a working knowledge of astronomy and anatomy: human and animal, setting simple fractures and performing some operations, one in particular being the removal of eye abscesses.

They were fearless in their pursuit of whales, walrus, sea-cows, sea-lions, and seals. They had the world's first weather bureau: After a hunter grew too old to hunt, he was often trained in the art of weather forecasting. Atmospheric pressure, air density, wind velocity, and temperatures were used along with centuries of observation of local weather conditions to enable the observers to render competent daily forecasts.

Spears, arrows, and javelins were used in hunting, as well as in warfare. The poison on their darts was the trade secret of a selected few. It was manufactured from putrid oil and the powdered root of monkshood. Combustible sulphur was used to start fires, with sparks being struck from rocks containing pyrite. They also mined copper and iron sulphides, oxides, synite, slate, sandstone, pumice, greenstone, and many other minerals, which they used as paint for their lamps, dishes, tables, tools, and weapons. The present archeological theory is that the iron weapons that were used among these people came with them across the Bering Sea. However, Dr. Fredericka de LaGuna disputes that point, stating that no comparisons have ever been made to identify placement.

The Smithsonian Institution, in Washington, D.C., is the only official repository for the few remaining Alaskan mummies. Large numbers of them were burned by early Christian missionaries jealous of all forms of "paganism." There are many more yet to be unearthed in the frozen northlands. Perhaps enough will be found in future excavations to determine once and for all the identity of this fair-haired people who long ago dominated what has since become the largest state in the Union.

## MYSTERIOUS INDIGENOUS PEOPLE

Spanish explorers of America's Pacific coasts were met by indigenous peoples physically unlike the Indian tribes encountered in the rest of the Continent. The controversial origins of these untypical natives was described in the March/April, 1997 issue of *Ancient American* by William Donato, head of *The Atlantis Organization* (Buena Park, California), and the world's leading authority on an underwater structure in the Bahamas known as the "Bimini Road." He and his decades-long investigation have been featured in several nationally televised documentaries, such as *The Discovery Channel's* "Secrets of the Deep: The Hunt for Atlantis" (1994) and "Arthur C. Clarke's Mysterious Universe: Secrets of Ancient Worlds" (1996); and "Truth or Dare: The Bermuda Triangle"(2004).

### WHO WERE THE "WESTERN WHITES"? BY WILLIAM M. DONATO

In 1576, when sailing off course from his route near South America, between Peruvian Callao and Chilean Valparaiso, Juan Fernandez encountered what he thought was the shores of a great southern continent. He claimed to have seen "the mouths of very large rivers...and people so white and so well clad and in everything different from those of Chile and Peru."

During the 16th century, Cabrillo described the people of *Gha-las Hat* (California's San Nicholas Island) as being more advanced than those on the mainland. He described the women as having "fine forms, beautiful eyes, and a modest demeanor," and the children as being "white, with light hair and ruddy cheeks." Their culture seems to have been a variant of Chumash-Gabrieleno. Old ship logs and other contemporary written accounts also refer to "the white-skinned" Native American communities on Santa Catalina Island. Catalina was called "Pimu" by the original inhabitants, and Santa Cruz Island was known as "Limuw." Incidentally, "Limuw" means "in the sea." A study of human crania cited by Dr. Jeffrey Goodman showed that the ancient Channel Islanders had the greatest affinity with a group labeled "archaic Caucasoid."

According to Yurok traditions, before their ancestors arrived at the Klamath River, the land was occupied by a white-skinned people they described as moral and civilized, and shared what they had with the Yurok, who remembered them as the *Wah-ghas*. Though we would like to give something substantive with respect to who these ancient people were, we cannot. No one knows who they were, where they came from or where they went. That they existed is an undisputed fact, as some of their physical remains still exist in museum collections in California and Nevada.

Though they resembled Caucasoids, they appear far too early to have been either Kelts or Vikings. The only facts we do know point to their culture as non-European. Were they descendants of Mu, also known as Lemuria, the lost "continent" of the Pacific? Their Channel Island names, such as Pimu and Limuw, hint as much.

## GIANT BEARS

Obstacles faced by the early inhabitants of North America were daunting in the extreme. Certainly, the most horrific challenge to their existence stood in the form of monstrous bears that dominated the land for thousands of years. During the conflict between brute strength and inventive intelligence, the survival of one or the other hung in the balance. The Curator of Anthropology emeritus at Waukegan, Illinois' Lake County Museum told just how close our species came to extinction on this Continent for readers of *Ancient American*'s February, 2000 issue.

 ### GIANT BEARS TERRORIZED ANCIENT AMERICA BY DR. E.J. NEIBURGER

Man has occupied the Americas for the last 50,000 or 60,000 years. His earliest habitation sites cluster in South America. But why didn't early humans settle in North America before colonizing distant areas farther south? Perhaps the answer may become self-evident in the following conjectured scenario from the distant past.

Boki finally completed the long walk over the cold and windy land- and ice-bridge later known as the Bering Strait. He and his paleo-Asian band moved south along the great water to a land beyond the glaciers. The land had dense pine forests and much game. A shadow also traveled with them. It was cast by a giant bear.

Boki and his band called the roaring creature "Gor." He was a terrible spirit, not like the more common brown or black bears. Gor was much, much larger than a big, shaggy Kodiak or ghost-white polar bear. He stood two or three times the height of the tallest man. His arms could spread the distance of two men placed head to toe. His claws were longer than a man's hand. Gor could not be killed. Many parties of warriors went out to battle him with traps, pit falls, and spears. None returned. He was a spirit with hide so thick it could stop the sharpest obsidian spear. They were unable to trap him, because his giant claws could lift his massive body out of any dead-fall pit or cave.

The paws were powerful enough to snap a tree as thick as a man's leg. No woven rope could hold him. Gor was always hungry and always near by. He followed the band of hunters wherever they camped. If they hid, he caught their scent and dug them out of their holes. He ran them down in the meadows, where he would swat the puny humans to the ground and crush their heads with a single bite. And he was clever. He often laid quietly until darkness fell, then swiftly lumbered into camp and took a human or two for dinner. Some hunters might stop to throw spears or torches at Gor. Others tried to outrun him, but always failed. Their band was growing smaller. But the monstrous bear was relentless.

Although the foregoing recreation was fictitious, Gor was not. *Arctodus simus*, the giant, short-faced bear of North America, did indeed exist. He roamed the upper reaches of the North American continent from approximately 36,000 Years Before Present to only about 5,000 years ago, at the end of the Pleistocene Age. Arctodus was a contemporary of Ice Age man, the mammoth and other giant mammals. Some scientists believe his presence was an irresistible pressure for early North American man to quickly move south and populate the warmer areas outside the monster bear's range in Central and South America. Arctodus was a giant. His fossilized bones belonged to a beast that towered 12 to 14 feet high when standing upright, 5 or 6 feet high at the shoulder when down on all fours.

Other fossils show he was 80 percent to 120 percent larger than the biggest modern Kodiak bear. Average polar or grizzly bears weigh about 500 pounds. The largest modern male polar bear is recorded at about 900 pounds. The largest Kodiak reached 1,150 pounds. Arctodus was much heavier. He was similar to a grizzly, save for his longer front legs and a pushed-in, shortened, broader muzzle. The Indiana fossil of a medium-sized Arctodus revealed a 9 foot front arm span, and an estimated weight of 2,575 pounds (776 kilograms). Fossils of this bear are a third larger than the Indiana fossil.

Extrapolating these findings, some fossil Arctodus individuals could have reached 3,500 pounds during their lifetimes, triple the size of the largest modern Kodiak bear. If we assume that the population size range of *Arctodus* was similar to that of modern bears (some individuals are twice the size of the average bear), then there probably were at least some 5,000 pound bears (twice the size of the Indiana fossil) that stood more than 20 feet tall. Fossils of Arctodus have been found in more than 100 locations, including the Yukon, Kentucky, Pennsylvania, Indiana, California, and northern Mexico. These types of slash-marks could have been made with a Clovis paleo-Indian spear point. It may be that the *Arctodus*-human interchange was not always a one way relationship.

As are modern bears, *Arctodus* was an omnivore; in other words, he ate everything—plants, as well as animals. Studies of his fossil remains show that he suffered many of the illnesses occurring in mammals today, including man. Because of his size and habitat, painful arthritis and fungal infections were common and, in all probability, kept *Arctodus* in a continuously irritated, mean mood. The enormous size and frequency of remains are the impressive aspects of this beast. Its wide distribution and physical power probably influenced the rapid human migration to Central and South America. Fossils of large animals are rare, and the recovery of 100 of them indicates a very large population, because only a minute percentage (one in a million) of any group of animals will become fossilized.

There were many Arctodus bears, and as the populations of mammoth, mastodon, giant beaver, musk ox, and sloths disappeared, man became a prime food source. How could such an animal, even if it was big, force large numbers of well-organized (tribal) humans, armed with spears, traps, and knowledge of killing large game such as mammoths, to literally run to safer areas in South America? The answer is quite simple. The bears were tougher than humans. Today, we have little experience in hunting bear with the weapons available to early Asian immigrant hunters.

It is a considerable jump from shooting a 600-pound Kodiak with a high powered, long range, semi-automatic rifle, as compared to running up to the enraged creature and poking a spear or arrow into his tough, thick hide. Even if one were about to penetrate the skin, a 5-inch-thick layer of fat covered the muscle. Five to 8 inches of muscle protected the vulnerable internal organs, so penetration power of a foot or so was necessary to inflict *Arctodus* with a fatal wound. Such weapon penetration technology was not usually available to the paleo-hunter; even if he chose to commit suicide with a close-contact assault.

The power of bears was well documented by Lewis and Clark in their report to President Jefferson (1807) concerning experiences with relatively small, but newly discovered grizzlies on their expedition to the Pacific coast. Lewis states, "The men, as well as ourselves, were anxious to meet with some of these bears. The Indians give a very formidable account of the strength and ferocity of this animal, which they never dare to attack but in parties of six, eight, or ten persons; and are even then frequently defeated with the loss of one or more of their group members."

On 5 May 1805, Captain Lewis reported a "monster" bear (later weighed at 600 pounds), which required ten shots—five of them through the lungs—to kill it." Even though severely wounded with nine shots from the .69 caliber Harpers-Ferry rifles, the grizzly chased the hunters down a 20-foot perpendicular embankment and into the river. The bear was finally killed with a 10th shot to the head. Such ferocity and danger involving relatively "tiny" bears as experienced in Lewis's report must be multiplied several times over for creatures as big as Arctodus.

Another problem encountered by early man was bear intelligence. The relative brain/body-size ratio of Arctodus was comparable to that of modern bears. This implies that Arctodus probably had the same intelligence of modern bears, who are really quite smart. Some recent news stories coming out of our U.S. national parks illustrate this point. Park bears are generally pests constantly looking for food. Hanging food from campground poles or trees became ineffective when the bears discovered how to chew the ropes and drop the food bags. Metal lockers were installed but the bears learned how to open the locks. Numerous cars were systematically vandalized by some bears who broke windows, tore off the doors, and got into the trunk area by removing the back seats. The record of this activity was a mother bear and her two cubs who "processed" 44 cars in one weekend.

Our Ancient American ancestors faced *Arctodus*—numerous, giant, ferocious, unstoppable, and intelligent bears. No wonder they quickly moved to Central and South America. They wanted to be out of range from the largest carnivore since the days of the dinosaurs!

For some unknown reason, about 5,000 years ago, *Arctodus* became extinct. Perhaps the scaled-down versions of flat-faced *Arctodus* (grizzly brown bears) or pointed-faced black bears were more efficient food gatherers in a post glacial, changing environment. It is also possible that new diseases finished off the big bears. We really do not know, but in the evolutionary-natural selection scheme, smaller-sized game often results in smaller-sized carnivores. Around 5,000 Years Before Present, North American game such as mammoth, musk, and ox, were relatively small. But before then, giant bears roamed North America, and human beings were their prey.

# MICHIGAN'S MYSTERIOUS PAST

Immense walls, pyramids, gigantic statues, and megalithic monuments such as those erected by Europeans during the Stone Age once dotted the landscape of America's Upper Midwest. Some still exist, hidden by dense vegetation or under water. Indigenous oral tradition assigns their construction to foreigners who raised these impressive structures in deep antiquity. On a quest for the identity of these long-vanished builders was Daniel Wood of Michigan's St. Joseph County Historical Society and the author of "Religious Motives for Columbus' First Voyage," as it appeared in *Discovery of the Archaeology of Spain and Portugal*. In his May/June, 2003 article for *Ancient American*, he reveals some of the hidden history of his native state.

## THE VANISHED BUILDERS OF BRONZE AGE MICHIGAN BY DANIEL WOOD

Somewhere deep within the misty twilight of prehistory, a band of intrepid explorers sailed up the St. Lawrence River. The Great Lakes were far warmer then than they are today, even balmy. The group encountered natives who probably offered various copper objects in trade. The explorers heard of vast freshwater seas at the source of copper. In time, the newcomers reached the south shore of Lake Superior.

These overseas' visitors, whose identity was so long ago forgotten, excavated hundreds of pit-mines along the coasts of Michigan's Upper Peninsula. They followed regular water routes and erected markers along the way. To avoid being caught in the hard winter, they built numerous stone calendars that would ensure they embarked for home well before the first snowfall. Regular mining continued for two thousand years. Then the mines were suddenly abandoned. While the forests gradually reclaimed the pits, native tribal peoples continued to regard the stone structures as hallowed places.

They offered tokens to the cairns' spirit-guardians in the hope of obtaining safe passage on the lake waters. French explorers learned of Michigan's freshwater seas and mountains of copper in much the same manner as their prehistoric forebears. They found stone giants guarding water routes from Detroit to Green Bay. Native Americans told both the French and the latter American pioneers that these and other rock shrines were built by another, more ancient, race. Many traditions yet exist regarding this lost race. The early 19th-century explorer Bela Hubbard noted an abundance of stone shrines in his memoirs.

During 1837, he visited a stone monument overlooking the Saginaw Bay. "Memorials of the native inhabitants were still frequent upon a swelling knoll overlooking the bay," he reported. "In the midst of a tract of country from which all the timber had been burned was a spot which seemed to have been dedicated to the evil Manitou. Here an altar was erected, composed of two large stones, several feet in height, with a flat top and a broad base. Around that area there were smaller stones, which were covered with propitiatory offerings; bits of tobacco, pieces of flints, and other articles that were of little value to the Native American, as, with religious philosophy, he dedicates to his Manitou."

While traveling along the south shore of Lake Superior three years later, Hubbard observed similar stone "altars." Of these he wrote, "We passed frequent memorials of the Indian inhabitants.... Sometimes we met a rude altar of stones, where bits of tobacco and other petty offerings were placed for the Manitou."

A very similar altar existed during historic times in Michigan's northern Gratiot County, on the banks of the Pine River. Copper, tobacco, and other gifts offered to the Manitou were placed atop the boulder. Earlier, the Jesuit missionaries observed stone slab altars throughout the Upper Great Lakes. They pulled them down believing their destruction to be a necessary precursor to conversion.

Charlevoix reported that an Indian maiden was tied to one such stone altar as a sacrifice. Fires were lit around her. Just before the flames consumed the poor girl, the chief shot an arrow into her heart. Warriors then dipped the tips of their arrows into the blood gushing from her wound to become empowered.

A veritable host of sacred rocks existed throughout Michigan, most of them natural formations that, because of their appearance or location, acquired an aura of sacredness for Native Americans. These included Red Rocks on either side of Keweenaw Bay; Doric Rock near Marquette; Portal Rock along the Pictured Rocks Lakeshore; the Vanishing Indian of the Huron Islands; and Rabbit's Rock.

Though mainstream scholars insist that Michigan's Indians did not work in monumental stone, it nonetheless seems likely that they were built by Native Americans. More troubling to define, though, are stone idols. All known examples occurred near strategic bodies of water, and the smallest were several hundred pounds. Six miles north of Rogers City, in Presque Isle County, two stone idols stood approximately 100 yards offshore at the mouth of the Swan River where dogs were sacrificed.

The Devil River Idols stood near Ossineke, in southern Alpena County, until the 1940s, when local fishermen appropriated them for use as anchors. These idols, each more than several hundred pounds, resembled human forms. The Indian name for the spot, *Shing-gaw-bawaw-sin-ek-ego-bawat*, meant "image stones," implying that they predated the Native Americans. The Native Americans did build large mounds near the mouth of the river, but the famed Jesuit missionary, Claude Jean Allouez, provided an even greater stumbling block for conventional researchers.

In Outassuac Country, an area now containing the Eastern Upper Peninsula and adjoining lands in Canada, he discovered that the natives were in possession of a most curious idol. There they venerated a statuette about 5 feet high that they "found in the country." They gave it "a beard like a European's, although the savages themselves are beardless. There are certain fixed days for honoring this statue with feasts, games, dances, and even prayers, which address it in diverse ceremonies."

Another strange idol looked out from the south shore of Alcona County's largest lake until it was lost at the end of the 19th century.

The so-called "Indian Worship" of Hubbard Lake likewise stood 5 feet tall and featured a removable head within which offerings were placed. Alcona County also once boasted of the sacred Black Rock, near Springport, as well as the more historic Mikado Earthworks and Black River enclosures. One wonders whether some of the other stone heads discovered throughout the state were once part of larger stone idols such as the Indian Worship.

The *Bab-o-quah*, a 4-foot-tall idol, once existed between Flint and Grand Blanc along an old Indian trail. A huge smiling boulder was unearthed along the Saginaw and Tuscola county lines. In 1938, yet another stone head was discovered at Merriweather, near Lake Gogebec. During 1669, members of French explorer Sieur de La Salle's party pulled down and destroyed a humanoid, painted idol that stood along the Detroit River. The natives believed that proper propitiatory offerings could guarantee safe passage on the waters. It seems the missionaries gave some credence to these claims and blamed the idol for some of their own misadventures.

The French missionary, Abbe de Galinee, wrote: "...we discovered a place that is very remarkable, and held in great veneration by all the Indians of these countries, because of a stone idol that nature has formed there. To it they say they owe their good luck in sailing on Lake Erie, when they cross it without accident, and they venerate it by sacrifices, presents of skins, provisions, and so on, when they wish to embark on it. The place was full of camps of those who wished to pay homage to this stone.... The Native Americans painted the idol to accent its crude human features."

Abbe de Galinee, along with fellow missionary, Father Dollier, blessed an axe and then set about destroying the idol. They joined a pair of canoes together to carry away the fragments up the Detroit River, where they were duly dumped. Father Galinee at once noticed a turn in their fortunes: "God rewarded us immediately for this good action, for we killed a roebuck and a bear that very day."

*The Jesuit Relations* record a virtually identical incident near the Oconto River in Green Bay, Wisconsin: "One day's journey up river from the Bay of Pauns, there are three or four leagues of rapids. At the falls is an idol that the Native Americans sacrifice to, a rock shaped by nature in the form of a human, but in which one can distinguish, from a distance, the head, shoulders, breast, and, more especially, the face which passersby are wont to paint with their finest colors. To remove this curse of idolatry, we had it carried away by main force and thrown to the bottom of the river, never to appear again."

Fortunately, James Scherz (Professor Emeritus, University of Wisconsin-Madison) and ancient copper expert Fred Rydholm have found a similar stone head on Mummy Mountain, in the Upper Peninsula. Precise measurements by Professor Scherz demonstrate that the stone head is aligned to the Huron Mountain Dolmen, facing the summer solstice. The dolmen, or artificially arranged stone monument, measuring 5.7 cubic feet and weighing 900 pounds, sits 1,600 feet atop Huron Mountain.

Four thousand years ago, it would have stood along the shoreline of a beautifully protected harbor, as a clear sentinel for mariners. Scherz believes that other stone structures in the immediate vicinity of the head were aligned with Mt. Bohemia by way of another, smaller dolmen in concert with a perched rock to calculate Lammas Day, August 1. He argues that most, if not all, of these sites were built by ancient traders as maritime landmarks. They indicated both direction and time.

Dolmens similar to those found on Huron Mountain have been located in Minnesota (Boundary Waters) and in Canada, where Rydholm is currently conducting research. A complex not unlike that at Huron Mountain only much larger, is reported along the Sanguiny River, at its entrance to the St. Lawrence. In Oakland County at least 40 cairns were discovered during 1987, not far from a large stone face.

In ancient times this complex probably overlooked a lake, long since dried up. Mainstream investigators continue to dismiss these sites as "glacial erratics," freaks from the Ice Age action. Their interpretation might be plausible if only a few such sites existed. But the sheer number of these structures, their clear analogies to counterparts in Northern Europe, and their obvious human design sink the Glacial Erratics Theory. Virtually all North American dolmens are located at strategic points along extinct water routes that existed during the Bronze Age, 3000 B.C. to 1200 B.C.

As previously mentioned, Michigan at that time was balmy by today's standards, and an Atlantic crossing was not nearly as perilous as one might think. By 7000 B.C., the Ice Age ceased to be the dominant factor in the environment of the Upper Great Lakes. A thousand years later, deglaciation was complete. Freed from the tremendous weight of the glaciers, the Lake Superior basin began a phenomenon known as "upwarping," which gradually increased the lake levels of Huron and Michigan.

The lakes of the Bronze Age belonged to the Nipissing Stage (3,000 to 1500 B.C.), a period when all three of the giant lakes were combined in one, immense body. Rising lake levels of the Nipissing Stage drowned prehistoric sites of the Lower Peninsula beneath as much as 400 feet of water. In the Upper Peninsula, however, ancient lake shore sites are now as far as 20 miles inland. This explains the dearth of Bronze Age sites in the Lower Peninsula: They are under water. The Bronze Age of the Old World and the Nipissing Phase of the Great Lakes occurred at precisely the same time.

Throughout this period, the entire region could have been navigated without portages. Thus, copper might be mined and transported without resorting to any burdensome overland routes. If we couple this fact with the purity of the copper itself, virtually free of the need for smelting, we may understand how the Michigan trade network was economically viable. The waters of Lakes Superior, Huron, and Michigan formed one enormous lake. Traders could follow the

North Bay outlet through Ontario or take the Chicago outlet to the Mississippi. Evidence exists that both routes were used. Large copper storage pits, for example, line both probable water routes.

The Torch Lake Pit is 50 feet across with a 20-foot burrow around its perimeter. This pit alone contained 20 tons of carbonate of copper and has been dated circa 1800 B.C. Pits have been found as far east as Sault Ste. Marie. Others still exist in southern Wisconsin. As many as 20 have been located in the ancient city of Poverty Point, Louisiana. The average Poverty Point pit measured 15 to 20 feet in diameter, with no regular shape prevailing. Purported to be America's oldest city, flourishing from 1500 to 500 B.C., the ancient metropolis had no real source of local copper. *Ancient American* editor Frank Joseph, has developed a provocative theory that a sophisticated copper entrepot grew-up at Rock Lake, Wisconsin. Now submerged below the lake, the city of Tyranena once acted as a collection and distribution center for Lake Superior copper, shipping it south along the Mississippi. Mr. Joseph personally coordinated research at the site, which included high-tech diving and side-scan sonar.

Underwater conical pyramids, effigy mounds, and other structures that would have stood along the ancient shoreline of Rock Lake have been positively identified. Research into the traditions of the Winnebago have revealed details of the "old foreign chiefs" of Rock Lake who dwelled in the city from roughly 3000 B.C. to 1200 B.C. Joseph believes that settlers from the Canary Islands, off the Atlantic coasts of North Africa, founded the town.

Michigan's numerous stone monuments are something more than glacial freaks. Stone circles have been located on Garden Island and Beaver Island in northern Lake Michigan. On Beaver Island alone, 39 stones form a 397-foot circle. A center stone, 4 feet high and 5 feet across, provides an axis with which the summer solstice may be observed.

Although Establishment professionals continue to dismiss the site as a natural formation, Ojibwa tribal elders maintain that the land was cleared prior to assembling the circle. Subsequent examination has established that the ground was indeed burned beneath one of the stones. Ojibwa oral tradition states that the "Ancient Ones" built the stone circle on Beaver Island, which has been tentatively date to circa 1000 A.D. Beaver Island also possesses seven medicine wheels, numerous petroglyphs, and several raised garden beds. Writing about Beaver Island, Professor Scherz reported, "While surveying rock barrels and pits near the extensive prehistoric garden beds on Beaver Island, we were told by Native Americans that ancient 'Thunderbird Lines' intersected at this old ceremonial site.

"They recounted how one such line went to the ancient mines on Isle Royale, and another south to Rock Lake, Wisconsin. Pamita, a local Native American teacher, said that rock structures now under water in Rock Lake were associated with other rock structures in Madison, Wisconsin, and with those on Beaver Island. He described the network of rock structures as long-range 'grid-lines' set up by wise men in prehistoric times. According to legend, other ancient lines arranged by the Ancients are marked by two giant, perched stones near Madison, Chamberlain Rock, and Spirit Rock. They would have been visible about two nautical miles apart. The geometry-based alignment is nearly north-south, and can be traced to other sites, such as the so-called 'Wisconsin Rapid Site' on the Wisconsin River, and then to the Ontonagon Site, near the mouth of the Ontonagon River, in Michigan. If this is not all a coincidence, it would seem that ancient wise men did indeed create a giant grid-system marked by rock structures between prominent, recognizable land-forms to aid long-distance travelers."

Numerous cairns have been reported throughout the state. Basically a pile of dry, unmortared stones, cairns were frequently erected over the dead in many ancient cultures. Others were built as crude observatories. Antiquarians Greg Bambenek and Glen Langhorst of Duluth, Minnesota term this later group as "cosmic cairns." They examined cairns at Canada's Thunder Bay that would have stood along the ancient shoreline 4,000 years ago. They concluded that the stones marked the summer solstice, both at sunrise and sunset. They believe that the cairns helped identify spawning season for the trout and whitefish in nearby shallows. In Michigan, the Black River Cairns of Negwegon State Park probably served similarly as guideposts and calendars for ancient travelers along the copper trade routes. Who actually built these structures is still open to question. Michigan's monuments closely resemble structures found throughout Northwestern Europe, home to the oldest monumental architecture in the world.

The mines themselves closely resemble those excavated in pre-Roman Cornwall. From the late fourth to early first millennia B.C., Atlantic crossings would have been less hazardous than they were in later times and should not be deemed beyond the scope of early civilized man. In fact, Bronze Age vessels were on par with those of the early Renaissance, and we know that Columbus himself visited the Canary Islands, Iceland, and Ireland (places of significance to Bronze Age Michigan), while planning his own historic voyage. Epigraphers have uncovered a number of stone inscriptions in Minoan, Phoenician, proto-Norse, and Keltic dialects throughout North America.

Conventional investigators once bristled at the very mention of these inscriptions, even accusing some epigraphers of mental illness for suggesting the inscriptions were made by pre-Columbian visitors from overseas. Recently, though, at least a few leading academics are re-thinking the work of retired Harvard professor Barry Fell and his followers, concluding that the controversial markings may have been made by arrivals from the ancient Old World after all.

Fell pronounced Michigan's Newberry Stone, composed of local clay and discovered in 1896, to be a Minoan commentary on agricultural omens. He identified the Escanaba Stone, found in the river of the same name in 1957, as a Keltic prayer-stone written in Ogam Consaine, a script in use throughout North Africa and Western Europe, most recently in Ireland, from about 2000 B.C. to A.D. 900. Fell's translation read, "A prayer on my behalf, let me not drown in the waters."

The Keltic tradition of prayer-stones continued in Scotland at least until the middle of the 20th century. Scottish soldiers were given small stones to carry in their uniforms, and sailors used to take stones from the Hebredean island of Iona to protect them from drowning. According to Fell, by 1000 B.C. Keltic mariners established small trading colonies along the eastern seaboard of North America, a land they called Jargalon, "the Land Beyond the Sunset."

In evidence of his interpretation, an Irish Keltic axe has reportedly been found on Garden Island, while numerous "Keltic Chambers" were picked up across the state. Also encountered are stone-lined caves featuring large stone lintels placed over each entrance, facing north. Plentiful in New England, Michigan has a few such caves, as well. One is said to be near Huron Mountain; another atop Beacon Hill, in Champion; two each may be found in Alger and Ontonagon counties; and one lies along the Escanaba River.

An uncorroborated report tells of a Keltic Chamber near Baldwin, in Lake County, surrounded by a group of cairns. Bronze Age Europe evidenced a powerful appetite for copper at the same time it was being mined in prodigious quantities throughout Michigan's Upper Peninsula. Likewise coincidentally, both climate and river levels favored this massive chamber. The circumstantial evidence is compounded by an abundance of material artifacts belonging to a nonnative culture. Their remains were and are situated at locations strategic to maritime commerce, and often reflect a concern for the summer solstice. Whoever the prehistoric miners were, they made every effort to vacate the mines before the onset of winter. In all reality, several different ancient groups probably visited and interacted with the lands and people of ancient Michigan. Enthusiastic amateur antiquarians dig, study, write, and report about the old copper mines. Meanwhile, the professional archaeologists turn a deaf ear to their findings.

But the sheer amount of evidence demands a new paradigm; the official framework for America's prehistory was erected on sandy soil, with no firm bedrock beneath to support it within a global context. Michigan has long been characterized as a boom or bust state. History records the commercial empires built upon her fur and timber resources. The state's 19th-century copper mines supplied as much as four-fifths of North America's demand for the mineral. And, of course, Michigan dominated the world's automobile industry for the better part of a century.

But another chapter to the state's boom and bust history must be added. Michigan copper helped build many of history's greatest empires. Because of its tremendous mineral wealth and freshwater highways, it occupied a prominent place in the Ancient World, both here and overseas. Popular recognition of this fact should thrust Michigan into the vanguard of future research into American prehistory. As Michigan was the focus of so much ancient attention, so it will be the focus of research in the future.

# CHAPTER 4:

# Pre-Columbian Visitors From the Pacific

## MAYA PYRAMIDS

Known on seven continents as the "Real Life Indiana Jones," David Hatcher Childress personifies the maverick archaeologist, bucking the academic establishment in a personal quest for the real story. At just 19 years of age, he left home to backpack his way around the globe, always off the beaten path, ferreting out answers to the enigmas of human origins beyond the reach of armchair explorers.

In 20 years of often life-threatening travel, from the overthrow of Idi Amin in Uganda to the murky depths of the Pacific Ocean in Micronesia, Childress accumulated vast personal experience of the modern and ancient worlds. This he distilled into his best-selling selling "Lost Cities" series, in addition to more than 15 other unconventional books about the deep past and alternative science. He heads up the World Explorers Club out of Kempton, Illinois, with branches in Peru and Australia. Childress was featured with Charleton Heston in the nationally televised "Mysterious Origins of Man," and appeared in "The Search for Atlantis" with Richard Crenna.

As early as the fourth issue of *Ancient American*, in January, 1994, Childress wrote of his encounter with a pyramidal anomaly in the jungles of Indonesia. It dramatized a very real link between Java and Mexico long before the first Spaniard ever set foot in Middle America.

## SEARCHING FOR A MAYA PYRAMID IN JAVA BY DAVID HATCHER CHILDRESS

I have spent a good portion of my adult life traveling around the world in search of lost cities and ancient mysteries. I journeyed all through Central and South America, and was familiar with many of the archaeological sites, especially those in Guatemala, such as Tikal and Quirigua, or Copan, in Honduras. I wrote about some of the mysteries of the Maya, postulating contacts between them and ancient Chinese and Hindus. Imagine my surprise, then, when I discovered what looked exactly like a Maya pyramid complex, complete with stelae, on a remote hillside in Java. I arrived in Indonesia from Australia, where I had been lecturing on evidence for Egyptian explorers and mining expeditions to coastal areas of that country.

After a week on Bali, I took a ferry to the main island of Java, the population center of this large southeast Asian island-nation. I made my way to Jakarta in the south-central hills of the ancient capital of the Moslem kingdom. From Jakarta, one can make easy day-excursions to such famous sites as Borobudur, the largest Buddhist structure in the world, hidden by a lava flow until the Dutch uncovered it in the early 1800s. One day, while sitting in a cafe near my hotel, I was looking through a postcard rack and was astonished to find a postcard of what looked exactly like a four-sided Maya pyramid in a jungle setting. There were even Mayan-looking stelae (carved marker-stones) around the pyramid. The site is that of Sukuh, an ancient pyramid-temple on the slopes of Mount Lawu near Sukakarta, in Central Java.

The amazing temple has stone stelae, and a step-pyramid that would match any in the jungles of Central America. I left Jakarta the next morning and took a bus to Solo, a large town in central Java and an ancient capital of one of Java's kingdoms. I checked into a hotel in the city center and began making inquiries how I might get to Candi Sukuh. I discovered it would be best to go early the next morning, so instead I took a quick trip to the famous Java Man site in a ravine a few miles outside of the city. The following morning, I took a local bus toward the mountain that the site is located on. For an hour, the bus meandered through terraced rice paddies, picking up villagers with products heading to markets.

At the small town of Karangpandan, I changed to a mini-bus headed up a minor but paved side road through the central Java mountains. I told the driver, and everyone else on the bus, in fact, that I was going to Candi Sukuh. They all nodded and assured me that they would tell me where to get off. As we rounded a hill and came to some houses along a thickly wooded section, the battered mini-bus screeched to a halt, and everyone pointed out the door. I grabbed my day-pack and bounded out into the morning sunlight. Immediately, a young man with a motorcycle helmet in one hand grabbed me by the shoulder with the other and asked, "Candi Sukuh? I take you on my motorcycle!"

I checked the directions and ascertained that the pyramid structure was at the top of a steep hill just where the bus had stopped. Apparently, it was a very strenuous, hourlong hike, but a road did not lead to the summit. I began bargaining with the motorcycle-guide

*Java's Candi Sukuh pyramid compares with its Maya counterpart, Uaxactun, or "Eight-Stone," named after an eight-year-cycle calendar found at the Yucatan site.*

and was content to hike up the hill myself, but I was also interested in seeing another nearby site, which I knew was too far to reach by foot. We struck up a deal, and soon we were off up the hill on his small motorcycle. The road was extremely steep, and it seemed that only a motorcycle or small 4x4 Suzuki jeep could make the ascent. There were the slopes of Gunung Lawy, an ancient, eroded volcano that has maintained its symmetrical shape over time.

The pyramid site was located on the knoll of a steep ridge, looking out to the west with a tremendous view of the surrounding countryside. I was amazed by the four-sided Maya-looking pyramid and the many statues that had been placed around it. A fence enclosed the main temple area, but a caretaker allowed me to enter through the gate. The structure is small, as are many Maya pyramids, only about 40 feet high. A stairway on the west side climbs the stepped terraces to a platform on the top. The pyramid, in fact, is virtually identical to those found in the ancient Maya site at Uaxactun, near Tikal. According to the guidebooks, Candi Sukuh is an ancient Hindu temple that was used up until the 15th century, when Islam became the religion of all Java, including the remote interior. Many guidebooks mistakenly call the temple a 15th-century site, though it is sure to pre-date the great Buddhist temple, Borobudur, which was covered by a volcanic eruption in the ninth century A.D.

It is probable that Candi Sukuh is thousands of years old, and may date back to 500 B.C. or even further. No serious excavation or dating of the complex has been done since the Dutch and Indonesian archaeologists turned it into a small park. One thing is certain: An extremely ancient flight of steps reached Rom the lower plains of Java to the temple-pyramid. The similarity to Maya pyramids has been noted by a number of Indonesian and other archaeologists. The popular Indonesian Handbook by Bill Dalton says this: "The shape of Candi Sukuh, with its steps leading to the upper part of the temple, is strikingly similar to the Mayan temple of Yucatan and Guatemala, which were being built at the same time!" Candi Sukuh is a controversial and mysterious structure to the Indonesians themselves, because it is a highly erotic temple, with statues of men holding their phallus, and a general sexual overtone to the complex.

One suggestion is that the temple might have been used for sex education! On the masonry floor at the top of a steep tunnel leading into the complex, a large, realistic penis faces a lovingly sculpted, swollen-in-excitement vagina carved in relief. It is believed that the temples are dedicated to the Hindu Bima, a giant warrior god of the great Hindu epic, the *Mahabarata*. A conspicuous statue at the temple is that of the winged god, Garuda, who name is also used for the Indonesian national airline. Most of the statues have been placed on the modern concrete slab, forming an inexplicable hodge-podge of sculptural styles, eras, and themes. One can see guardians holding their clubs in on hand and their penises in the other, marker-stelaes with ancient south Indian script on them, statues of Bima, or pylons with the story of Garuda. All in all, it is a baffling site, out-of-place in Indonesia, even by Indonesian standards.

Everyone who sees Candi Sukuh remarks on its obvious similarity to Maya architecture. Could there be a link? Though it may be possible that a lone sailing mission from Central America somehow washed ashore on Java and a temple was built in their honor in Maya style, it seems doubtful. Rather, it appears more likely that the ancient Hindus had some role in both the early development of Indonesia and Central America. It is well-known that ancient Hindu explorer/traders began penetrating the Indonesian archipelago many thousands of years ago. Indian chroniclers wrote of Indonesia as early as 600 B.C., and the Hindu epic of the "Ramayana" (probably much earlier) also mentions Indonesia. The early Nagas of South India, Burma, South East Asia, and Indonesia were great traders who set out through Indonesia in their large ships and theoretically sailed beyond Indonesia into the great Pacific Ocean. They might have explored the north coasts of Australia and coastal areas of New Guinea. Then they set out to the various island groups in the Pacific, beyond to Central America.

Diffusion anthropologists, such as Thor Heyerdahl, Barry Fell, and myself, believe that ancient Hindus, Dravidians, Babylonians, and Cambodians sailed in large ships along the Indonesian archipelago, and then set out into the Pacific Island groups by either going north or south of New Guinea. It is well-known that ancient Hindus explored and colonized Indonesia many thousands of years ago. The question that suddenly arises is whether the ancient Hindu Indonesians were in contact with the Mayas and influenced their pyramid-temple structures. Anthropologist Gunnar Thompson makes a good case for Taoist influence coming to Central America in his book, *Nu Sun, Asian American Voyages, 500 B.C.* Thompson starts his case by describing the ancient Shang Dynasty of China, showing its symbols and motifs (the yin-yang is the most famous, but there are many more), and then relating them to known Maya art and sculpture. In many parts of Southeast Asia, Taoism replaced Hinduism as the dominant philosophy of the time. Did Taoism supplant an earlier Hindu-style religion that had been in contact with Central America at an earlier time than 500 B.C.?

It is theorized that a succession of ancient civilizations ventured out from Indonesia into the Pacific, including Egyptians, Sumerians, Hindus and Chinese. The famous anthropologist, Peter S. Buck, who wrote the classic book *Vikings of the Pacific*, believes that the Polynesian race (of which he belonged) was descended from Indo-Malaysian groups. They obviously arrived on Pacific islands via catamaran boats. As far as the temple of Sukuh goes, its amazing parallel with early Maya temples in the Peten jungles of Guatemala, might prompt someone to ask if this design originated in Central America. Or perhaps some other, third locale? The similarities between Maya practices, such as pyramid-building, the use of stone markers known as stelae, and hieroglyphic writing, has been discussed in many diffusionist publications. Is the Sukuh pyramid proof of contact between Asia and Central America?

In looking at nearby islands around Java, one finds evidence of ancient sea-farers with a high degree of culture and science. The Indonesian island of Celebes, northeast of Java, is home to the huge and ancient megaliths of Tana Toraja. These lichen-covered stones are similar to the menhirs of Western Europe. They are certainly of a megalithic-building, maritime culture that move throughout the western Pacific region from Indonesian islands, out past New Guinea, and into the island archipelagoes of Fiji, Micronesia, the Samoas, Tahiti, the Marquesas, and the Americas. In an article for the prestigious journal, *New Scientist,* entitled, "Pacific Islanders were the first Farmers" (*New Scientist,* December 12, 1992, p.14), author Leigh Dayton points out that archaeologist J. Golson, formerly of the Australian National University, has found ditches and crude fields in this area of New Guinea.

The implication is that humans were tending plants here between 7,000 and 10,000 years ago. Dayton further points out that on Buka Island in the Solomons, while excavating Kioly Cave, archaeologists M. Spriggs and S. Winkler unearthed small flaked tools with surfaces displaying small, starch grains and other plant residue. Evidently, these tools were used for processing taro. Further, the starch grains resembled those of cultivated, rather than wild taro. The date for the find was an astonishing 28,000 Years Before Present! Dayton points out that a site at Wadi Kubbaniya, Egypt, has been dated at 17,000 to 18,000 years old by G. Hillman of the Institute of Archaeology, London. This site also had grinding stones and tuber remains, but the Solomon Island discovery was 10,000 years older!

Another new discovery is that of a Candi Sukuh-like pyramid and even a stone sphinx on a remote island off New Guinea. The site is known to even a nearby logging company, but no one to the outside world in general. This giant pyramid has only been seen by helicopter pilots and a few natives of the island. It is another example of the Hindu/Maya connection in the early Pacific. So far, no photographs of the site have come forth. No one yet knows the age of this New Guinea pyramid and its "sphinx" on a remote island near the Solomons. When some of the more than 400 gravel hills on New

Caledonia were excavated in the 1960s, they had cement columns of lime and shell matter carbon-dated by Yale and the New Caledonia Museum. They came back with a date that was set before 5120 B.C. These weird cement columns can be found in the southern part of New Caledonia and on the Isle of Pines.

Lapita pottery that is found throughout the Solomons, New Caledonia, Vanuatuy, and as far as Fiji, Tonga, and Samoa, is dated to 4,000 Years Before Present. A major site in the timber- and metal-rich Solomon Islands would make an excellent sea-colony to explore and trade across the Pacific. Here we find a connection with the Aroi Sun Cult and pyramid-building religion of the Polynesians. Their sacred island and cult-center was Raiatea, where they built massive platforms and step-pyramids by the sea, and erected gigantic statues.

In other words, the archaeological evidence abundantly supports a cultural connection from Java, home of the Candi Sukuh site, out across the Pacific Ocean to Middle America, with its comparable stone temple-platforms. Ancient pyramids still exist all over the world, from China and Indonesia to the Pacific Islands, and across the Americas. From Maya pyramids in Indonesia, or Indonesian pyramids in Central America, ancient man and his architecture spanned the globe.

# CHINESE TREASURE

Long before Columbus set out on his transatlantic voyage of discovery, Imperial Chinese vessels three times larger than his *Santa Maria* were cruising throughout the Pacific. These immense ships, imminently more sea-worthy than anything floated by Renaissance Europeans, were said to have reached the other side of the ocean at a continent referred to as Fu Sang, a land some investigators believe was North America. As though in support of their conclusion, a precious object dated to early

15th-century China was found on the West Coast and described in the December, 2003 issue of *Ancient American.*

## ANCIENT CHINESE GOLD IN CALIFORNIA BY ARTHUR D. PALMER

In 1957, Mr. Orval Stokes and several family members were hunting in the Susanville area of northern California. They had recently moved into the area and were enjoying some of the beautiful scenery, as well as the recreational hunting that was available. Even so, he had so far failed to "bag" the buck he dreamed of finding. He sat on a rock for more than an hour, patiently awaiting a good target to either appear on its own or to be flushed out into his area by other family members. Orval got up to stretch cramped muscles after carefully setting his rifle against a tree, then took a few steps and stubbed his boot on what appeared to be an automobile hubcap sticking out of the ground.

Prying it from the dirt, he realized that the object was heavier than any wheel-cover and stuffed it in his backpack. Returning home, he found the encrusted plate more difficult to clean than anticipated, so he put it aside and more or less forgot his discovery. Several years later, he made a more serious attempt with a stiff bristle brush. After a good scrubbing, the item was still dark, but he could now discern some images on the bottom. Applying a mild acid solution brought out an unsuspectedly bright sheen of bronze, brass, or gold. Unimpressed, he put it aside for another 40 years until a young Chinese couple happened to move into the neighborhood. When they heard about Orval's "discovery," they asked to see it. The husband was astounded to behold the plate, which he instantly recognized as part of a Ming Dynasty treasure. "It has been stolen and must be returned!" the man exclaimed.

*The Ming Dynasty plate found in California holds many mysteries. Did an Imperial Chinese mariner beat the Spanish to California?*

But having found, not stolen the object, Orval was not inclined to give it up to Communist China and locked the artifact in his gun-safe. On reconsideration, he approached Yixian Xu, professor of Chinese history at Idaho State University. He closely examined the plate and found a faint inscription that he was able to translate with little difficulty. The words read, "Made in the reign of Xuan De (1426-1435) of the Ming Dynasty (1368-1644)." Orval's Chinese neighbor was correct: The object was authentically Ming Dynasty; its metallurgical composition is perhaps a bronze-gold alloy.

Less certain is how it arrived in a remote, seldom-visited area of the Susanville area. Some Yurok Indians say they have Chinese blood in their veins. Could a Chinese treasure-ship have come aground off the Northern California coast sometime in the early 15th century? Perhaps Orval Stokes's discovery is physical proof of transpacific visitors to our continent from Imperial China decades before the arrival of conquerors from Christian Spain. A thorough search of the area in which he found the plate might yield additional pieces of a discovery more valuable than gold.

# MYSTERIOUS BEAR STATUE

The fortuitous discovery made by a small, pioneer girl playing in the dirt may shed light on transpacific visitors to the American Northwest long before 19th-century settlers reached the same area. This revealing, unique artifact was described in the May/June, 2002 issue of *Ancient American.*

*The Puyallup River Bear left by visitors from ancient Japan.*

2002 © Photo by Gary L. Wilson
digitalfx@swbell.net

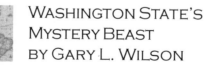

## WASHINGTON STATE'S MYSTERY BEAST
### BY GARY L. WILSON

Around 1840, a family of early settlers arrived in the Pacific Northwest, in what would eventually become the State of Washington. While digging a well, the parents noticed that their 4-year-old daughter was playing with something she lifted from the pile of loose, freshly excavated dirt. At 1 5/8" tall and 1 1/2" wide at the base, it was the representation of a bear-like creature, standing on its hind legs spread far apart, its clenched claws apparently grasping spherical objects. The weighty, solid figure was apparently composed of several metals, including bronze and—judging from traces of verdigris—copper. The base was incised with characters ascribed to no known culture, although the glyphs are plainly Asian. Attempts at determining their positive identification or the age of the artifact itself have been consistently negative.

Its Tacoma-area discovery near the Puyallup River, which leads directly into Commencement Bay in the Pacific Ocean, suggests the item may have been brought to Washington State by overseas' visitors in the ancient past, considering its subterranean find. The beast appears to be dancing, and perhaps belonged to a bear-worshiping group who were pre-Asian inhabitants of Japan, a Caucasian people known as the Ainu. Professor Gunnar Thompson devotes an entire chapter (Chapter 2, "Japanese Voyagers") of his classic encyclopedia of cultural diffusion, *American Discovery, the Real Story*, to abundant evidence for the arrival of travelers from ancient Japan along America's Pacific Northwest shore.

For example, lead tools from prehistoric Japan have been found at a site in Ozette, part of the Olympia National Park, another coastal site in Washington. The bear was likewise a sacred animal for the Haida and Tlingit, but no British Columbian tribes created metal figurines before historic times. Although no parallels close enough to make useful comparisons with the object's script are known in Asia, it may nonetheless represent proto-Japanese glyphs so far found nowhere else. Any modern or local provenance for the object seems ruled out by the circumstances of its discovery and lack of affinity with resident native cultures.

According to Dr. Thompson, Japanese sailors began arriving along the Pacific coasts of America 7,000 years ago. Given the rather high level of the figure's metal craftsmanship, a date closer to 1200 B.C. seems more likely. If so, then the little dancing bear may have been brought by Ainu or early Japanese visitors across the vast Pacific Ocean, down Puget Sound and up the Puyallup River at a time when the Trojan War was raging on the other side of the world. In any case, there must be something special about the mysterious little object, because it has been continuously treasured, handed down from mother to daughter across the generations of the same pioneer family whose little girl picked it out of the dirt more than one hundred fifty years ago.

# CORN LINKS 2 WORLDS

Gunnar Thompson graduated *Magna Cum Laude, Phi Beta Kappa*, with High Distinction in Anthropology from the University of Illinois, Urbana, in 1968. Despite his impressive academic background, university authorities "invited" him to leave their graduate program, because they found his belief in pre-Columbian contacts between the Old and New Worlds "unacceptable." Forced to change careers, Dr. Thompson earned a Ph.D. in Rehabilitation Counseling at the University of Wisconsin, in Madison, then went on to become assistant professor in Counselor Education at the University of Hawaii, Honolulu. But he never abandoned his research into prehistory, publishing his first book, *Nu Sun, Asian-American Voyages, 500 B.C.*, in 1989, and his widely acclaimed *American Discovery, the Real Story*, five years later.

In his article for the October, 1998 issue of *Ancient American*, Dr. Thompson traced the global distribution of corn during pre-Columbian times to establish the impact of India on the native peoples of the New World.

## SEEDS OF PARADISE
## BY GUNNAR THOMPSON, PH.D.

During the 1992 Columbus Quincentennial celebration, the Smithsonian Institution sponsored a special exhibit called "The Seeds of Change." According to Smithsonian curators, the 1492 Columbus voyage inaugurated the spread of New World plants across the Atlantic to the great benefit of mankind, an event often billed as "The Great Encounter," or "The Great Exchange." At the very front of this 2.5 million-dollar exhibit was a spectacular, grand archway made up of 14,000 ears of corn, or "maize," the most important food plant to reach the Old World from the Americas. Within two decades of the Spanish mariner's return to Europe, or so we are told, maize agriculture had spread throughout the world.

Orthodox historians justify the fame and glory bestowed upon Columbus by reminding us through such grandiose exhibits of the mariner's illustrious achievements. The only problem is that maize cultivation was already present in Europe, Africa, and Asia many centuries before Columbus was even born. The antiquity of maize in Europe goes back at least to Roman times. During the first century A.D., Pliny the Elder described several plants that were first domesticated in the New World. These included "henbane," or tobacco, and maize, which Pliny called "India Millet." As early as the 16th century, Spanish historian Joseph De Acosta realized that a maize-like plant was known to the ancients: "The millet that came from the Indies into Italy, 10 years before Pliney wrote about it, hath some resemblance unto mays (maize), for it is a grain, as he says, that grows in reeds and covers itself with the leaf, and hath the top-like hairs, being very fertile; all of which things agree not with millet" (Markham, 1880, 231).

Spanish archaeologists have confirmed that maize was present in the Roman Empire. Miguel Oliva found remains of the grain inside third century silos at Ullastret, along the Mediterranean coast. This "Indian mays" was a marginal crop in Spain and Italy up to the time of Columbus. Spaniards called it *panzio,* or "panic-grass." A contemporary of Columbus, the famed historian, Peter Martyr, compared *panic-grass* growing around Milan and Granada to the New World plant ("*mahiz*") that Columbus had brought back from Hispaniola in 1493. Martyr noted that the same kind of grain, the size of peas, was "found in abundance among the *Insubres* (people of

Milan, Italy) and the people of Granada (Spain)." His account was found in a letter written to the Cardinal of Sfroza and later published in his book, *Decades*. By the time of his third voyage in 1498, Columbus wrote that "there is already much maize growing around Castile." This seems rather quick for a foreign plant to replace traditional forms of agriculture. Orthodox historians have interpreted this to mean that Spanish farmers had already adopted the "new" grain from Hispanolia; but it is more likely that Columbus simply used the Indian name in place of *panzio*.

Several varieties of maize reached Europe during the Middle Ages. The principle conduit seems to have been from Asia Minor across the Mediterranean Sea in Arabian or Turkish merchant vessels. This grain was invariably called "grano de turkey," "turkie korn," "Mecca corn," "Saracens' corn," or some other variation of "Turkey grain" expressing the belief that the origin of the shipment was from the Middle East.

Botanist Leonhard Fuchs (1542) published the earliest known illustration of the maize plant in Europe with the caption, "Turchish corn," and the scientific name, *Turcicum frumentum*. At this point in time, Fuchs was convinced that Turchish corn originated in the Middle East, from where it was shipped to European ports. There is no historical indication of any suspicion among the botanist's associates that this common feed grain might be a New World import. A variety of other names given to the plant suggest multiple sources for early maize in Europe. Along the shores of the Adriatic Sea in Italy, a mysterious import (probably maize) was known as "grana de Brazil," or Brazilian grain. This name was mentioned in a commercial contract (dated 1193) between the Duchy of Ferrara and a neighboring town.

Irish legends from the same time period tell of a land called "Hy-bresail" across the North Atlantic, suggesting an early import of maize from the East Coast of North America. Icelandic explorers called the New World grain they found near Wineland, "self-sewn corn." This was recorded in a saga from the 11th century. Back home,

Scandinavians called the grain "turkie korn," possibly because it was fed to turkey fowl. This New World bird also reached Europe in ancient times. Thus began a tradition in the northern countries that *turkie korn* was unfit for human consumption; yet it made excellent feed for fowl and pigs. The earliest reported name for maize in Portugal was "milho marroco"—or "corn of Morocco"—which suggests that the Portuguese first got maize from North Africa.

Inhabitants of some German cities called the grain "Welsh korn," and it was so named in Hieronymus Bock's 1572 book of plants. Many Europeans identified two kinds of corn at the same time: There was both "panzio" and "mahiz" in Spain; England had "Turkic Korn" and "Indian corn"; Germany had both "Welsh Korn" and "Indienisches Korn"; the French had "bled d' Turquie" and "bled d'Inde." Here, "Indian" referred to the so-called "New India" that Columbus identified across the Atlantic—and that he had named in accord with Roman traditions. Such multiple names are not consistent with orthodox assumptions that maize was introduced from a single source, such as Spaniards returning from the New World. However, these names are consistent with different kinds of maize being introduced from different sources or at different times.

Botanists and historians did not have to deal with the issue of the original habitat of maize until the early 17th century. Until that time, people generally assumed that the continents were all joined together, making it easy for plants to become dispersed over land. However, by the late 1500s, it was becoming clear to geographers that the continents of the Western hemisphere, Amerigo Vespucci's "New World," were effectively separated from the Old World by great ocean barriers. Soon, botanists realized that plant domestication had to occur on either one side of the world or the other. The issue of where maize domestication took place was a perplexing problem. Europeans had a tradition that maize was first known as a plant from the Middle East; yet it was also clear that maize was an ancient feature of the New World.

Over time, there emerged two diametrically opposed factions: those who believed that maize was independently domesticated in both hemispheres, and others who insisted that maize was a New World domesticate totally unknown in the Old World until after Columbus. Supporters of the "dual-centers of domestication" paradigm included such famed botanists as Bock, Ruellius, Fuchs, Sismondi, Michaud, Gregory, Lonicer, Amoreux, Regnier, Viterbo, Donicer, Tragus, Tabernamontanus, Bonafus, St. John, DeTurre, Daru, DeHerbelot, and Klippart. They were close enough in time to accept the Turkish names for maize and traditions of Turkish imports as evidence that the grain originated in the Middle East. The botanist Tragus compared Turkish corn to plants described by Pliny and Theophrastus in the first century.

It was also apparent that maize was a traditional crop of New World civilizations; thus, two centers of domestication were indicated. Accordingly, in 1588, Tabemamontanus identified two kinds of corn: Turkish corn and Indian corn. His Indian corn was a new variety brought back from the New World, which was sometimes referred to as "India Occidentalis" or "India Nuovo" which means New India. This new variety had what he called "prop roots" and larger ears; thus, it was distinguishable from Old World varieties. The belief that the grain was known in both the Old and New Worlds is reflected in the scientific name that Linnaeus gave the plant in 1753. He called it *Zea mags*, combining a Greek word for grain (*zea*) along with the native Arawak "*maiz.*"

Opposed to the dual-center model was a growing number of botanists who insisted that maize was a New World plant that couldn't possibly have reached the Old World until after Columbus. Religious doctrine certainly played a role in their theory, for it was now popular to think of the New World as totally isolated until after the God-ordained mission of Columbus opened the way for exploration and conquest. Members of this group believed that maize could only be domesticated in one center. Strong similarities between maize found in America and Europe were regarded as proof that the plants had common parent varieties. It was also clear that maize played a central role in native American cultures, as opposed to Europe, where it was served principally used for animal feed. Therefore, it seemed evident that maize was older in the New World, and this was judged to be the single center of domestication. The Old World name for maize, "Turkic corn," was dismissed as a colloquial expression: Presumably, anything imported or of sub-standard quality was identified with Turkish merchants. So the name was regarded as a post-Columbus anachronism.

The botanist, Matthioli, was the first to ascribe a New World origin to maize in 1570. Rebart Dodoens followed in 1583, and, in 1588, Camerarius added his description of maize as an American plant. Those favoring a New World origin for maize explained the apparent and sudden spread of the new grain throughout Africa and Asia as proof of the importance of the Columbus voyage. The conclusion, based solely on tricky rationalizing, was neither logical nor supported by either physical or historical evidence. It merely served to put a positive spin on claims by the opposing camp that such a rapid and abrupt change in traditional agricultural practices was a blatant impossibility.

Loyalists of the "Columbus-Was-First" doctrine led the march to revise history by condemning the so-called "mistakes" of their theoretical adversaries and predecessors. The botanist, Herbert Prescott, lamented the popular French name for maize, *ble de Turque*, or "Turkish grain." He called it an "error" due to contrary evidence that maize was a New World domesticate. The famous Swiss taxonomist, Alphonse DeCandolle (1890), also branded the French term "an error." He based his argument on the central importance of the plant to native American culture and its similarity to the Mexican grass-teosinte. Certain assumptions also played a role in his belief regarding the origin of maize. He erroneously assumed that the oceans were effective barriers to maize diffusion until after Columbus. And he surmised that the plant was such an improvement over earlier grains that it spread throughout the Old World within two decades of the Columbus's voyage—simply because farmers appreciated a good value when they saw it.

This theory of the "rapid spread" of maize was nothing more than DeCandolle's own fantasy. Unfortunately, this fantasy was resoundingly adopted as a canon by anti-diffusionists. Any evidence that served to challenge this doctrine was condemned "out of hand." Those who brought forth such evidence were accused of disloyalty or scientific naivete.

An alternative to the conundrum is suggested by cultural diffusionists: The evidence seems to indicate that maize was carried across the oceans in ancient times, perhaps quite frequently. If the dual-centers of domestication model had been correct, then New World maize should have been significantly different from Old World varieties of corn. But all the major varieties of maize have been found in both hemispheres. If the New World isolation model had been accurate, then there should be no evidence of maize in the Old World until after Columbus. However, evidence of maize in Asia and Africa before 1492 is quite sufficient to set aside the theory of cultural isolation.

During the British colonial period in India, schoolchildren learned that maize was first brought to the subcontinent by the Portuguese, circa 1498, along with the other benefits of European civilization. At one time, historical accounts seemed to confirm this belief. *Milho* (the Portuguese word for maize) is mentioned in naval records of the region as early as 1503. Documents include inventories of grain used to feed sailors in the Portuguese fleet that sailed on the Indian Ocean.

*This 13th-century statue from India offers an ear of corn with its left hand, proof that the plant was known in the Sub-Continent long before it was supposedly first introduced to the outside world from America by the Spaniards.*

So, it would appear that a scant 11 years following the Columbus voyage, Portuguese mariners acquired the grain, brought it down the coast of Africa, introduced it to Hindu farmers, who were also taught maize agriculture for the first time, and within a short time thereafter, the grain was raised in such vast quantities that there were sufficient harvests to feed the Portuguese fleet. Considering such a seemingly miraculous achievement, it is no wonder that orthodox historians might honor Columbus for changing the world by bringing maize back from Hispaniola. However, it is now clear that this concept of maize introduction into India resulted from religious myopia and sloppy scholarship.

Mohammed Azhar Ansari and Jaweed Ashraf are among the new breed of scholars who have questioned these antiquated paradigms and the academic ineptitude of doctrinaire scholars. Ansari wondered how it was possible for Hindu farmers to change crops so radically. Ashraf noted that European scholars had completely missed ancient sculptures of maize plants on Hindu temples. And they had failed to identify vernacular names for maize in ancient religious and medicinal texts. Sculptures of Hindu deities holding maize ears are abundant in northern India, and they soon attracted the attention of American geographers. Stephen Jett provoked the wrath of isolationists with his 1976 illustration of a Hindu goddess holding an ear of maize. Orthodox scholars reacted by insisting that the item in her hand must be "a stack of beads, candy, or a pomegranate."

That speculative rationale fell apart under the thorough research of Carl Johannessen and Anne Parker from the University of Oregon. Their examination of scores of Hindu statues confirmed that the plants depicted in stone carvings had all the characteristics of maize: elongated husks, parallel rows of kernels, and silk strands at the top. Some of the items included hybrid forms of maize with two sizes of grains. Their shapes also conform to the same variety of shapes that are characteristic of maize—bulbous, conical, and elongated. Similar maize ears are present in the local markets.

Sculptures on Hoysala temples can be dated by historical accounts to the 12th or 13th centuries; thus, they are unquestionably of pre-Columbian age. According to Ashraf, the oldest sculptures of maize at Sanchi, India, date to the second century B.C. In 1995, archaeologist Dr. John Jones traveled to northern India to photograph maize sculptures. His field report is indicative of the conflict that still rages in Hindu universities between adherents of colonial-era misconceptions about maize and more recent appraisals of the evidence: "When I was at Halebid," he stated, "some Indian professors approached me to ask where I was from. Several were botanists. Excitedly, I showed them some of the carvings on the temple, and I asked their opinion of the food being held by the carved figurines. After a short discussion, they said 'corn.' I then told them of the issue of corn being a Western hemisphere plant. This created more discussion amongst themselves in the local language."

Unintentionally, Jones had ignited a controversy among the group of Hindu scholars. According to the popular version of history inherited from British colonialism, maize was regarded as a Portuguese import that transformed Hindu agriculture. However, the professors that Jones met at Halebid were well aware that the temple itself dated to the 13th century! After Jones pointed out the obvious contradiction, they must have realized at once that it was impossible for stone masons to have carved statues with ears of corn more than two centuries before the grain was supposedly "introduced" by the Portuguese. What other errors, they must have wondered, were taught as part of the official academic doctrine?

The plant sculptures on temples at Halebid, Mysore, Khajuraho, and Somanthpur are undoubtedly varieties of maize. But this plant is not portrayed here as an agricultural item—it is a sacred one! And this explains one reason why Western scholars failed to notice references to maize in ancient Hindu documents. They began with a bias towards Portuguese introduction of the plant, so they only looked for references to "*milho*" at the time of Portuguese contact. They relied on revenue documents and completely missed references in religious and medicinal texts, because they didn't bother to consider non-dietary uses of maize in Hindu culture. Furthermore, they were not proficient in the local languages (Hindi and Sanskrit), so they disregarded the ancient Vedas and Puranic texts. Jaweed Ashraf's study of maize in the ancient texts was reported in the *Annals of The National Association of Geographers of India* (1994). He traced regional names for maize backwards in time beginning with vernacular names for maize in the 16th century: *juarijwarijunhari* and *makka*. Juari Mata was the Hindu goddess of fevers; *juari* (maize) was a medicinal used in the treatment of fevers. Thus, it is only expected that maize ears would be found in temples dedicated to the goddess. The 16th century *Padrrivat of Akbar* has "juhar-i" as a royal garden fruit and a food item of the Mogul army. Another name, *lohjara*, was recognized as *maize* in several Hindu dictionaries. The 14th-century physician, Hakim Diya, used a medicine which he called *makka* or *bhutta*.

These Hindi words are still used to refer to maize in some regions of India. An Arabian traveler from this period, Tahir Maqaddasi, reported that *durah* was used on the west coast of India. This *durah* was synonymous with *khundrus*, a Hindu herb mentioned in a Greco-Arabian medicinal (the *Canons of Avicenna*). *Dura* is a common Arabic word for maize; thus, *khundrus* can also be regarded as a name for maize. The medieval dictionary of Mohammed Husaini calls *hanta* a synonym for *khundrus*. At this point in time, the plant was widely regarded as a medicinal or a garden fruit in most of India, whereas it was an agricultural crop in the mountain regions of the north. Sanskrit translator Hakim Bhua Khan (1491) identified *mak* or *makka* as the Ayurvedic medicine for fevers used between the second to eigth centuries. Sanskrit lexicons, Puranic texts, and palm-leaf manuscripts also mention a plant called *markata* or *makataka,* which is an early version of *makka* (maize).

The fifth century B.C. text *Apstharnba Sarutasutra* mentions a plant called *markataka,* the earliest recorded name for maize in India. Hindu religious texts call maize one of the 12 original plants bestowed by the gods; it is known as "the Fruit of Rama," the highest god. Such a deep religious identification of maize constitutes a strong argument that the grain or fruit was an ancient plant in India. Likewise, Tibetan traditions indicate great antiquity for maize. Among Lamanists, maize is said to be the "first" plant domesticated by mortals. It plays a central role in rituals celebrating the birth of Buddha. Such traditions are hardly consistent with claims that the plant was introduced by Portuguese traders in the 16th century. Geological and archeological findings have confirmed the ancient presence of maize in India. Radio-carbon dates for *Zea mays* pollen found in earthen cores from Kashmir fall between the third and 10th millennia B.C. Dr. Vishnu-Mittre, an Indian archaeologist, reported maize imprints on potsherds dated to 1435 A.D. at Kolhapur.

The historical record of Chinese plants is very poorly developed, thus we can only speculate on the origins of maize in this region of the world from a few brief texts. The second century B.C. *Chronicle of Ning Po* mentions a grain that paleo-botanist Heinrich Bretschneider (1870) identified as maize. Court historian Wang Yu Kie's sixth century account of the mysterious voyage by the Afghani monk, Hui Shen, to a land called Fu-Sang might be a description of maize circa 500 A.D. According to Yu Kie, the monk returned from an overseas' voyage with seeds from a new plant that had leaves similar to an oak, a stalk similar to a sugarcane, and a reddish, pear-shaped fruit (maize?). The chronicle of Anwhei, dated 1511, mentions maize as a "barbarian grain." A few decades later, a wood-block illustration in the *Pen-tsao-kung-mu* book of plants called maize "a gem-like sorghum" or "a cereal from Szechwan that was like a precious stone" (*shu-cho-yu*). Inhabitants of other provinces called maize "imperial wheat."

The Portuguese name, *milho*, is absent, even though orthodox historians assume Portuguese traders introduced the "new" grain. Whether or not outsiders inspired the agricultural use of maize, there is evidence that it was already a religious or medicinal plant. Statues found in Buddhist caves dating to the sixth century have garlands over their shoulders that were made to look remarkably similar to maize cobs. Maize is definitely featured on a ceramic mural in Shanxi Province, where a footlong yellow cob with kernels has long leaves at the base. California State University Professor, Sidney Chang, identified the mural as a ninth- or 10th-century design. In 1422, Chinese naval officers reported seeing "extraordinary large ears of grain" on voyages to Africa and India. Thus, the khan's mariners had ample opportunity to bring home samples of maize already growing in the Old World.

In his taxonomy of plants, Swiss botanist Alphonse DeCandolle observed that maize kernels had been recovered from an ancient Egyptian sarcophagus. But this he regarded as so impossible that he explained away the evidence as "the dastardly attempt of Arabs to mislead science." However, the recent identification of such New World plants as cocaine and tobacco in the mummy of Ramses III cautions against assuming that Egyptians were ignorant of maize until after 1492. M.D.W. Jeffreys has dated the introduction of maize at Ife, Nigeria, to about 1000 A.D., based on the impression of maize cobs on potsherds. Other than the kernels found inside the Egyptian sarcophagus and the Ife potsherds, the only other evidence we have to go on is linguistic.

Maize was so widespread in central Africa at the time of Portuguese colonization that some orthodox historians assumed the grain had come via overland routes from Egypt and the Sahara. Although some names suggest that maize was an occasional Portuguese introduction, most native names for maize, along with deep cultural traditions, indicate that maize was present in more ancient times. The earliest Portuguese reference to maize in West Africa is found in the chronicle of Valentim Fernandez (1502), who reported seeing *milho zabuffo* along the coast. Later writers compared this plant to *mehiz* of the West Indies. One writer even included a sketch of a plant (as maize) in the 1554 book, *Del navigatione e viaggi*.

The plant was known in West Africa as *misr*, the Arabic word for "Egypt." In a letter dated 1514, the trader Goncalo Lopes mentioned his receipt of "red corn" from Sierra Leone. John Locke, a 16th-century mariner, described a "wheat" on the west coast of Africa in 1554 that had ears with more than two hundred kernels the size of peas. British seaman Andrew Battell (1591) wrote about "wheat" in Angola that was also known as "Guinea wheat," a common European name for maize in Guinea. The natives called this grain *masa maputo*. Maize was called *clough-eub* in Zanguay and *makkary* in Fuli along the Niger river.

In both places, maize was a central part of the culture and religion when the tribes were first visited by European explorers in the 17th century. In 1746, British botanist Thomas Ashtley described four kinds of maize growing in Angola. One variety, called *massanga*, had ears a foot long. The other varieties were called *masambala, masinpeta* (or Guinea wheat), and *masamambala* (great millet). Another variety, *mazza* (or *mazza maput*), was known to the Portuguese as "Congo corn"; it was fed only to hogs. Duarte Lopez saw this plant in the Congo in 1591. Phonetic similarities between Hindu-Persian *makka*, West African *mazza*, and West Indian *maize* provide linguistic evidence of ancient transoceanic contact.

Orthodox historians contend that the African term, *mazza*, was derived from Portuguese slave merchants who brought the West Indian word, *maize*, along with the domesticated plant after 1492. However, the common Portuguese term for maize was and still is this word that seems to provide evidence for a 16th-century Portuguese role in maize diffusion—but only in a few places. One of these was South Africa, where natives called maize *mielie*, or *mealie*, a term that was probably derived from Portuguese *milho*. In 1798, the explorer Lacerda reported maize growing deep in eastern Zambia. He called the grain *milho grosso* in his field notes. Subsequently, translators compared this *milho grosso* to the Hindu *diowarri*, the Persian *durrah*, and New World *maize*. Apparently, they were all the same kind of plant.

The shippers of Medieval Europe's "Turkie korn" obtained their seeds and supplies from even more distant sources. Maize was known to the Turks as *misr* ("grain of Egypt") or *kukuruz* ("barbarian grain"). Arabs called maize *dhurah India* ("sorghum of India"), Abysinnian sorghum ("Ethiopian grain"), *bandum-i-makka* and *hanta-i-rusia* ("corn of Russia"); in Egypt it was called Syrian sorghum. Persians called maize *ghendum, ghendumi-makkah, haldah, duram-i-makka, kakui, Jao-i-barhana*, and *gandum-isahrai*. Another Persian name for maize suggests that at least one variety came from Russia, and this was mentioned in a 15th-century text. Presumably, this Russian corn originally came via Hanseatic merchants sailing across the North Atlantic.

Maize was part of the ancient, Greco-Arabian medicinal tradition of Avicenna. One of the medicinal names for maize was *hantah-i-rumi*. Medieval medicinal dictionaries regarded *hanta-i-rumi* as an equivalent to *khundrus* ("maize in India"). A medieval dictionary, the

*Nasiral-Mualyin,* mentions that *khundrus* is the Arabic name *foqowar* ("maize of India"), and this plant is known in Persia as *durah-i-makka.* The plant is described as follows: "fruit is a head of sweet white grains. The plant grows as tall as a man and resembles sugarcane." Al-Ber-uni's 1358 medicinal says that the fruit is "a cob of red, white, or yellow grains the size of peas." These characteristics identify the plant as maize. Other forms of "corn," such as millet, barley, wheat, and sorghum have smaller grains, and lack the variety of colors.

The oldest evidence for maize yet found comes from Mexico, where botanist Paul Manglesdorf has estimated the age of fossilized pollen at nearly 80,000 years old. The pollen was taken from geological core samples drilled down two hundred feet below Mexico City. In the nearby Tehuacan Valley, archaeologist Richard MacNeish found corn cobs which were radiocarbon dated to 5000 B.C. Equally important, botanists have identified two native grasses, *teosinte* and *diploperennis,* which strongly resemble the maize plant. By the time of Columbus, native varieties of maize had spread throughout both North and South America. On Haiti, Columbus found a grain that the natives called *mahiz,* a common name for the plant in the Caribbean region. Elsewhere, maize was known by a variety of native terms. In Virginia, it was called *pagatowar.* Near Boston, it was known as *nokehick* or *nasaump.* Natchez natives called it *boota copassa.* It was *sagamite* to the Iroquois. One name for maize in Brazil, *milho de Guinea,* was probably introduced along with African slaves in the 16th century. The name suggests that maize and slaves taken from Guinea were brought to Brazil. This is only one historic example of Old World maize being brought to South America, a place that already had its own local varieties of the grain.

Columbus might have brought samples of maize back to Spain in 1493. Strangely, there is no historical basis for the Spaniards or other Europeans raising crops from New World seeds until the mid-16th century (or long after Portuguese colonists supposedly introduced the "new" plant along the coasts of Africa and Asia). Native American corn, or "Indian corn," may have provided a greater yield than varieties of corn already growing in Europe. That judgment seems likely from the illustration by Tabemamontanus (1588), which shows the cobs and kernels of Indian corn from the Caribbean region to be much larger than those taken from Europe's traditional maize or "Turkish corn."

Neither the isolationist paradigm nor the dual-origin model sufficiently explains the remarkable fact that maize seems to have maintained parallel diversity in both hemispheres and also to have retained genetic compatibility among both populations. This could not be possible if maize plants were effectively isolated over a span of several thousand years.

One of the arguments put forth to support the origin of maize in China or India is the presence of primitive forms of the plant that developed during the early stages of domestication. Presumably, if maize had been imported by the Portuguese, there would be only modern varieties represented, and they would have European names such as "Portuguese millet." Supporters of the isolationist paradigm have argued that such primitive form—still growing in marginal areas—do not constitute proof of Asian domestication, because the same kinds of maize are also found in the Americas. In this instance, the isolationists assume that the primitive forms, as well as more modern maize varieties, were taken by the Portuguese to India and China. The logistics required for the Portuguese to have imported all the varieties from different areas of the Americas to Asia, while simultaneously preserving the genetic uniqueness of each variety. That would have been a formidable endeavor. Perhaps too formidable to even warrant consideration. Furthermore, there is no historical basis that this simultaneous, multi-variety introduction of maize ever took place under the auspices of Portuguese mariners.

In order to overcome the deficiencies in earlier theories of maize origins, we offer a new paradigm for maize: It is an inter-hemispheric domesticate that has been cross-fertilized on numerous occasions, as it was being domesticated in various cultural centers and simultaneously transported across the oceans at the hands of ancient explorers. This periodic separation for a time and then reunion of divergent forms undoubtedly contributed to the tremendous variety of maize plants that we are blessed with today.

# CHAPTER 5:

## The Vikings Have Landed!

## NEWPORT TOWER

Featured in Henry Wadsworth Longfellow's epic poem, "The Skeleton in Armor," Rhode Island's gaunt tower has stood at the center of an often hotly debated controversy for at least 200 years. Although mostly indepen- dent investigators point out its similarity to other structures in Medieval Scandinavia, mainstream academics, (eschewing any Norse connections), claim it was simply a flour mill once owned by the notorious traitor, Benedict Arnold. Writing in the July/August, 1996, issue of *Ancient American*, Paul Chapman poked holes in official explanations for the old building and showed how the father of mod- ern cartography helped confirm its pre-Colonial origins. In addition to Chapman's insightful articles for *Ancient American* during the 1990s, his *Norse History of America* was used as a textbook at Harvard and cited for its excellence by the editors of *U.S. News & World Report*.

*Rhode Island's enigmatic structure bears an uncanny resemblance to Medieval counterparts in Scandinavia.*

## THE NEWPORT TOWER: COLONIAL MILL OR VIKING LIGHTHOUSE? BY PAUL H. CHAPMAN

An official report that persuaded the academic community that the Newport, Rhode Island, Tower is of colonial origin is deeply flawed. In fact, it contains enough internal information to negate its own argument. In an attempt to identify the stone Tower as either the workmanship of Scandinavian visitors to America a thousand years ago or establish it as merely a Colonial Period structure, archaeologist William S. Godfrey, Jr., was commissioned to excavate it, which he did in 1948 and 1949. His findings were subsequently published in *American Antiquity* (2, 1951): "The Tower could not have been built before the latter half of the 17th century. The Norse theory can no longer be entertained."

But in researching my book, *The Norse Discovery of America*, I found that Gerald Mercator's map of 1569 actually indicated the Newport Tower at Narragansett Bay. Because Mercator published his map some 67 years prior to the colonial settlement, it stands to reason that the Tower could not have been of colonial origin. Unlike Yale's famous *Vinland Map*, Mercator's has both an identified cartographer for its source and a long history on record. It remains at the Prince Hendrick Maritime Museum, in the Netherlands. Mercator was a well-known mapmaker and leader in his field. The popular "Mercator Projection" method of constructing a map is named for him. His mention of the Tower in his pre-Colonial map seemed to be irrefutable evidence that the structure was in existence prior to the arrival of 17th-century Europeans.

Despite the Mercator find, however, Establishment experts continue to cling to obsolete theories. In 1982, the Chicago Historical Society's Archaeological Institute of America co-sponsored a symposium entitled "Vikings in the West." One of the papers presented was "Viking Hoaxes," by Brigitta Wallace. My new observations received no attention, and Godfrey's 32-year-old interpretations were dusted off. His flawed report was reverently held up as some kind of academic classic of debunking, and even elaborated upon and enlarged with no regard to its myriad of inaccuracies. In supporting Godfrey, Wallace stated that "the excavations also proved, once and for all, that an ambulatory surrounding the tower had never existed."

But Godfrey's report refers to a "possible posthole having been found in the trench which extended out from a tower opening." This may or may not have been a fence post hole, as was postulated, but one cannot rule out its having been a post for an adjoining structure. The Mercator map shows just such an adjoining structure. In any event, post holes are not required for buildings; we've had houses in America without such well into the 20th century. Dr. Godfrey dutifully dug a trench through the ground under this structure, and reported the details of his work, even including the hard evidence that contradicts his own analysis. But he was blinded to the truth he himself unearthed. Godfrey's colleagues, who welcomed his report, were, not surprisingly, likewise closed-minded or woefully ignorant of its contents. Even today's archaeological and historical communities in general still blindly accept this overrated individual's opinion, as flawed as it is, simply because he was the "expert" who proclaimed it. As Christopher Fry remarks in his play, *The Lady's not for Burning*, "What is official is incontestable."

What exactly is wrong with Godfrey's report? Surprisingly, he begins by conceding, "The weight of evidence favors the Norse theory." But then catches himself, and hastens to add, "The weight of authority favors the Colonial theory." In other words, Godfrey confesses that he ignores evidence that happens to contradict the academic powers-that-be. His admission is a revealing comment on the pathetic condition of modern archaeology. The only authority cited for the Tower's Colonial origins, however, was then Governor Benedict Arnold's will, which "mentioned the Tower." Godfrey goes on to quote from this will: "My stone-built wind-mill." Such a statement of ownership, contained in a person's will, does not constitute proof that Arnold constructed the Tower. If he had, we could assume that personal pride would have him say, "The stone wind mill I built." Arnold's will is a paltry piece of evidence on behalf of any Colonial provenance and utterly insufficient to prove the Tower's actual identity, one way or the other. More valuably, it reveals a preconceived bias.

A proponent of the Norse origin presented a map of the Narraganset Bay area, drawn in 1634, showing a settlement marked "Old Plymouth" on the eastern shore of the bay. Godfrey belabored him, saying that the author's "claim, 'it is exactly in the position now occupied by Newport,' is unsubstantiated...no support other than his basic interpretation, which is probably in error." Godfrey was nit-picking. As regards an "exact" location, "Old Plymouth" does show on the eastern shore of the bay. Newport is on its eastern shore. The position, though it may not be exactly correct, is certainly right within the degree of accuracy of the map.

Next, Godfrey condemned as a "documentary misconception" any belief that the Plowden Petition of 1632 referred to the Newport Tower. This petition requested a grant of Long Island and part of the mainland, and mentioned "a round stone tower." He argues, "Holland's contention that this refers to the tower in Newport is difficult to believe. By no interpretation of the petition would Rhode Island be considered mainland adjacent to Long Island."

In fact, however, present-day Rhode Island is diagonally across Block Island Sound from Long Island. Seventeeth century maps were not always configured north-south, and often coastal maps were lined up with the coast. Accordingly, even present-day Rhode Island would be portrayed as "adjacent."

Godfrey insisted that Narragansett Bay is not the "Vinland" of the Sagas. Here, at least, I am inclined to agree with him. The navigational research presented in my book shows Vinland located elsewhere. But this is a moot point. The *Vinland Sagas* cover a brief period of approximately 15 years, and the Norse were known to be sailing out of Greenland for a period close to five hundred years. Other settlements must be considered as possibilities.

Godfrey writes with regard to details of the Newport Tower's second-floor fireplace, "Many architects and antiquarians have debated these items fruitlessly, and on physical characteristics the Tower remains enigmatic." I have shown the position of the fireplace (including its second-floor location), and the shape and size of the window on the opposite wall, casting a beacon light from the fire down the channel. Thus the Tower served as a lighthouse. However, I was not published until after Godfrey had written his paper.

Now we come to the faulty reasoning that led the archaeologist to misconstrue his own work. He describes his discovery in the trenching operation as a blue clay on bedrock, with yellow clay next. Above this was loam containing Colonial artifacts, and then "what were probably the remains of an original gravel floor...we thus confirmed a layer of brown earth under the earliest floor." By the author's own account, the gravel was discovered during the course of the digging of the trench. Neither was it widespread across the floor. It had been found in only three places. Yet, he speculates that this was "probably the remains of an original gravel floor."

First, he assumes the gravel was throughout this upper level. Next, he assumes that it was flooring material; and finally, he assumes it was the original floor. Evidence exists for none of his assumptions. Godfrey overlooked or was in ignorance of the use of clay as a flooring material. The Norse, in their sod houses, utilized clay for floors. On a research visit to the Faeroes, I found one such house still standing. It was surprising how neat and clean the floor appeared, similar to linoleum. As for the top soil to which he refers (the brown dirt), it would seem far more likely that it was an accumulation since the structure's original construction. Likewise, the archaeologist's assumption that the three scattered spots of gravel represented the original floor simply cannot be accepted. A floor should go wall to wall, and there is no indication that it did so.

Second, there is no reason to believe gravel would have been used as flooring in the first place, when a perfectly good clay was already located there. Another explanation for the spots of gravel seems more logical. Construction work was done within the tower during historical times upon at least two occasions, as noted by Godfrey. In addition there were two more obvious construction projects on the outside: a cement walkway and an iron fence imbedded in concrete. Each of these would have required gravel, and in the days before cement mixer trucks, gravel was brought along with the sand and cement to a construction site then stored where possible in a sheltered area. The Tower could have served such a purpose.

They then concluded that because the Colonial artifacts found in the top soil were below the floor level, the structure was Colonial. Unfortunately for these conventional investigators, the entire thrust of their report was based on this gravel assumption. In the center of the Newport Tower, treasure hunters once dug a pit, reportedly 4 to 5 feet deep. Theirs was not the only instance of an on-site disturbance. The archaeologists themselves named another area the "barbecue pit" because of the large quantities of bones and charred wood found within it, the refilling of which they described as "haphazard." During the period 1930 to 1948, maintenance crews "dug out the center of the Tower, and at the end of the 1948 season, added topsoil."

But the most significant of the prior investigations is revealed not in the archaeologist's diggings, but in another written report that he cites. This refers to "Catherwood's measured plans of 1837, which show 16 inches of the north column drum exposed." The importance of Godfrey's "floor level" line of reasoning becomes apparent. He was only looking for selective evidence to substantiate his Colonial Origins Theory, which alone interested him. Having already dismissed any consideration of a possible pre-Colonial provenance for the Newport Tower, his agenda focused exclusively on finding proof for his politically correct assumptions. Godfrey writes, "to observe this area I pried several loose stones at the column base, but it was impossible to tell whether they were the top-most foundation stones of the plastered drum. In the brown earth, protected in its position by one of the stones which we removed, was a small gun flint and a fragment of plaster. These objects were in the brown earth under the edge of the column."

The author previously argued, and with good reason, that "it must have been necessary to fill in the construction trench (around the foundation stones) before the above ground building was begun, for the foundation stones were not mortared or fitted in any way. Apparently this refilling was done before the foundations were capped with mortar." Continuing, he writes "excavations on the inside of the vertical columns disclosed that the yellow-olive clay which refilled the construction trench, as well as a very thin layer of loam, actually covered part of the foundation stones before the mortar cap was poured...on these prepared mortar surfaces, the columns were then built, the stones perhaps roughly shaped after setting and the drum then plastered."

As can be seen from the previous, the plastering of the walls and drum took place after the foundation stones had been backfilled and mortar capped. For a piece of the plaster to have made its way underneath could have happened only during some sort of excavation. Any such opening would have also enable the "small gun flint" to enter the same area.

The case for a Colonial construction date of the Newport Tower has not been proven. Establishment archaeologists, historians, and anthropologists who have accepted Godfrey's conclusions at face value need to have a further look at his evidence. In whatever year its foundation was laid, the Newport Tower's pre-Colonial origins are certain. And though nothing else like it was erected in New England, its close resemblance to structures built along the coasts of 11th-century Sweden underscore its identity as a Viking Age lighthouse for Scandinavian voyagers from across the North Atlantic.

## MAINE COON CAT

An *Ancient American* article that attracted attention from as far away as New Zealand and Holland, and drew reader response for years after its first publication in the September/October, 2002 issue described a New England feline with a pre-Columbian pedigree. Sally, the Maine Coon in question who posed for the original article, has since moved on to Valhalla, but her memory and the impact of her kind on the prehistory of our continent lives on.

## THE VIKING CAT THAT DISCOVERED AMERICA BY FRANK JOSEPH

DNA research is not only revolutionizing police work, but uncovering otherwise unknown historical information with no less revolutionizing consequences for our understanding of the past. A case in point is the unexpected solution of an old controversy surrounding the Maine Coon Cat. The breed has long perplexed biologists, because they were unable to explain its unique appearance or trace its origins. The animal derived its modern identity from the state in which it is primarily found, although smaller populations appear in the Atlantic coastal regions of New Brunswick and Nova Scotia.

Somewhat larger than the average housecat, specimens of 10 or more pounds are common. But the beast is best known for its unusual hind-quarters, which resemble those of a raccoon; hence, its name. Moreover, its bushy tail, brown and white striped markings, together with an occasional tendency to wash its food, helped to promote its reputation as the result of unions between cats and raccoons. But such crossings are biologically impossible, because raccoons are not felines, but canines related to members of the dog family.

In an attempt to trace the genetic origins of the singular Maine Coon Cat, scientists subjected it to DNA testing last year for the first time. The results were as clear as they were surprising: The Maine Coon is the direct descendant of an unknown, domestic breed that went extinct within the last few centuries and the *skaugkatt*, or "Norwegian Forest Cat," brought to our continent from Scandinavia 1,000 years ago. As the Website for the Cat Fanciers' Association explains, "These are the cats that explored the world with the Vikings, protecting the grain stores on land and sea, and are believed to have left their progeny on the shores of North America, as a legacy to the future. Is their Norse name accurate? Yes, the *skaugkatt*, meaning 'forest cat,' really did come out of the Scandinavian forests in the last 4,000 years."

*The Norwegian Skaugkatt from which Sally descended is known in Scandinavia as the "Mountain Fairy Cat" for its singular ability to scale vertical cliff faces.*

Because the large animals are determined hunters, they were invariably taken aboard Viking expeditions to keep the long-ships free of vermin. When the Medieval Scandinavians landed along North American coasts, some of the "wegies," as they are commonly nicknamed in Britain and the United States, jumped overboard, and mated with that unknown domestic breed that no longer exists. The living descendants of those early days in Viking America are today's Maine Coon Cats. Their majority presence in the state that gave them its name suggests that the Norse did more than briefly establish a settlement at L'Ans aux Meadows, as mainstream scholars insist, but went on to colonize other parts of the Eastern Seaboard. Concentration of the Maine Coon's population in that state implies that the Vikings' elusive Vinland was in Maine after all.

The Maine Coon's descent from Norway's Forest Cat is unmistakable. The *skaugkatt* is somewhat larger; its fur texture is not quite as silky; the head shape is slightly different; tufts, not seen on its American counterpart, sprout from the tips of its ears, and, most noticeably, its hind legs are straighter. But physical and behavioral comparisons leave no doubt that it is the ancestor of the Maine Coon Cat, as confirmed by DNA research. In a happy coincidence, the *skaugkatt* was designated Norway's official cat by King Olaf late in the last century, about the same time the Maine Coon was named the official cat of the Pine Tree State. Connections between the two are valid evidence for Medieval Norse in America, centuries before Columbus. Anyone who wants to meet a direct descendant of the first Viking visitors to our continent need only make the acquaintance of a Maine Coon Cat.

## RUNESTONE HOAXES

Of the several alleged Midwestern runestones, all allegedly carved by Vikings before the 16th century, specimens in Minnesota and Oklahoma are the most famous. But for conventional thinkers, the year 1492 represents a permanent barrier over which no one from the Old Worlds of East or West could have crossed to America. Hence, any contrary "evidence" must be, *ipso facto*, false—part of a conspiracy to fool respectable scholars. Such a closed-minded attitude is the precise opposite of scientific thought, which is based on a suspension of judgment until all relevant facts have been presented. Even so, it is precisely this kind of academic myopia that dominates Establishment archaeology, at least in the United States.

In the opening sentence of his article for *Ancient American's* November/December, 2002 issue, Dr. Haines concedes that "it is now generally accepted" that the Norse arrived in the New World long before Columbus. He fails to mention, however, that the Establishment critics who currently dismiss the Minnesota and Oklahoma runestones as fraudulent are the same naysayers who for years denigrated the merest suggestion of a Viking presence in Labrador, until they were overwhelmed by the evidence. Moreover, his theory that the Oklahoma runestone was actually made by late-16th-century German farmers is patently wrong because: (1) the Heavener inscription was chiseled in Old Norse and (2) it would have made no sense for the immigrants, who spoke only German and a smattering of English, to have carved a monumental territorial marker in a dead language they could not understand!

Contrary opinions, such as those espoused by Dr. Haines, are nonetheless welcome by *Ancient American* readers, who believe the truth may be ascertained only if all points of view are freely considered.

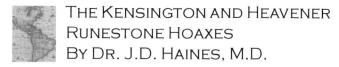

## THE KENSINGTON AND HEAVENER RUNESTONE HOAXES
## BY DR. J.D. HAINES, M.D.

It is now generally accepted that the Vikings were the first Europeans to set foot in the New World. But were they also the first white men to discover Minnesota and Oklahoma?

Though Leif Ericsson is believed to have sailed from Greenland to Baffin Island, Nova Scotia, Labrador, and perhaps Newfoundland, further explorations into the North American interior seem unlikely. When Ericsson returned to Greenland in 1012 A.D., he called his discovery "Vinland," because he had observed grapes and wild wheat growing there. His journey was described in the book *Greenlander's Saga*. Recent archeological research has confirmed authentic Norse artifacts in the Arctic, Labrador, Newfoundland, and the Gulf of St. Lawrence, substantiating the old histories. Beginning in 1837, evidence of Norse explorations far into continental America was first proposed. The two sites were in the New England area at Cape Cod and Newport, Rhode Island, and deep into the Midwest, at Kensington, Minnesota, an incredible 4,000 miles (as the crow flies) from Greenland.

Interest in Norse visitors to present day America peaked in 1837 due to the publication of *Antiquates American*, by an Icelandic-Danish antiquarian, Carl Christian Rafh. The romantic image of bold Nordic warriors conquering the New World stirred the public's imagination. Over the next 150 years, a total of 52 sites, 69 artifacts, and up to 100 inscriptions were cited as evidence of Viking explorations throughout North America.

Two of the most famous sites in the American Midwest are the Kensington Stone, in Minnesota, and the Heavener Runestone, in Oklahoma. Initial enthusiasm over the discoveries has greatly diminished among all but the most blindly devoted of believers. Unfortunately, both of these hoaxes have been formally memorialized by state museums, so the joke is now on the taxpayers. The stories of the Kensington and Heavener Runestones are instructive as examples of the influence of pseudo-science today.

In 1898, the Kensington Stone was discovered on the Minnesota farm of Olof Ohman. He was a Swede who had immigrated to America in 1879, and bought his farm from a Norwegian. Ohman claimed that he found the curious tablet-like stone bearing ancient runes buried on a small wooded knoll. The stone was supposedly tangled in the roots of a tree. The runic text featured on the stone describes a party of 30 Scandinavians traveling westwards from "Vinland" (presumably Maine or Labrador) to what is now north-central Minnesota. The inscription reports that 10 people in their group were massacred. All this was supposed to have taken place in 1362 A.D.

The discovery of an authentic runestone in Minnesota was highly unusual, because the custom of erecting runestones had not been transferred from Scandinavia to Iceland and Greenland. The stone itself was also unique, in that the runes were cut with a chisel and punch, with all cuts clear and sharp. In Scandinavia, runes were always pecked with a pointed hammer. In addition, the runes were arranged in the fashion of a book page, rather than the typical Scandinavian practice of carving runes around the periphery of the stone. When Ohman made known his discovery, the runestone was shipped to Northwestern University, where Dr. G.O. Curme examined it. The professor claimed that the message was written in modern Swedish and incorporated recent runes. He also commented on the freshness of the cuts, which lacked patina, like the rest of the stone. Curme dismissed the stone as a joke and returned it to Mr. Ohman. It was later revealed that Mr. Ohman had been trained as a mason and that some of the runes showed peculiarities similar to the dialect of Sweden where Ohman was from. Ohman also owned two books of runes and knew how to read and write runes, as did many 19th-century Swedes.

The stone would have been most likely forgotten, if not for an ambitious book salesman and amateur historian, Hjalmar Holand. Nine years after Ohman's find, Holand set out on a lifelong crusade to convince the world that the stone was authentic. Up until his death in 1963, Holand never wavered, continually seeking corroborating evidence including artifacts, documents, and other runestones in the area.

Ohman did not admit to having carved the stone himself, but there may have been a legal reason. After acquiring the stone, Holand attempted to sell it to the Minnesota Historical Society in 1910. Holand's asking price was an exorbitant $5,000. Ohman objected to the sale, prompting the historical society to launch an official investigation, which included the authenticity of the stone. If Ohman had carved the stone himself, he undoubtedly would have feared that the hoax would be exposed, making him guilty of fraud against the state. In these circumstances, it is understandable that Ohman would not have admitted to carving the stone. The following year Ohman accepted $100 from the historical society for the stone but refused to discuss the matter further for the rest of his life. Following Holand's death, two American researchers, Alf Monge and O.G. Landsverk, added a new twist to the runic translations. They claimed that the runes contained hidden messages in the form of cryptograms.

The Kensington Stone fostered new discoveries of artifacts on the east coast and Midwest. So-called Norse battle-axes were later found to be early American lumbering tools. Particularly amusing were the discovery of 30 small "halberds" throughout the U.S. When it was observed by critics that the halberds were too flimsy to be used in battle, proponents quickly dubbed them as ceremonial halberds. Holand vigorously defended the halberds as authentic. When no similar examples could be found in Scandinavia, he pronounced them so rare that even Scandinavian museums did not have examples. Research showed that the halberds were actually 19th-century tobacco cutters distributed as part of an advertising campaign for the Battle Axe Tobacco Company. The cutters were manufactured by the Rogers Iron Company in Springfield, Ohio. After having outlived their usefulness as plug tobacco cutters, they were removed from the hinged attachment to a cutting board and used as hatchets. Some were reportedly popular for decapitating chickens. The Kensington Stone is very similar to another rune stone hoax, this time in Oklahoma. A stone with strange carvings was supposedly known to Choctaw Indians after their removal to eastern Oklahoma, in the 1830s. The stone was rediscovered by white settlers, who established the town of Heavener, in 1894. The stone was locally known as "Indian Rock," because the carvings were presumably made by a Native American.

It was later determined that the carvings were runes, prompting local resident Gloria Farley to embark on a lifelong crusade to prove that the inscription was made by Vikings who had journeyed to Oklahoma nearly 1,000 years ago. She reported the runestone to the Smithsonian Institution, whose directors responded that, although the runic text had been made by someone familiar with Scandinavian grammar, it was doubtful that Vikings inscribed it. Farley persisted in her belief, however, and was aided by historian Ole Landsverk and cryptanalyst, Alf Monge.

The Heavener inscription consists of eight runes, which reads; GAOMEDAT, or GNOMEDAL. By reversing two runes that appear to be different from the others, the inscription becomes GLOMEDAL, or "Glome's Valley." GNOMEDAL can also be translated as "Sun Valley," "Monument," or "Boundary." Alternatively, the inscription could be G. Nomedal. Nomedal is a Norwegian family name.

Monge, the cryptologist, proposed that the inscription was a cryptogram for the date 11 November 1012 A.D. This explained why two runes were from one Norse alphabet and the other six were from another. Monge claimed that Norse markers were known to mix alphabets to conceal dates in crypto puzzles. Several other runestones were found near the towns of Poteau and Shawnee, giving rise to a theory that the runestones were boundary markers. If this is accurate, the translation of Gnomedal as "boundary" may be the correct one.

Even though all attention directed towards the Heavener Runestone has centered around supposed Viking origins, Leslie McRill advanced a theory in 1966 that seems much more plausible. French explorers claimed the entire Mississippi Valley for France in 1682. New Orleans was established in 1718, and became the capital of the French Colony of Louisiana four years later. Louisiana covered the central third of the present-day United States, including all of Oklahoma. Captain Jean Bossu of the French Marines described two German villages upriver from New Orleans in 1751. He had been sent to assume command of a duchy or grant in the Illinois country. Captain Bossu stated that the German villages had earlier settled further up the Mississippi and on the Arkansas River.

As Bossu wrote, "These two villages, peopled with Germans, are the remainder of a grant made in 1720 to Mr. John Law, a

Scottish financier and gambler who formulated a wild Louisiana business speculation scheme in France that led to a financial panic known as the bursting of 'The Mississippi Bubble.' The colony was to consist of Germans and Provencals to the number of 1,500; the ground for it was four leagues square, and near a wild nation called the Arkancas (sic); the colony was erected as a duchy...But Mr. Law failed, and the India Company took possession of the goods."

Leslie McRill maintains that because the French were establishing duchies or grants out of New Orleans, the Heavener Runestone may well have been a marker for such a grant. Dr. Muriel Wright of the Oklahoma Historical Society agreed. Danish archivist, Kaj Monrad, noted that the rune for "n" is written as a Swede would write it. Interestingly, Captain Bossu notes that a Swedish captain supervised the two German villages. Bossu names him as a "Mr. Arntsbourg, who was at the Battle of Poltava with Charles XIII."

There is abundant proof that the French explored and traded along the Arkansas River and its tributaries in present-day Oklahoma during the 1700s. It is also known that the French visited present-day Le Flore County, where Heavener is located. It seems entirely possible that someone familiar with runes, such as Swedish Captain Arntsbourg, inscribed the stone as a boundary marker for one of the French duchies. The alternative of Vikings sailing from Greenland to the Gulf of Mexico, up the Mississippi River, then up the Arkansas River into Oklahoma 1,000 years ago seems highly unlikely. Especially when the only evidence is eight runes carved on a rock.

The French left behind numerous remnants of their culture in North America, as did other Europeans. Yet nothing that can be scientifically verified confirming a Viking society has been uncovered. Experts universally agree on one point; the inscriptions were not Native American in origin. Gloria Farley has claimed that the white settlers in the Heavener area were illiterate and incapable of carving runic inscriptions. This is of course false, as numerous Europeans wrote extensively of their explorations in this part of North America in the 17th and 18th centuries. The proponents of the Viking origins for the runestones have employed virtually every form of flawed reasoning, including appeal to myth, shifting the burden of proof, argument by authority, irrefutable hypotheses, and others. These are all common methods of pseudo-science favored by proponents of myths and hoaxes.

In a testament to the unending quest for the tourist dollar, both the Kensington and Heavener Stones are the centerpieces of state parks. This despite numerous doubts that have been cast on the Viking hypothesis. The myth of the Vikings in the Midwest will persist as long as verifiable scientific fact and logical reasoning are absent from the beliefs of their proponents.

# 15TH-CENTURY RUNESTONE

Contrary to ill-founded opinions of the Kensington Runestone as a transparent hoax, application of the hard sciences with state-of-the-art research technology has confirmed the 15th-century Norse provenance of its inscription. Also, its re-examination reveals internal evidence for of the runic text's authenticity unknown to scholars in the 1890s, when the Stone was discovered. News on the latest disclosures about the controversial artifact appeared in the December, 2000 issue of *Ancient American*.

*The Kensington Runestone's age could have been determined shortly after its discovery in 1898. But examiners at Washington, D.C.'s Smithsonian Institution scrubbed it clean of all datable evidence.*

## MINNESOTA'S RUNESTONE IS AUTHENTICATED BY HAROLD BLAUZAHN

On 8 November 1898, a Swedish immigrant was clearing his Minnesota farmland near Kensington, about 120 miles northwest of Minneapolis, when he made an unusual discovery. Entwined in the roots of an old, dead poplar tree was a peculiarly shaped boulder of graywacke granite, a kind of hard feldspar. Measuring 36 by 15 inches, and 6 inches thick, the rectangular slab was covered on two sides with lines of strange letters. They were runes from a syllabary used by Vikings during the Middle Ages.

Scholars in the archaic Scandinavian languages were able to translate the inscription, which described a company of Norsemen arriving in what is now Minnesota from across the North Atlantic Ocean, 130 years before Columbus supposedly discovered the New World. A revised translation first presented by linguistic expert, Dr. Richard Nielsen,

Contributing to this catastrophe were predatory merchants of Germany's Hanseatic League. Theirs was a corporation of Baltic states formed into an economic alliance for the acquisition of large, valuable territories from the ailing Swedes and Norwegians. In 1360, Keyhoe said, the Hansa took over the vital sea-ports at Bergen and Skahne, rendering the Scandinavian kingdoms almost bankrupt. It was then that the Swedish and Norwegian monarchs began developing long-distance trade routes as far afield as Novgorod, in the Ukraine, and Byzantium.

To make matters worse, they learned of an Oxford friar who published a book about his travels to Greenland and unknown territories further west. Concerned that the English would beat him to the discovery of new resources, Norway's king, Magnus Eriksson, issued a royal decree in 1355, ordering a fact-finding mission to investigate conditions of Greenland's Norse colony and beyond. Headed by Count Paul Knudsen, the expedition returned in 1364, just two years after the date appearing on the Kensington Runestone. The report he delivered to the new king, Hakon Magnussen, described his adventure as a "journey of discovery."

To underscore this historical context in which the Kensington Runestone was inscribed, Keyhoe remarked that similar runestones are most abundant in Sweden, where they were likewise erected as memorials to the dead. So too, the text of the Minnesota runestone tells of a mixed company of Swedes, some of whom died at the hands of American aboriginals. Some 5,000 runestones are known throughout Scandinavia, most of them in Sweden.

Researcher Barry Hansen spoke at the Conference of the "bullet-proof" testing he organized to unlock the Kensington Runestone's secrets. The professional geologist he engaged was Scott Walter, who said his investigations revealed that most if not all of the artifact's runes had been individually "gone over" with a modern tool sometime after the object's discovery at the close of the 19th century, probably to make the weathered letters more easily discernible. This tampering caused skeptics to declare that the inscription had been newly created.

But Walter's microscopic scrutiny of the runes showed that the modern scratches were made on top of the original runes carved centuries earlier, as indicated by oxidation residue surrounding each of the written characters. Comparing variously weathered areas of the Stone's exterior likewise suggested a date for its inscription anterior to the 1898 discovery by at least several hundred years. Another new find comprised a series of chisel marks someone made to break the Stone free from a larger boulder, something the old Minnesota farmer was unlikely to have done on behalf of a hoax from which he received only lifelong scorn, not profit.

Dr. Nielsen demonstrated that arguments most commonly used to fault the Runestone's Norse provenance actually helped establish its artifactual identity. Opponents of its pre-Columbian authenticity insisted that certain words, numbers, grammatical marks, and individual letters of the inscription were not found among Scandinavian runic writing until historic times. The English "fromm" for example, appears in the Kensington text, but was allegedly unknown to 14th-century Scandinavians. Nielsen, however, found contemporary Swedish manuscripts that do indeed use "fromm." The letter "J," too, supposedly never appeared as a rune, until Nielsen produced several 14th-century examples.

Conventional scholars argued that the highest runic number was only 19. Yet, the number 22 is cited in the Minnesota inscription. Dr. Nielsen presented 14th-century runes going as high as 26.

An early expert in Old High German pointed out what he took for umlauts over several of the Kensington runes and concluded that the Stone must be fake, because umlauts were not introduced until the 17th century. The double dots do not represents umlauts, however, but were part of a grammatical convention in use throughout the 1300s.

Perhaps the most persuasive of Dr. Nielsen's evidence was that of an "E-dialect" evidenced by the Kensington Runestone inscription. Olof Ohman, the Swedish immigrant who found the Stone and was subsequently accused of faking it, spoke an "A-dialect" used in his native Rosander; he was ignorant of the "E-dialect." The text mentions a mixed crew of Goths, or men from Gothenland and the island of Skahne, where the "E-dialect" was spoken.

In a paper distributed to Conference members before his presentation, researcher Arne Brekke pointed out that no less than 11 Medieval rune-forms on the Kensington Stone were unknown to scholars in Ohman's day, but have since proven correct. Also, a dozen old Swedish words (some only recently found) not published in any Middle Ages lexicon of the late 19th century appear on the Runestone. It additionally features Medieval manuscript abbreviations unknown to Scandinavian experts in 1898. In order for Ohman to have faked the Runestone, he would have had to induce "Mineralization within the carved out runes after they were carved," said Brekke, and "induced mica degradation on the split side of the Stone to match a five hundred-year effect."

In 1974, when a hedge was constructed for a memorial plaque in the place where the Stone was found, workers uncovered rock fragments of the same material as the Kensington Runestone. They were located about 60 centimeters (23.62 inches) below the ground surface. This is a clear indication that the Stone was cut in the place where it was found, and long before Ohman's time.

In a statement faxed after the Conference, Barry Hansen declared that "the Kensington Runestone has 24 rune-forms which were 'strange' according to the experts, who then concluded that it was a fraud. All were later proven to have been in use on the island of Gotland in Medieval times. Several of them were unknown to any expert in the world in 1898. These experts claimed that the forger (an uneducated farmer) 'invented' them, when the experts themselves could not explain them. The Kensington Runestone has about a dozen words that were claimed by numerous experts to be 'impossible for the 14th century, and, therefore, the Runestone is a fraud.' Those words have now all be found in the Medieval records of Dalsland, Bohuslan, and Vastergothland (all in the same area of western Sweden), and verified in the peer review process. If no expert in the early days of the controversy knew, then how did the forger?"

"The Kensington Runestone displays a pentadic numbering system for the date and six other number groups. This was declared to be impossible. It has now been shown to not only have been possible, but likely for someone from Gotland in the 14th century." Hansen said further testing is planned for the immediate future. "Over the next few years, we hope to look closely at mica degradation, mineral formation, coatings and alterations using scanning electron microscopy, differing weathering of calcite-graywacke, incipient weathering with 3-D laser imaging, differential mineral absorption as a result of standing up-right in the ground, a root stain on the backside of the Kensington Runestone, detailed analysis of the effect of iron tools used to carve the stone, origin of the original Greenbelt graywacke boulder, and more."

Though additional testing must reveal more information about the Kensington Runestone, its professional skeptics, in their traditional refusal to consider data contrary to consensus-reality, will just as surely refuse to budge from entrenched opposition to its Old World inscription. But their intransigence is rendered irrelevant by the facts, which confirm that the controversial Stone is an authentic monument to Norse sea-farers in Minnesota long before Columbus landed on the beach at San Salvador.

## HEAVENER RUNESTONE

Cyclone Covey, Ph.D., is Professor Emeritus at Wake Forest University, in Winston-Salem, North Carolina. One of the very few academic luminaries courageous enough to brave the opposition of his scholastic peers, he has been an outspoken proponent of cultural diffusionism for more than 40 years. The "futhark" he mentions in his article for the May/June, 1994 issue of

*Ancient American* is the name of the runic alphabet, comprising its first five letters; the third and fourth were combined in a single glyph. At least three different "futhark" sets are known, and were created centuries apart. Their appearance on the Heavener Runestone points up the Norse authenticity of its single, inscribed word.

## OKLAHOMA'S GIANT RUNESTONE BY DR. CYCLONE COVEY

During the 1830s, soon after the forced removal of aboriginal tribes into Indian Territory, Chocktaw hunters roaming Oklahoma's vast, vacant, forested hills came upon a huge, mysteriously inscribed stone in the idyllic vale of Poteau. There it had stood immemorially hidden in its remote ravine for more years than anyone could guess. In the following century, a local girl first hiked to the stone when no path yet led the 2 miles uphill from her home in Heavener. A precocious youngster, Gloria Farley realized that the large characters carved on the "Indian Rock" were not ordinary letters. They were runes belonging to the written language of Northern Europeans in the Middle Ages.

In 1951, after moving back to Heavener from Ohio, she renewed her childhood interest in the stone by clearing away obscuring lichen growth, measuring the protective semicircle of 40-foot-high, overhanging cliffs, and began a serious study of this "ancient billboard," as she described it. The huge stone in question was an upright gray slab of very hard, fine-grained, Pennsylvanian Savanna sandstone, 12 feet high, 10 feet wide, and 16 feet thick. According to geologists, it once fell off the cliff above and landed in its present position many thousands of years ago.

*The one-word inscription of the Heavener Runestone could only have been left by someone conversant in Old Norse.*

The large runes, 6 1/2 to 9 1/2 inches high, stretch horizontally nearly 2 yards across the west face of the smooth rock face. Tool marks, one-quarter to three-sixteenth inches deep, were detectable although the sharp-chiseled edges had been rounded by long-term weathering, despite the natural shelter. Gloria's name and investigation of the "Heavener Runestone" were already famous throughout Oklahoma by the time I examined the *cause celebre* of her life in May, 1965. That was before it was fenced off in a state park. A few days later, I beheld a replica of the Ruthwell Cross and other large British runestones in the National Museum of Scotland that bore the same and similar characters as their Oklahoma counterpart. Even then, no special acumen was required to recognize that the Heavener engraving consisted of letters from the older, 24-rune *futhark*, not the later 16-rune *futhark* or any combination of the two.

Two years following my first visit to Heavener, Norwegian cryptologist Alf Monge claimed to have identified six of the Oklahoma runestone's letters from the older, longer futhark, together with but two from the later set, in order to decipher the inscription as a medieval crypto-puzzle signifying a specific date: November 11, 1012, or St. Martin's Day. A former army cryptanalyst, Monge went on to assume that every alleged runestone in North America similarly recorded important dates, all of which fell in the 11th century, because Thorfinn Karlsefni's saga-attested expedition to Vinland took place after 1000 A.D. By that time, however, the old style of certain Heavener rune-forms had already fallen out of use for nearly 500 years.

Minnesota's Kensington Runestone is unquestionably inscribed with the year 1362 A.D., and its grisly message is consistent with 14th century style runes. But the Heavener Runestone is in third, to 5th century style. Monge interpreted its single, inscribed GNOMEDAL to make his date come out right. In 1961, the expert in Viking culture, Frederick Pohl, himself of Norwegian descent, translated GNOMEDAL from the Old Norse as "Gnome Valley" (*dal* is "valley" in Norse), perhaps a reference to the relatively gnome-like aboriginal inhabitants of the Poteau Valley in which the Heavener Runestone is found. Other investigators decided the inscription was not a word. It makes a quaint, appropriate name for a miniature vale or dell, such as gnomes (Indians that Vikings referred to as *Skraelings*, a term meaning "Screechers").

Runes in the same evolving styles were written in differing dialects: Norwegian, Swedish, Danish, and Anglo-Saxon. The discovery that Anglo-Saxon was still spoken in isolated pockets of Sweden astounded 19th-century philologists. How to get Anglo-Saxon writers to Oklahoma during the Heavener rune-style of 200 to 500 A.D. beats me. The eminent scholar of Danish history, Dr. Richard Nielsen demonstrated what should never have come into question; namely, that the Heavener inscription uses a single alphabet. Yet, he had to stretch it to a 10th-century precedent in order for it to read GLOMETHAL, deciding D is "th" after a vowel, which does not make any difference, because *thal* and *dal* mean the same thing: dell or vale.

*Glom* (usually *Gla*) is a proper name in a 1014 A.D. Norse saga for a "ghostly looking man," related to the Old Norse *glamr* for "moon," the modern Swedish *glama*, "to stare," and the English "glamour." Nielsen went on to suggest that in some dialects *e* might have replaced standard *a* for genitive, thus his solution: "Glom's Valley." He did not fail to point out that Glomdal and Glomstad exist as place-names in Norway. Right or wrong in his transliteration/translation, Nielsen realized the Heavener Runestone dated to possibly 800 A.D., or a little before or after, stretching the date to catch the beginning of Viking expansion, which, however, commenced after the new *futhark* had come into vogue.

The Heavener form of *n* and *o* changed in England during the course of the fifth century. If the Heavener inscription is Anglo-Saxon, then it should date before 500 A.D. At least it derived from the style of that period. The celebrated navigator/linguist Paul Chapman, transliterated the Oklahoma runes in retrograde: LADEMONG in a novel reading of the old *futhark* characters. Assuming them to be Norse, he recognized a closer relationship to Old English *laeden*, "to lead," than to the Old Icelandic *lada* (modern Icelandic *leida*) or the Danish *lede*. Norse *lada*, Chapman found, alternatively means "to invite" or "bid," whereby the word would mean something such as "Come barter," or "Trading Post." Dr. Berry Fell, in *Saga America*, strangely read the *O* as *R,* and the word as *Gnrmedaedt,* and was unwontedly baffled as to its meaning.

At least four of the Heavener-region runestones lie in a northwest-southeast line, Gloria Farley perceived, lending credence to the smaller runic specimens as boundary markers. The Warner Stone, found during December, 1972, by a boy in a field near Dirty Creek, an Arkansas tributary, between Warner and Muskogee in east-central Oklahoma, consists of three characters, of which only the *X* corresponds to *futhark* runes. They could nevertheless read OCHS in Greek or QATTA in Libyan. The Poteau Runestone, which Wes Thomas relocated in February, 1959, after seeing it 45 years before on a ledge about 10 miles north of the Heavener specimen—higher on the same Mt. Poteau—shares the first three characters, the fifth, and sixth with the Heavener inscription, also perhaps the seventh, an *L* in forward, instead of reverse position, and "stung" with an added, little cross-stroke. The word seemingly reads GNOIEAELD, which sounds Norse or Anglo-Saxon enough.

The approximate dozen runic inscriptions Farley tracked from the Arkansas side of the Arkansas River, west perhaps 200 miles, include an elegantly carved specimen at the highest elevation of Tulsa; another on a hillside boulder near the North and South Canadian confluence 75 miles west of Heavener; and the Shawnee Stone, which was found buried face-down in August, 1969, near a small branch of the North Canadian River, 125 miles west-northwest of Heavener. Two more runic inscriptions were reported 200 miles west of Heavener. Farley was able to relocate both, which ignorant homesteaders may have destroyed as they did to many verified artifacts. Often buried or lichen-covered, inscriptions are hard to find and read as it is.

The red Permian-sandstone Shawnee Stone reads in unequivocal futhark: MYRDOC, which might be the name of a man buried in the immediate vicinity or, as Chapman discerned, an unnamed man murdered there: *Myrda* in Old Icelandic means "to conceal a murdered body." The Byfield, Massachusetts runes are in the same style and read: NIOIC. *N* and *O* are in common with the Heavener inscription; the *C* is the same as the Shawnee rune text; and an identical *I* is found among the Poteau and Tulsa Runestones.

The Heavener sequence so nearly matches Byfield in style that Gloria Farley thought the same hand carved both of them a year apart. The regional dispersal of these Oklahoma runestones and the conformance of their shared stylistic elements with original Norse runestones in Scandinavia points out their Medieval (or earlier) provenance. All were, moreover, discovered near important watAerways that could have carried a people skilled in navigation deep into the interior of Oklahoma and to the sea.

Despite its dismissal as a transparent hoax by conventional archae-ologists emotionally unable to tolerate contrary evidence, the Heavener Runestone is secure today in its own park, protected from all ignorant persons who would harm it. Whether its single word proclaims a thousand-year-old trading center or a valley of gnomes, the "ancient signboard" is enduring testimony to the arrival of the Northmen in what is now Oklahoma, centuries before Christopher Columbus was born.

# CHAPTER 6:

# East Meets West in Ancient America

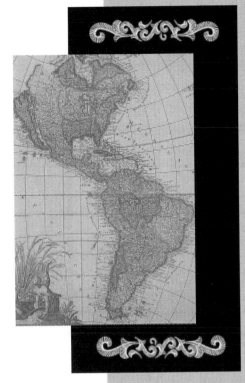

## DRUGS IN ANCIENT AMERICA

It would appear that South America has been the world's supplier of narcotics far longer than assumed, according to this especially provocative article in the January/February, 1995 issue of *Ancient American*. Its author, a biology researcher in Austin, Texas, reveals a direct, surprising link between the Andes Mountains and the Nile Valley.

 ### THEY CAME FOR THE COCAINE BY A.J. JULIUS

Were South Americans providing drug-plants to inhabitants of the Nile Valley 3,000 years ago? Did trade-routes connect the ancient empires of the

Egyptians and the Inca? Not according to most modern historians, because theories of transoceanic contact and diffusion have suffered from a supposed lack of supporting hard evidence. However, a recent report from scholars in Germany is rekindling the debate.

Researchers at the Institute for Anthropology and Human Genetics at the University of Munich have detected cocaine and nicotine in the tissue of Egyptian mummies. These surprising results are difficult to explain. Cocaine and nicotine are members of a chemical class of compounds known as alkaloids. Plants containing alkaloids have been culturally and economically important for thousands of years. Nicotine is found in a number of plants around the world; the same cannot be said of cocaine. Coca plant (*Erythroxylum*) was unknown in the Old World until after the Spanish expeditions to South America during the 15th and 16th centuries. Since then, it has been cultivated in other parts of the world. Nearly a year after the report appeared in *Naturwissenschaften* ("Natural Science," 1992), the journal published several controversial letters received from the scientific community. Some felt the editorial staff had been sloppy in reviewing the manuscript, and that the project was either a bizarre hoax or an experiment gone wrong. The researchers were attacked because they failed to include proper controls, and the possibility of instrumental error was not sufficiently ruled out. Dr. Franz Parsche, one of the mummy researchers, responded, "... our analysis provides clear evidence for the presence of alkaloids in ancient human remains."

The investigators offered no explanation for how the drug compounds came to exist in the mummies but defended their results as correct, citing the known reliability of the analytical methods employed. Several explanations were offered by scientists. Some mummies might have absorbed tobacco smoke while being studied and displayed in museums. Perhaps the drug reactions resulted from residual pesticides used during preservation and storage. Several scientists noted that unknown chemical reactions might have occurred in the mummified skin, hair, and bone tissues tested. The composition of

Egyptian mummification chemicals is not well-known, but we do know that the procedure varied somewhat over time. This uncertainty supports the valid existence of these drugs in the mummies. Materials tested were dated from 1070 B.C. to 395 A.D., and all were positive for cocaine and nicotine.

On one hand, it is unlikely that the embalming techniques of the Egyptians were so static more than 1,500 years, so as to produce the same long-term chemical results. On the other hand, it is uncertain how long cocaine and nicotine are stable in mummified remains. Perhaps native plants (unknown today) that contained cocaine, nicotine, or related alkaloids, were used by the Egyptians. Such plants could have been medicinally important or consumed in the normal diet. Nicotine is found in many members of the plant family *Solanaceae,* which includes food and drug-plants such as tomato, potato, tobacco, and jimson weed.

If the drugs were not of local origin, and they are not "artifacts" in the mummies, only one possibility remains. The findings would be good forensic evidence for pre-Columbian transoceanic contact. Because the mummies tested covered a broad timespan, such contact would have been well established and regular, unless plants could be returned to Egypt and propagated. Coca is a well-known anaesthetic and stimulant. If the occasion should arise, it would be a likely candidate for transfer between ancient medical practitioners. The useful properties of the plant were known to South Americans before the Inca. Today, inhabitants of the mountainous regions of Peru and Bolivia use coca much as their ancestors did. Leaves are chewed with powdered lime (calcium carbonate, traditionally from crushed shells or ashes). The lime creates alkaline conditions in the saliva to extract the cocaine and other alkaloids more efficiently.

Egyptian medical writings go back 4,000 years and were advanced for their time. Egyptian doctors were in demand throughout the known world. Although they practiced surgery and had a diverse apothecary, as far as we know, their understanding of anesthetics and stimulants was poor. There are no writings or artifacts that clearly refer to or depict New World herbs or procedures, such as coca leaf-chewing. Research suggests that dispersal of medicinal knowledge was slow in ancient times.

"We should not put our interpretation of these drugs as they are used in modern societies to the Egyptians," argues Dr. Parsche, "further experiments are in progress to clarify some of these issues."

Clarification is needed. Mummies are not rare and there is ample material available for testing. Further research may help us understand this biochemical enigma; until then, the mystery of the Egyptian drug-mummies remains unsolved.

# EGYPTIANS IN PRE-COLUMBIAN AMERICA

There is no physical evidence to support arguments for ancient Egyptian influence in pre-Columbian America, or so the advocates of cultural isolation insist. Among their most articulate, well-informed spokesmen was Eric Lurio, a prominent New York illustrator and artist/author of *A Fractured History of the Discovery of America,* a satire on cultural diffusionists. The "Davenport Tablet" he mentions in *Ancient American*'s January/February, 1995, issue was purported to depict an Ancient Egyptian Djed festival, the raising of a sacred column, allegedly found in western Iowa during the late 19th century. Most archaeologists condemn the "artifact" as bogus. That same characterization, according to Mr. Lurio, might be applied to all claims for overseas' visitors to America before Columbus.

POINT: NO EGYPTIANS IN
ANCIENT AMERICA
BY ERIC LURIO

The main if not only reason the advocates believe in Egyptian contact with the Mexicans-Andeans is the existence of pyramids. Almost every book and article claiming that the Ancient Egyptians made contact with the Ancient Mexicans and Andeans use pyramids as their prime pieces of evidence. The sole exception to the rule was Barry Fell, who based his "proof" of Egyptian contact on the notorious Davenport fraud. The use of a proven hoax for evidence, as Fell did, tainted the rest of the evidence presented.

Gunnar Thompson, in his latest book, repeats this lie and those of others. The Maya and the Aztecs had pyramids, the Inca had pyramids, and the Egyptians had pyramids, they say, so there just had to be contact. The pros, except for Thor Heyerdahl, dismiss this out of hand, usually in a paragraph or two. Did they or didn't they? In this article, we will examine the evidence to see which side is right.

In order to explore the question properly, we have to ask two others: Did the Ancient Egyptians actually get all the way across the Mediterranean, then all the way across the Atlantic, then all the way across the Caribbean, and the Gulf of Mexico, then all the way across Mexico and a goodly portion of the eastern Pacific to Peru? And if they did, did they arrive at the time the Mexicans and Andeans began to build pyramids? Let us survey the evidence.

First, there is wood. Advocates of contact, such as Thor Heyerdahl, claim that wood was, if not completely absent, then so rare that Egyptians used papyrus reed-boats almost exclusively for both trans-Nile and international travel. It was this assumption that inspired the failed "Ra-I" Expedition in 1969 and its successor a few years later. These expeditions, which are often cited as evidence of contact, are irrelevant, because, well, Egypt did have trees after all. Akashia, pine, and juniper trees, though not that common, were not all that rare either, and akashia wood was the primary material for crafts larger than a personal rowboat, which were generally made of reeds. But akashia, although far superior than reeds, is not the best possible wood. So the Egyptians went to what is now Lebanon to get the cedar for which that country was famous.

The best known example of a cedar ship is Cheops', which was found under the Great Pyramid itself. The ancient trade in cedar wood is extremely well documented and was a primary reason why Egypt conquered and reconquered Canaan over the millennia. More often, the Canaanites would deliver it by land across what is now Israel and the Sinai, or sometimes by sea in their boats. But once the Egyptians sent a fleet of their own all the way over to the Lebanese coast to get the valuable wood themselves. The Pharaoh at that time (Shahure, circa 2460 B.C.) was so proud of his achievement, that he put the whole story on the walls of his pyramid. Why would Shahure have been so proud of a mere trip to Lebanon, if Egypt had gotten all the way to Peru?

The question is even more puzzling when one remembers that Numidia, west of Lybia, had lush, extensive forests filled with cedar, spruce, and pine. Roman shipwrights used Numidian timber almost exclusively for centuries, destroying most of the forests and Hannibal's elephants in the process. Had the wood-hungry Egyptians known of these Numidian forests, oh, the stories they would have told! But of any Egyptian colonies west of the Nile Delta, there is not a trace. Egyptian and Egyptian-like artifacts, which are found down the Nile Valley all the way to northernmost Kenya, are unknown west of easternmost modern Libya, prior to the Phoenician explorations in the 9th century B.C. As far as I am able to determine, the earliest Egyptian mention of Sicily and Sardinia occurred when the so-called "Sea Peoples" attacked Egypt during the reign of Ramses III (1184 to 1153 B.C). The question of how the Egyptians could have made it passed the Straits of Gibraltar without even knowing about such abundant, valuable resources so close to home is an important one that must be answered.

The other major problem is timing. Did the Andeans and Mexicans start building pyramids while the Egyptians were building theirs?

To explore that question, we have to know about their respective pyramid-building traditions. The first Egyptian pyramid is Zoser's. It was built by his vizier, Imenhotep, no earlier than 2750 B.C., and most likely a century later. Ancient sources tell how he invented the pyramid as a series of "mastabas," or tombs, one on top of another. There are none earlier in all of Africa. The Egyptian pyramid tradition continued for more than a millennium, until the end of the XVIIth Dynasty, around 1570 B.C. Later, the Egyptians began burying their pharaohs in artificial caverns in the Valley of the Kings. No pyramids were built in Egypt after that, although the XXVth Dynasty (715 to 660 B.C.) erected some in Meroe, Nubia. The XVIIth Dynasty ruled Upper Egypt, while the Hyksos, invaders from Asia, occupied Lower Egypt. Their royal pyramids are small, pathetic stuctures that compare to the Gizeh monuments as outhouses might with the Empire State Building.

*Critics of ancient Egyptian influences in America are hard-pressed to explain objects such as this one on the side of a monumental statue at the Maya ceremonial city of Copan. The knotted loop depicted here, in Honduras, was also revered in the Nile Valley as "Sa," a stylized life-preserver signifying "protection" and associated with "the Great One," Taurt, divine protector of the dead.*

Now, what about Mexico? The Aztecs and the Mayas were not the first Mexicans to have pyramids. Mesoamerican Civilization began to flourish around 1200 B.C. Its earliest center at San Lorenzo was built on a huge artificial mound. Although the place was destroyed in 900 B.C., remains of pyramid mounds have been discovered there. Another major center was built at San Lorenzo about a century later. The pyramid there, more of a conical mound, is the oldest one still in tact in Mexico. Notice that the Olmec Civilization came into existence at a time when pyramids had not been built in Egypt for more than 3,000 years. A very long time for Egyptian architects to wait, don't you think?

The Andean Civilizations of Peru present very different problems. For one thing, pyramid-wise, the Andeans got there first. Let me make that a bit clearer: The oldest Andean pyramids are older than the oldest Egyptian ones. The oldest Andean pyramid is located at Aspero, along the Peruvian coast, about halfway between Ecuador and Chile. It is called the *Huaca de los Sacrificios*. The structure is about 30 feet high and carbon-dating of its mud-bricks at the summit have an average date of 2857 B.C. The base is considerably older. The latest possible date given is 2800 B.C. This is a minimum of 70 years earlier than the earliest possible date of Zoser's pyramid. (Zoser was king from 2638 to 2609 B.C.) The gap is most likely greater. The *Huaca de los Sacrificios* was built during a period archaeologists call "Pre-ceramic IV." The reason it is called that is because the Andeans of the time didn't know how to make pottery. The first pottery in the area dates from centuries later.

Egypt, however, had pottery almost 2,000 years prior to its first pyramid. This argument alone is enough to rule out the possibility of contact. The development of pyramidal architecture in the Americas could not have possibly been due to contact with Egypt, because of factors of distance, Egyptian ignorance of the Western Mediterranean and, most importantly, time.

Other alleged evidence of contact, such as Thor Heyerdahl's "Ra Expeditions," are irrelevant or, as in the cases of the Davenport

Stone, outright frauds. The worst of these frauds is a bogus word list that has appeared in such books as *They Came Before Columbus* and *American Discovery*, from which I quote: "...Mayas had their underworld kingdom called Mani. Mexican and Peruvian names for the sun-god (Ra) are phonetically the same as the Egyptian Ra, meaning 'sun-god.'" For the record, let me state that the Maya underworld was Xibalba, the Inca sun-god was called Inti, and the solar deities of the Mayas and the Aztecs were known as Ki and Tonatiuh, respectively.

Sorry, folks! It just ain't so.

# EGYPTIANS ON AMERICAN SHORES

Gunnar Thompson's response to the acerbic critique Eric Lurio published in the same *Ancient American* issue was, by contrast, good-spirited and generous. It nonetheless poked a great many holes in his arguments against all possibilities for a Near Eastern influence in pre-Columbian America. Dr. Thompson also opened fresh evidence that must cause even the most hard-bitten skeptic to wonder if the Dynastic Egyptians did not, after all, actually arrive on the shores of our Continent thousands of years ago.

### COUNTERPOINT: EGYPT'S ROLE IN ANCIENT AMERICA BY GUNNAR THOMPSON, PH.D.

Mr. Lurio's article against cultural diffusionism from Ancient Egypt to America has some good points. He is correct in stating that Peru's earliest adobe pyramids predate stone pyramids in the Nile Valley. He is also correct in stating that Egyptians had wooden ships, hence, his criticism of Thor Heyerdahl's selection of totora reeds for construction of Ra II, which made a successful voyage from Morocco to Barbados in 1970.

Mr. Lurio also mentions several well-known facts about pyramids in Egypt and America. However, his information is inadequate and his conclusions are erroneous. His insistence that Egypt's sun-god, Ra, was unknown to ancient Americans is merely a false assumption; it is not a fact. Egyptian names for the Sun in ancient America are clearly established. Egyptian artifacts have been found in American archaeological sites under controlled circumstances, and Egyptian influence is apparent in the arts, architecture, writing, and religious practices of ancient America.

Mr. Lurio begins his argument with a claim that *American Discovery* relies on pyramids as the "prime piece of evidence" for Egyptian contact. After such a statement, I seriously doubt that he has read my book, *American Discovery, the Real Story*. Indeed, the Chapter on Egypt states, "Only two New World pyramids (Panche and La Venta) evoke images of Egyptian pyramids." Two examples out of several thousand New World pyramids hardly support Mr. Lurio's preconceived idea that pyramids are a central part of my argument for Egyptian contact. How is it that Mr. Lurio missed my statement on page 85 saying, "Native architectural traditions were well enough established to resist Egyptian influence"?

Contrary to Mr. Lurio's claim, *American Discovery, the Real Story* details evidence of architectural inspiration for pyramid construction in the Americas coming via Indo-Sumer and China. Numerous native burial mounds and some earthen pyramids were probably indigenous phenomena. Mr. Lurio is correct in doubting Egyptian influence on Peruvian architects; at least we are in agreement in that respect. The evidence suggests to me that early adobe pyramids in Peru, as well as cotton textiles, bottle gourds, and reed boats, are most likely the results of contact with Indo-Sumerian travelers by the fourth millennium B.C.

Although it is true, as Mr. Lurio states, that Inti, Ki, and Tonatiuh were native names for the sun-god, they were not the only names. Isolationists must realize that "half-of-the-truth" does not constitute the whole story of native cultural development. Old World

The famous mid-14th century B.C. bust of Egyptian Queen Nefertiti depicts her wearing a hat decorated with the double-loop insignia representing a united kingdom.

The pre-Columbian statue of an unidentified, prominent Toltec lady shows her wearing a hat not only similar to Nefertiti's, but decorated with an identical double-loop emblem.

diffusion is a significant part of the story. We must seek the whole truth if we are going to begin to fathom what took place in antiquity. Mr. Lurio's attempt to deduce what happened based on logic, limited information, and faulty assumptions is an entertaining but fruitless exercise.

There were many tribes in the New World, and they had many names for the sun-god. Some of those names have been lost because of the ravages of disease on native populations and the fading memories of passing generations. However, the Egyptian name of Ra (or Re) for the sun has survived the millennia as testimony of Egyptian cultural influence in ancient America. Archaeologist Curt Muser reported the "Re" glyph at Teotihuacan, Mexico, which is the site of the enormous Pyramid of the Sun. This important glyph includes a scroll and an eye motif inside a circle. Both Muser and Mexican archaeologist Alfonso Caso identified the "re" glyph through ethnographical research as *ojo de reptil,* or "eye of the serpent." Native artists at Teotihuacan placed "re" glyphs at the center of solar symbols to represent "the eye of the sun." Egyptian artists used a similar symbol consisting of the *Udjat* ("Hawk-Serpent Eye") placed inside a symbol of the Sun. It was called *Ra* or *Re,* the "eye of the sun." Presence of similar symbols with identical names is strong evidence of cultural diffusion. Thus, two reputable archaeologists, Curt Muser and Alfonso Caso, have established that some of the inhabitants of Teotihuacan knew their sun-god by the Egyptian name, Re, although later Mexicans chose different names for the deity.

Thor Heyerdahl perceived the Egyptian sun-god's name (Ra) in the title of a Peruvian culture-hero, Kon-tiki Vi-ra-cocha. This name and Peruvian use of reed-boats led Heyerdahl to suspect cultural diffusion between Egypt and Peru. His goal in sailing a reed-boat across the Atlantic was to prove that Ancient Egyptians, using the most primitive technology, could have succeeded in reaching the Americas. Reed-boat technology was available to inhabitants in the Middle East by the 10th millennium B.C. Although most Egyptians used wooden ships by the third millennium B.C., huge reed-ships were still in use on the Red Sea as late as the first century A.D. Smaller reed-boats are still popular among peasants in North Africa, Asia, and Peru.

Isolationists often complain about a so-called "lack of artifacts" to bolster their claims of "no contact before Columbus." However, this complaint often cloaks overly restrictive admissions criteria and outright ignorance.

One of the most important finds of Egyptian artifacts occurred in 1914, in El Salvador. Since then it has been largely ignored by academicians in the United States. During the course of controlled archaeological excavations under the direction of Professor Miguel Angel Gonzalez, workers uncovered two Egyptian statuettes buried far below the surface. One of the statuettes is of a pharaoh's sarcophagus (or mummy) wearing the crown of Osiris, god of resurrection. The other appears to be the Mother Goddess, Isis. An inscription on the male statuette approximates the cartouche of Pharaoh Osorkon (22nd Dynasty, circa 1000 B.C.). Photographs of these artifacts were published in *Historia de la Nacion Mexicana* (1940), that was written by the Jesuit priest-historian, Manuel Cuevas. He was convinced of the authenticity of the artifacts and their importance to ancient New World history. Yet, the bias of Yankee scholars against anything that might support pre-Columbian contact with the Old World resulted in a failure to consider this evidence.

Over the passing years, vital clues to the puzzle of New World cultures such as these have been virtually lost due to a conspiracy of ignorance fueled by academic arrogance among tenured professors. I "re-discovered" the artifacts inside Cuevas's book during one of my many forays into the stacks of the University of Hawaii Library. The book had been sitting on a shelf unopened, gathering dust for the past four decades. Manuel Cuevas suggested in his *Historia* that ancient Mexicans had contact with Egyptians or with merchants who made voyages to the Nile. He believed that Egyptian inspiration played a role in the construction of the Pyramid of the Sun at Teotihuacan. He compared the Mexican pyramid to the Pyramid of Khufu (Cheops) at Gizeh, which has the identical geographic orientation and the same base-dimensions.

However, the Mexican pyramid is not merely a replica of the Egyptian monument. It has unique characteristics that reflect the native tendency of adapting foreign ideas to better suited native culture. The pyramid was only half as high as its Egyptian counterpart, and it had stairways with a temple on top. It also played a more active role in native culture, as it was the center not just for rituals, but also for public markets. Presence of the "Re" glyph on ceramics at Teotihuacan lends support to Cuevas's theory of some Egyptian inspiration behind the New World monument.

As do his colleagues, Mr. Lurio insists that the time lag of many centuries between construction of Egyptian pyramids and those of America is sufficient to preclude the possibility of diffusion. Although the theory of diffusion in this case is admittedly conjectural, it is presumptuous to suppose that Egyptian influence was impossible. Indeed, Khufu's monument continues to inspire those who look upon its massive building blocks. Recently, one American entrepreneur built a pyramid-shaped hotel in Las Vegas as a result of his exposure to Khufu's lingering legacy. So, the rulers of Teotihuacan might have decided in 300 B.C. to build a city of pyramids to rival those of Egypt after hearing about the Nile monuments, long after the original architects passed away.

Other evidence of Egyptian contact continues to accumulate. In 1994, George Carter noted the presence of tobacco and cocaine in ancient Egyptian mummies. These native American plants were tentatively identified by a team of German microbiologists. Other researchers found the American tobacco beetle in King Tutankhamun's tomb. Barry Fell demonstrated a probable Egyptian influence in Micmac glyphic writing. My own *American Discovery* included an illustration of Libyan writing on priestly robes at the Maya ceremonial center of Bonampak, in the Yucatan. Libyans served as surrogates for Egyptian interests in distant lands, such as Central America. Isolationist scholars have entirely over-looked this Libyan writing at Bonampak, because it does not "fit" into their preconceived notion about what Mayan writing is supposed to look like. Nevertheless, the foreign script is plain to see on Bonampak murals and in many textbooks having photographs of these murals.

The most enduring Egyptian influence appears to have been in native religious practices and the arts. Egyptian motifs on native art include the serpent apron of fertility seen on Maya statues, the Aztec sun-god (Tonatiuh) holding an incense burner in the same manner that Egyptian sun-gods (pharaohs) hold incense burners, and Mixtec serpent headdresses that parallel those of pharaohs and queens of Egypt. Some Olmec statuettes have stylized beards below their chins that mimic the false beards of Egyptian pharaohs. All of these artistic traditions have unique religious roots that defy isolationist assumptions of "independent derivation" or "coincidence." They substantiate diffusionist theories of pervasive Egyptian cultural influence in ancient America.

Mr. Lurio is correct to point out inadequacies in the diffusionist position that have resulted from hoaxes, romance writers, and lack of research. However, what he refers to as "lies" seem to reflect his own dogmatic academic training and lack of understanding. Discovering the secrets of the past requires extra effort on the part of true explorers. Although academic scholars can rightfully boast of specialized field research, my own training in anthropology and exposure to the sacrosanct dogma of academia have taught me that some of the most thorough researchers are to be found among the ranks of the cultural diffusionists.

Meanwhile, vested academicians often exude an attitude of "ignorance is bliss," as they toil in isolation from other scholars. Hopefully, Mr. Lurio will come to appreciate and celebrate the great beauty of America's multicultural heritage. That heritage is abundantly evident from the artifacts, loan-words, traditions, physical characteristics, symbolism, maps, writing systems, transoceanic epidemics, and agricultural practices of ancient peoples. Much of the evidence has been found by maverick scholars and non-professionals outside the exclusive club of orthodox American archaeology.

Keep your skepticism, Mr. Lurio. But cultivate an open mind.

## WAUBANSEE SCULPTURE

The industrial city of Chicago is not usually associated with the prehistory of our country. Yet, one of its foremost museums displays an absolutely unique work of art that may have been left by visitors from the Near East more than 2,000 years ago. If so, their monumental contribution to Chicago's riverfront could be no less archaeologically enlightening than it was originally macabre, according to this article in the August/September, 1998 issue of *Ancient American.*

*The controversial Waubansee sculpture.*

CHICAGO'S GREAT STONE FACE
BY FRANK JOSEPH

In the heart of Chicago's Loop, along the south bank of the Chicago River, once stood a large and curious stone. On one side was expertly sculpted the face of a man, his eyes closed and mouth open, with a chin-beard.

At the top of the stone was a depression like a small trough. Three inter-connecting holes bored through the hard stone linking the trough appeared on either side of the artwork and through the parted lips of the face. The relief sculpture measured 1 foot wide and 17.5 inches high, incised to a depth of 1.5 inches. Its top hollowed to 4.5 inches deep, 18 inches long by 9 inches wide, the three-thousand-pound granite block originally dominated a sand dune overlooking Lake Michigan. Geologists believe the pre-sculpted monolith was either deposited there by a glacier (which would date it to about 10,000 years ago), or part of the Canadian Shield, an area of rock at least 750 million years old.

In any case, this unique stone face formerly peered outside the stockade of Fort Dearborn, an early U.S. Army settlement that would eventually grow to become the Windy City. Daniel Webster stood on the stone while he harangued the fort's inhabitants, in 1837. When the military outpost was torn down near the close of the 19th century, the one-and-a-half-ton object was removed from its original location at what is now Wacker Drive and Michigan Avenue to the Sanitary District's headquarters on the near-north side. Some years later, it was freed from this undignified setting and found its permanent, far more appropriate home on public display at the museum of the Chicago Historical Society. It may be seen there today as part of the Fort Dearborn diorama recreation behind the main lobby on the first floor.

In 1881, a Mr. Henry Hurlburt became the first writer to describe this strange stone. He speculated that it had been carved by some unknown Fort Dearborn soldier with time on his hands and who wanted to sculpt the likeness of Waubansee, chief of the Potawatomi Indian tribe. With no real records or documentation of any kind at his disposal, Hurlburt had only aging hearsay on which to base his conclusions. The recess at the top of the object, he assumed, must have been used as a mortar in which maize was ground, although why anyone would need a 3,000-pound mortar was and remains unanswerable. Both his paltry explanations have long since been rejected, but the name stuck, and the massive artifact is still known as the "Waubansee Stone."

Aside from the fact that granite is among the most difficult mediums in which to sculpt, the face is clearly the master-work of a very gifted stonecutter who devoted considerable time and labor to his task—hardly in keeping with the duties of a common frontier soldier. And given the mutual hostilities that existed at the time between natives and settlers, it seems unlikely any White man, particularly a soldier, would have felt inclined to spend so much effort memorializing an Indian chief. More likely than speculations about some nameless serviceman with nothing better to occupy his time, the scant source material about the Stone implies at least that it was already waiting on its sand dune for the soldiers who built Fort Dearborn. Also, a glance at the top depression is sufficient to show that the oblong, somewhat concave hollow makes for a most unsuitable mortar.

But if no 19th-century Chicagoan was the sculptor, neither was any Native American. The Plains Indians rarely worked in stone, certainly never in granite, nor on the scale and refinement displayed by the Waubansee Stone. Moreover, Amerindians are beardless, and the carved face appears to sport a goatee. But if some anonymous soldier did not fashion it to memorialize a chief, and the hollowed top was never used as a mortar, who was the superb artist responsible?

Why was it made? And just how long was the stone standing at the mouth of the Chicago River? Although to answer these questions we may possess no more documentation that did Hurlburt, evidence of another kind is available to us in the form of modern archaeology. And the object itself will speak to us in its own way, if only we have the patience to listen.

The Waubansee Stone on display at the Chicago Historical Society.

Let us first consider its original position on the south bank of the Chicago River, just in from the Lake Michigan shore. The spot represents, as it has since the earliest known voyages, a natural portage before sailing westward along the Illinois River system into the Mississippi. Louis Joliet and Pere Marquette stopped there in 1673, and Robert Cavalier, Sieur de la Salle, built a supply store at the same place nine years later. Ships still dock near the Michigan Avenue bridge, the original site of the Waubansee Stone. These historically affirmed the usage of the location as a point of landing. This fact comprises our first clue to the object's intended function. Its identification as a mooring stone is suggested by its former riverside position, where so many vessels have been known to dock at least since the 17th century. The Stone's two side holes are large enough through which to pass a ship's line. At 3,000 pounds, the granite block could easily secure a large vessel tied to it.

Reinforcing its designed purpose as a mooring stone was the 19th-century rumor of a similar block (virtually identical in size but without any sculpted image) about one hundred feet west of the Waubansee Stone that also stood at the river's edge. This companion piece was supposed to have been pushed over into the water during construction of the first Michigan Avenue bridge, during the 1850s. In any case, another, similarly massy stone a ship's length down the river bank underscores its purpose as a mooring by which vessels were tied fore and aft.

But for whose vessel? Certainly, a pair of one-and-a-half-ton monoliths would not have been required to secure an Indian's birch-bark canoe. Perhaps the answer lies in a closer look at the Waubansee Stone's singular details.

In addition to its alleged function as a mortar, the hollow at the top of the stone was once assumed to have been a baptismal font, and, indeed, the oval depression naturally fits an object the size and dimensions of a baby. This speculation begins to approach the truth, which may be, however, a ghastly inverse of baptism. Following the function suggested by the Waubansee Stone, we begin to find its parallels a world away from prehistoric Chicago or its Amerindian natives.

The Phoenicians were an ancient Semitic people, also known as the Canaanites, whose origins were in what is now Lebanon. In the years following the Trojan War, during the first decades of the 12th century B.C., they began building what would eventually become a vast, mercantile empire created largely through their unquestioned abilities as the foremost sea-traders of their time. Their ships sailed around the African Continent, to every part of the known world and beyond, to areas of wealth they kept secret, such as Antillia, "the Farthest Land," somewhere outside the "Rocks of Melchart," today's Straits of Gibraltar. The precise location and identity of this land—rich in all kinds of mineral wealth—has never been satisfactorily determined, although growing numbers of investigators, most notably the famous cryptoanalyst Cyrus Gordon, believe Antillia was synonymous for the Americas, specifically, Brazil.

As we reported in a recent issue (number 17, "New Discovery of Ancient Map Puts Phoenicians in the Americas"), Dr. Mark McMenamin, professor of geology and paleontology at Mount Holyoke College, in South Hadley, Massachusetts, demonstrated last winter that the Phoenicians included representations of the Brazilian coast on some of their minted coins. Although these coins are physical proof that the ancients knew about South America, they are only the latest in an accumulation of evidence going back more than three centuries. A stone covered with Phoenician letters was discovered in Brazil about 120 years ago.

According to author Gunnar Thompson, the "inscription was found by Brazilian slaves during the early 1870s. Called the *Parahyba Text*, it recounts the voyage of Phoenician merchants, who traveled from Sidon in the 6th century B.C. The *Parahyba Text* was branded a fraud after its publication. However, subsequent research confirms that the inscription is authentic. Passages that were once thought to be erroneous have been verified from identical inscriptions on *bone fide* Phoenician artifacts. The inscriptions included ancient expressions and grammatical forms that were unknown during the 1800s. Cyrus Gordon, a Semitic language scholar at Brandeis University, has ruled out the possibility of forgery, because the archaic language was only recently decoded. In 1641, Jesuits living near Minas Gerais, Brazil, reported bronze figurines with strange writing. Antiquarians at the Vatican identified the inscriptions as Phoenician. In 1754, missionaries reported the ruins of a stone city in the Amazon jungle also having Phoenician inscriptions."

That the Phoenicians knew of and traveled to Brazil seems clear. But what was to prevent them from sailing to North America, specifically, to Lake Michigan at the Chicago River? The same abundance of evidence for the Phoenicians' presence in Illinois does not match their ancient landfalls in Brazil—except, perhaps, for one, very powerful artifact. Such a disparity is hardly to be wondered at, when we compare underdeveloped Brazil, where archaeological materials may be left undisturbed, with industrially over-developed Chicago.

An integral part of the Phoenicians' religion was infant sacrifice to appease the gods, especially Molloch, their boon-granting deity, and win their favor. The child was taken to a *tophet*, a kind of rude sacred site often out of doors, featuring a stone altar with a depression at the top very much like a baptismal font. There, the baby's throat was ritually cut, and the sacrificial blood allowed to run through the infant-sized hollow connected by a tunnel to the sculpted face of Moloch and to its open mouth. Then the blood of the ceremoniously murdered child would have spilled into a river or sea as an offering to the water-gods.

The Waubansee Stone's resemblance to a *tophet* is suggested by its eyes, closed in death. Even this unusual, characteristic convention recurs in surviving Phoenician art, such as the bronze head of a man with his eyes closed from Ugarit. And as the sculptors of the Chicago find, Phoenician artists favored frontal, full-face portraiture. Outstanding examples are the so-called "Mona Lisa of Nimrud" and the ubiquitous ivory carvings of "the woman in the window" found at Carthage, the Phoenicians' greatest city in North Africa. Interestingly, the face of the Waubansee Stone wears a chin-beard, a personal grooming detail of which Phoenician males were inordinately proud, but something certainly unknown to the beardless Native American Indians.

A possible scenario suggested by the Waubansee Stone includes a Phoenician sailing vessel loaded with timber, copper, and other materials—skirting the western shores of Lake Michigan on a southerly heading. The ship turns into the mouth of the Chicago River, where hawsers are thrown from bow and stern to hands waiting ashore at an improvised portage. The lines, passing through holes in the two granite mooring stones on the south bank, secure her fore and aft. Later, at some auspicious moment, an infant, possibly purchased in trade with local Indians, is placed in the hollow at the top of the Waubansee Stone. There, its throat is cut. Sacrificial blood courses through tubular channels in the stone and out the open mouth of the sculpted face (possibly meant to portray Moloch himself), into the river. It is a most important ritual dedicated to the gods for safe passage home during the long, perilous voyage to the Mississippi River, down to the Gulf of Mexico, and out across the Atlantic Ocean toward Africa and Carthage.

Any precise dates for these conjectural events is impossible to come by. Phoenician power lasted about 1,000 years, from around 1200 B.C. to the Second Punic War (218 to 202 B.C.) Whenever such awful dramas may have taken place, the Chicago Historical Society might possess the most valuable artifact in the pre-Columbian history of North America. If only the face of the Waubansee Stone could speak, what wonders—and what horrors—it might tell!

# CHAPTER 7:

## Out of Africa

### DID WEST AFRICANS PRECEDE THE SPANIARDS TO AMERICA?

Evidence for West Africans in the New World before the Conquistadors arrived has been steadily accumulating ever since their leader, Hernan Cortez, landed on the eastern shores of Mexico, five centuries ago. They appear to have been long preceded by ancestors of the same race shackled in the fetid bowels of Spanish slave-ships. But as Willard P. Leutze pointed out in his article for *Ancient American*'s April/May, 1996 issue, blacks not only populated Mexico in pre-Columbian times, but, in sharp contrast to their 16th-century plight, were sometimes elevated to god-status.

ANCIENT AMERICANS:
RED OR BLACK?
BY WILLARD P. LEUTZE

The shortest distance across the Atlantic is from West Africa to the eastward bulge of South America. Any raft or canoe caught by ocean currents off the coast of West Africa will be carried inexorably to the eastern shores of America. Dr. Thor Heyerdahl's *Ra-II Expedition* of 1971 dramatically demonstrated the transatlantic power of these currents and affirmed that an ancient American landfall from Africa was not only possible, but probable. Less adventurous, conventional archaeologists sniffed that the only thing he proved was that Norwegians made good sailors. In point of fact, however, Heyerdahl showed that virtually any waterborne craft shoving off from the North Atlantic shores of Africa would inevitably enter the Caribbean.

His was essentially the same transatlantic route Christopher Columbus used to "discover" the New World, less than 500 years before. Similar voyages were immediately undertaken after him. Spanish sailors referred to this mid-ocean crossing as the "Sea of Ladies" for its tranquil, unchallenging passage. By either accident or design, it stands to reason that, in time, some West African living on the shores fronting this peaceful, direct current would have survived a voyage to Mexico or South America.

Physical evidence for this supposition has been found in abundance by a German anthropologist. Beginning in the 1960s, Alexander von Wuethenau collected dozens of Mesoamerican clay and stone effigies clearly meant to depict Negroes. These finds were critically scrutinized by renowned archaeologist J. Erik Thompson as part of the peer review process. He concluded that von Wuethenau's figures represented travelers engaged in commerce. Thompson stated that the Maya god of merchants was Ek, or "black," Chuah. This immortal was also the divine patron of chocolate, because cocoa beans were valued as universal among the Maya, who associated them with traders. The Maya were additionally fond of word-plays, and to have a dark-skinned deity as the god of chocolate struck them as entirely appropriate. They, of course, made books of bark illuminated with illustrated glyphs and had great libraries documenting the arts, sciences, and histories of their civilization. Among the pitifully few volumes to escape the fires of Christian intolerance were what came to be known as the Dresden and Madrid Codices. Both works feature painted images of a black man with decidedly African facial features carrying a spear. He has been identified as Ek Chuah by William Gates, translator of Bishop Diego de Landa's 16th-century *Yucatan Before and After the Conquest.*

According to Ann A. Morris, in her multi-volume description of *The Temple of the Warriors at Chichen Itza,* the interior painting of a man was "all too typical of the Negro, and unlike the Maya to be readily taken for accident."

That blacks were still present in remote corners of Middle and Central America when early Spanish explorers arrived is attested by Pedro Martir, Spain's court historian, in 1530. Describing the discovery of the Pacific Ocean, he quotes Nunez de Balboa saying that, at the Isthmus of Panama, he and his fellow Spaniards "met Negro slaves from a region where nothing but Negroes are bred, who are ferocious and extraordinarily cruel. We believe that in former times Negroes, who were out for robbery, navigated from Africa and, being shipwrecked, established themselves in these mountains. The Indians have internal fights full of hatred with the Negroes."

However, mainstream archaeologists and conventional historians believe the existence of West African blacks in America dates back at least as far in time as the Mayas, who flourished from 200 B.C. to 900 A.D. Indeed, at least enough of these "native" American Negroes were still in existence to be personally observed by Balboa and his fellow Conquistadors. It would seem, then that black history in America did not begin with slave ships of the 16th century, but under less shameful circumstances, enough for the deification of a Negro man as the god of commerce, in the far deeper past.

# TERRA-COTTA HEADS

Assertions that blacks resided in North America long before Renaissance Europeans arrived are based on more than myth or hearsay. Physical evidence exists in the form of two pre-Columbian portraits owned by a prominent Mexican museum, as described in the June/July, 1996 issue of *Ancient American*.

## WEST AFRICAN IN PREHISTORIC MEXICO BY DIANE WIRTH

Mexico's Museo de Antropologia de Jalapa showcases two pre-Columbian works of art that appear to portray individuals of West African origins. Both terra-cotta heads have large lips and flared noses, features not found among Middle America's indigenous populations. One head is either bald or shaven, another anomalous trait, because baldness is not a genetic characteristic common to native American Indians. Nor was shaving hair from the entire head, a custom not indulged in by Mesoamerican cultures. The face of the other figure wearing a cap shows evidence of deliberate scarification, a ritual practice known to many tribes of Africa's Gold Coast, but never in pre-Columbian Mexico. Curators were unable to provide any further information about the two heads, which are clearly of negroid race: The terra-cotta itself has been fired black.

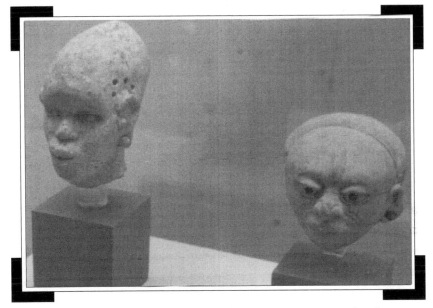

*The facial features of these Mesoamerican terra-cotta heads cannot be misconstrued as typically "Indian."*

Both museum pieces share a room with other sculptures from the Veracruz area, on the Atlantic coast, where ships following the Canary Island Current sweeping across the mid-Atlantic from West Africa would have been carried into the Gulf of Mexico from Ghana or Senegal. In any case, numerous other portraits of West Africans in Mesoamerica were reproduced by the German anthropologist, Alexander von Wuethenau, during the 1960s and 1970s. Although some of his photographs were made of sculptures from private collections and cannot, therefore, be verified, his book, *Unexpected Faces in Ancient America*, publishes black and white photographs of the same terra-cotta heads still on public display at the Jalapa Museum. There can be no question as to their authenticity. They are abundant physical proof for the presence of West African blacks in Mexico long before the arrival of modern Europeans during the early 16th century.

# HUMAN HEAD SCULPTURES

Colossal human heads of sculpted stone have been dug out of the ground in northeastern Mexico since the early 1860s. They are outstanding not only because of their stark realism, but for the unmistakably African features of the faces they portray. What can explain the monumental depiction of these men from the opposite side of the Atlantic Ocean? An article in the January/February, 1995 issue of *Ancient American* attempted to answer that continues to bedevil archaeologists, professional and amateur alike.

## THE GREAT STONE HEADS SPEAK
## BY FRANK JOSEPH

Nearly 150 years ago, the head of a stone giant was unearthed in a jungle near the Mexican town of Tres Zapotes. Even more striking than its huge proportions or the excellence of its workmanship was the face, obviously the portrait of a real person, but unlike any Native American. Instead, it bore the unmistakable features of a black African. Since that first amazing discovery, an additional 17 examples have been excavated, mostly around the ancient ceremonial center with its volcano-like earth-mound at San Lorenzo, in southern Vera Cruz.

Although not uniform in dimensions, weight, or even the individuals they depict, all were executed on a titanic scale in basalt, a stone not found locally. The nearest source lies among the Tuxtla Mountains, where archaeologists uncovered an unfinished head, proof that the huge portraits were sculpted there, then transported, incredibly, more than 50 miles to San Lorenzo. The largest specimen stands 9 feet tall and weighs 40 tons. All the heads were produced by the Olmecs, founders of the oldest Mesoamerican Civilization, which flourished from 1500 to 800 B.C.

at the Midwest Archaeology Conference, in Minnesota, reads, "We eight Goetalanders and 22 Northmen are on this acquisition expedition far west from Vinland. We had properties near two shelters one day's march north from this stone. We went fishing one day. After we came home, I found ten men red with blood, dead. Ave Maria, save us from evil! I have 10 men by the sea to look after our ships 14 days' travel from this site. Year of the Lord 1362."

The Goetalanders cited in the inscription were from the Swedish island of Gotland. Vinland was located in what is presently the state of Maine. Condemned almost universally as a self-evident fraud by conventional archaeologists for more than 100 years, the Kensington Runestone, as it came to be known, is still championed by a smaller number of less closed-minded professionals. They insist that proper testing should be undertaken before its identity as a modern hoax or a prehistoric artifact be conclusively ascertained. They were particularly motivated by the renowned Smithsonian Institution in 1999, when its cynical directors planned to exhibit the Runestone around the country as an example of bogus archaeology.

Interestingly, the Washington, D.C. Institution has been accused by more than one researcher of deliberately destroying material evidence unfavorable to current belief-systems in Columbus as the sole discoverer of America. Instead of joining the traveling carnival show run by the Smithsonian medicine men, curators at the Kensington Runestone Museum, in Alexandria, Minnesota, turned over their controversial artifact to real scientists for serious study. Some results of present testing were presented for the first time during the Midwest Archaeology Conference held at St. Paul's Raddison Hotel, 10 November 2000. Among the presenters was archaeologist, Alice Keyhoe, who pointed out that the date inscribed on the Stone, A.D. 1362, represented a moment in time of complimentary significance. Just 13 years before, Scandinavian populations had been decimated by the Black Death. One-half to two-thirds of the inhabitants of Northern Europe died within 24 months of its onset in 1349.

Unable to deny the African facial features of the great heads, early researchers concluded they were portraits of blacks brought by Arabs and sold as slaves to the Olmecs. Others wondered if the monumental sculpture represented African warriors from Atlantis. Recoiling from any suggestion of transatlantic influences, post-World War Two archaeologists simply denied the obvious. They insisted that the black stone faces were not negroid at all, but typically Amerindian. Only some of the features, they guessed, had been purposely flattened to facilitate transportation, a process that inadvertently gave the portraits a vaguely African appearance. By the 1970s, some anti-Establishment investigators claimed that the colossal artwork depicted black royalty from Egypt or tribal chiefs from Ghana, who became the African culture-bearers and ruling elite of Mesoamerica's premiere civilization.

It seems clear that these interpretations of the Olmec heads are racially and politically motivated theories, which more reflect the times in which they were current than any truly honest, unbiased, or straight-forward attempts at a solution. The scientists (Mexicans, North Americans, and Europeans) who studied the Tres Zapotes' finds, beginning in 1862, could not believe blacks were capable of producing anything even remotely civilized, anywhere, at anytime, and so naturally assumed the heads were depictions of slaves. But no one would go to the extremes of labor in sculpting, transporting over many miles, and setting up 40-ton memorials to the lowest-ranking people in society. And after the date-parameters of Olmec Civilization were determined, any speculation about Arab traders had to be discarded.

The fourth century B.C. Greek philosopher, Plato, wrote that Atlantis was a multi-racial state in its last days, but outside of this single reference to non-Atlanteans at the island-civilization, nothing in any of the abundant literature on the subject connects blacks with the sunken capital. Although the re-adjusted date for the final destruction of Atlantis, 1198 B.C., coincides with a sudden florescence in Olmec Civilization, the first of the stone heads was not sculpted until almost 300 years later.

Entirely theoretical assumptions that the sculpted faces were intentionally flattened to avoid chipping or breakage during removal from the Tuxtla Mountains are handily dismissed by one stone head in particular on display during the 1992 traveling exhibit staged by Mexico City's Anthropological Museum at the Chicago Art Institute of Chicago. The visiting specimen had a long, protruding nose and sharp edges to the facial features.

Dogmatic isolationists are emotionally unequipped to consider any foreign contacts in pre-Columbian America, and are, consequently, so heavily into denial, they reject the evidence of their own eyes. That the giant heads nonetheless depict black men is self-evident, not only in the deliberate portrayal of facial features, but in the ancient sculptor's choice of the medium used; namely, black basalt. Nor are the stone heads the only Mesoamerican representations of identifiably black African personages. They appear throughout stele carvings and statues in the round, with the best and most numerous examples on public display at La Venta Park, in Villahermosa. Although the majority of these portrayals of blacks in ancient Mexico are found in Olmec art, other outstanding specimens include the Vera Cruz carving of a black African head with closed eyes; the ceramic head of a woman with undeniably negroid features, found at the great pyramid-capital of Teotihuacan; and Toltec obsidian ware from Tula representing a negro boy as cup-bearer. Such abundant cultural evidence was underscored by the bones of negroes identified by the Polish forensic scholar, Andrzej Wiercinski, at Monte Alban, Tlatilco, and Cerro de las Mesas, important archaeological sites in Mexico. These human remains establish beyond doubt that blacks inhabited Middle America in pre-Columbian times.

But how did they get there, and when? The Florida researcher, Kenneth Caroli, offers evidence to show that Olmec Mexico might have been the legendary Punt (later known as King Solomon's Ophir), a distant land of fabulous wealth visited by expeditions ordered at Pharaoh's command. Were the blacks traveling as sailors, warriors, or even royalty, memorialized by the great stone heads? Indeed, trends to popularize Ancient Egypt as a black African civilization occur throughout America's entertainment media and even our schools.

Such a characterization is contradicted by the famous bust of Queen Nefertiti and the two best-known pharaohs—Ramses II, whose well-preserved mummy has thin, red hair, and Tutankhamun, a blond. Indeed, Tutankhamun's tomb included palace furniture that portrayed Negroes as servile or conquered, such as a rocking chair that shows a black captive bound to the rocker itself. On the soles of the king's sandals were depicted blacks, which Pharaohs could forever tread upon. Pygmies, the only blacks apparently welcome in Egyptian society, were highly valued as entertainers. According to A.A. Sayce, a classic authority on the subject, the dynastic inhabitants of the Nile Valley were a Caucasian people, short and sturdy of stature, with fine, brunette hair, often grey-eyed. Of essentially Hamitic stock, they were a homogeneous blend of what W.B. Emery, the distinguished excavator of Saqqara, called "the Master Race," a mysterious people (remembered as the *Smsu-Hr*, or "Followers of Horus"), who suddenly arrived from the west, settling in the Nile Valley around 3100 B.C.

Later, in the New Kingdom, with the imperialist expansion of Ramses II, significant numbers of foreigners began to become part of the native population for the first time. Particularly during the XXIInd through the XXIVth Dynasties, when native Egyptians could not even sit on the throne, the flood gates of immigration were thrown open, so that, by the time Egypt was reduced to a Roman province under Caesar Augustus, one could no longer speak of an "Egyptian people" any longer. With the Islamic conquest of the seventh century, racial transformation was complete, and Egypt became an Arab state. Although they still ruled their own fate, the Dynastic Egyptians were very race-conscious, often depicting clear divisions of foreign humanity into the black Nubians, the fair-skinned Kheftiu (Minoans), the callow Asiatics, the hook-nosed Semites, the bearded Lebu (Lybians), and the Europoid Hanebu, or "Sea Peoples."

As early as the 12th Dynasty, in the Middle Kingdom, about 1900 B.C., Senwosret I erected an inscribed nilometer (a device to measure the river's various flood stages) at the Third Cataract. It survives today and quotes him as having commanded, "No Negro shall pass beyond this point into my realm." That admonition stood for the next 20 centuries, until long after the decline of Pharaonic Egypt had become irreversible, and the divided country was taken over by Nubian potentates, in 712 B.C. Known as the Ethiopian Period, the XXVth Dynasty was to last a scant 41 years of unrelieved chaos, culminating in catastrophe: the subjugation of Egypt by Assyrian hordes. These late usurpers—Shabaka, Shabataka, and Taharka—were the only blacks to wear the *nemes*-crown of pharaoh, but they were powerless to actually rule Egyptian society, awash as it was then in civil turmoil and political decay.

Clearly, they were in no position to launch any voyages to Punt, be it America or down the block. Indeed, the last recorded expedition took place during the reign of Ramses III, five centuries earlier. The last of the African-faced Olmec heads was made 100 years *before* the black XXVth Dynasty was founded. These dating comparisons and the unrest of the Ethiopian Period, when Nubian "pharaohs" were supposed to have dispatched sea-traders to Middle America, obviate any likelihood that the stone heads portray black Egyptians.

In fact, the ancient Mexican artwork far more resemble West Africans. That remarkable resemblance belongs to a peripheral ridge following the outer curvature of the lips, a genetic trait that typifies Ghana negroes and is reproduced on the Olmec stone faces. But here, too, the dates cancel each other out. As mentioned above, the Olmec heads were not carved after 800 B.C., while Ghana society flourished from the 14th century A.D.

*Was this West African portrayed in monumental art by the ancient Olmecs because he was a king, favored slave, sacrifice, or champion? Photograph by Claudette Nichols.*

Supporters of black ancient Egyptians or later West Africans arriving in prehistoric America nevertheless claim that Olmec art memorializes powerful negro regents. But of the 18 giant heads, three portray distinctly Amerindian, decidedly *non*-African faces, such as the long-nosed example visiting Chicago, mentioned above. If the big sculptures portray a line of black kings who ruled pre-Columbian Mexico, how do these Native American versions fit into the picture? Worse, virtually all the other depictions of blacks in Olmec art portray them as servile (such as Alvarado's sandstone stele), cringing before bearded Semitic types, or contorted in castrated agony (the Danzante figures of Monte Alban). These are hardly the representations of all-powerful monarchs, but more reminiscent of the subservient Nubians portrayed in Egyptian art.

Although West African faces dominate the colossal stone heads, they are not the only foreigners sculpted in Olmec art. A middle Pre-Classic wooden mask originally encrusted with jade decoration, found in a Guerrero cave (presently at New York's American Museum of Natural History), is so overtly Asian in appearance, an observer might be inclined to assign it to a specific Chinese dynasty. It is by no means the only such example.

Even more common are the profiles of distinctly Semitic faces, often wearing artificial chin-beards, such as the stone relief of an important official on Stele 3, in La Venta Park. The Olmecs were great collectors of jade, the precious mineral that probably drew wealth-seeking merchants from both Occident and Orient, thereby creating the puzzling mix of early Mesoamerican culture. Perhaps the blacks were just part of the crowd of foreigners in search of Mexico's blue-green treasure. Or maybe they were something more, after all.

The proponents of West African origins for the disembodied stone portraits liken their headgear to the crowns worn by Ghana chieftains. Though both are kind of a cap, real similarities go no further and differ fundamentally in all other details. Moreover, the symbol of Olmec authority was a turban or high, conical hat, while headgear worn by the great stone heads appears to have been a simple, leather helmet. Too inelegant for royalty and unsuited for war, it would have provided adequate protection for a player during some sporting event, such as the Olmecs engaged in at their ball-courts. If this game was anything like the kind celebrated by the much later Aztecs (and scholars believe it remained essentially unchanged from Olmec times), its connection with persons depicted in the basalt sculptures may be our key to solving the mystery of the stone heads.

Known as *Tlachtli*, the Mesoamerican ballgame was far more than popular entertainment. Opposing teams sometimes played for weeks or even months at a time. The object was to kick or butt a solid rubber ball through an impossibly small hoop. Attracting the focus of the whole community, the games were serious religious events, wherein cosmological precepts were reenacted through sport, with the ball representing the struggle of the Sun to keep on its heavenly course. All participants were highly honored sacred athletes, especially the leader of the winning team. His reward for victory was to be sacrificed on the high altar of the sun-god. He was decapitated, his head or skull preserved in a public place of honor, while his soul flew up to the blessed regions of the solar deity.

In view of these ritual ballgames apparently inaugurated by the Olmecs, the most plausible explanation for the colossal stone heads is that they are portraits of and memorials to Tlachtli's victorious, decapitated team-players. The larger-than-life sculptures represent the ritually sacrificed heroes of the ball-courts, an interpretation that at once accounts for their monumental size, their football-like helmets and disembodied portrayal. But what accounts for their African faces?

If we look around the world at the time the great stone heads were made (from decades immediately preceding the 10th century B.C. to no later than 800 B.C.), we find that Solomon, ancient Israel's greatest king, was operating a huge commercial fleet manned by Phoenician sailors. Their ships ventured far to bring him the wealth of fabled territories, such as the legendary Ophir. If that far-off land of precious minerals (jade?) and abundant gold was Mexico (which does indeed provide an uncanny match for biblical descriptions of Ophir), then the anomalous Semitic profiles and Near Eastern apparel of the figures depicted on Olmec stele probably belong to sea-traders hired by King Solomon. The Phoenicians had important commercial dealings with black Africa, as evidenced by Hanno's well-documented expedition to Sierra Leone and the Cameroons. Edey writes that the Admiral "was interested in solidifying African trade," and blacks regularly served aboard Phoenician vessels. When they made port-of-call at the Mexican Ophir, several of the black crewmen may have been won over to the Olmec religion and its ritual ballgame.

Judging from the faces portrayed on the stone heads, there were no converts among the Phoenicians. Natural athletic prowess combined with a new spiritual fervor (supplemented by mind-altering drugs) and the deification by a whole society, resulted in the black foreigners becoming Tlachtli players, whose reward for being on the winning team was decapitation. Their bold faces still look out at the world they left, nearly 3,000 years after their fatal victories.

# CHAPTER 8:

# Pre-Columbian Europeans on Our Shores

## MURAL QUESTIONS KING'S HISTORY

An accidental discovery made in an obscure English town brought back to life the image of a royal personage being killed in North America. What made the old painting special, however, was its seventh-century origins and the renowned identity of its portrayed victims as revealed in *Ancient American*'s October, 2001 issue.

### WAS KING ARTHUR MURDERED IN AMERICA? BY JAMES MICHAEL

In 1972, in the little town of Stoke Dry, England (near the Welsh border), workers removed the whitewash from an old church's wall. There they found the mural of a young king shaven in the British, now called "Welsh," tradition. It depicted the king struck by the arrows of savages whom the townspeople referred to as "Native Americans."

Discovery of the perplexing mural was a surprise to the towns-people, who knew nothing of the events it portrayed. Some of them jumped to the conclusion that "It is proof the Vikings made it to America, came back to Britain dressed as Native Americans, and killed King Edmond!" But Edmond died in 860 A.D., 140 years before the Icelandic Sagas tell us the Vikings sailed.

Centuries ago, Stoke Dry occupied an area controlled by the sons of Madoc, the seventh-century Welsh monarch and their descendants. The young king depicted in the discovered mural was Arthur II, Madoc's brother, who was killed on the North American continent. His corpse was mummified, then shipped to his Welsh homeland for burial.

Although these events have long been generally forgotten, the name "Stoke Dry" still preserves something of their memory. No one would give such an evil, dastardly name to a town, unless they wanted to memorialize a particularly important incident. "Stoke Dry" translates from Old British as the "Evil Bow."

## LANGUAGE OF THE DARK AGES

Sixth century men had both motive and means to escape their European homelands, then falling under the deepening shadow of the Dark Ages. Some of them did so by sailing in leather boats to the other side of the Atlantic Ocean; the proof of that voyage was documented in a stone inscription until its recent vandalism. With its ignorant destruction, future generations have been deprived of a valuable treasure from their country's prehistory. The *Ogam* mentioned in this December, 1999 article from *Ancient American* refers to a written language used mostly by Irish monks from the sixth through 14th centuries.

## THE LOST ANCIENT IRISH INSCRIPTION OF KENTUCKY BY M.C. EDWARDS

Throughout America, inscriptions carved on rock shelters and in caves are still being found. Known as *petroglyphs*, they were once thought to have been made by American Indians. But recent studies by leading experts in ancient Old World languages discovered that not all the carvings were the work of indigenous people.

An outstanding example from the Laurel Branch of Goose Creek, in Clay County, Kentucky, appears to have been etched by Irish monks who arrived in North America about 500 or 600 A.D., nearly 1,000 years before Columbus re-discovered America. One such monk may have been St. Brendan. Known in his own time as "the Mariner," he was an Irish Christian monk, who founded the monastery at Clonfert County, Galway, about 560 A.D. During the reign of Pope Pelagius (555 to 561 A.D.), Brendan was said to have completed two transatlantic crossings, and monastic records of the period document that he discovered a new land far to the west. His voyages were said to have lasted several years, with as many as 17 men accompanying him. Religious strife at the time inspired many Europeans to seek escape from their homelands, even faced with the perils of the ocean. Irish monks, anxious to preserve the dying embers of civilization from an encroaching Dark Age, would have been the first to entrust their fortunes on the gamble of overseas' expeditions.

Although suggestions that anyone completed voyages to America before Columbus are anathema to conventional scholars, the trans-atlantic crossings undertaken by Dr. Thor Heyerdahl in his authentic replicas of Egyptian reed boats established that such journeys were not beyond the capabilities of sea-farers during ancient times. More pertinent to the story of our Clay County inscription, archaeologist Timothy Severin sailed across the North Atlantic 23 years ago in a leather boat identical to the coracles employed during the sixth century Irish monks. He showed that St. Brendan and his followers did indeed possess vessels capable of successfully completing round-trip voyages to North America. Severin's expeditions were described by the *National Geographic Magazine*'s "The Voyage of Brendan," December, 1977.

Their message nevertheless appears to have been carved in Gaelic and a Keltic script known as *Ogam* under a rock cliff at the Clay County site. In 1987, Dr. John Payne of Berea, Kentucky, sent his photographs and drawings of the site to California's Epigraphic Society, for analysis by Dr. Berry Fell, Professor Emeritus at Harvard University, and author of several books describing pre-Columbian contacts in the Americas. He interpreted the incomplete inscription as follows: "Do not sulk nor be downhearted, singing joyous carols more suitable to a monk."

Kentucky's Keltic inscription differs only slightly from the Ogham of Old Irish manuscripts. Another Gaelic inscription at Boone County, West Virginia, may be the longest such inscription written in *Ogam* anywhere. It seems to be a statement about the birth of Christ. Yet another, briefer specimen at Wyoming County, West Virginia, similarly deals with Christmas and is reportedly aligned with the winter solstice. The Kentucky and West Virginia sites were originally featured in a series of articles published by *Wonderful West Virginia*, March, 1983. Since then, opposing investigators have wrangled back and forth over their authenticity. But Professor Robert Meyer, an authority on Old Irish dialects and Professor of Keltic Studies at the Catholic University of America, confirmed in an interview with West Virginia Public Television, that the American Ogham was the work of Irish monks of the sixth century A.D.

Tragically, the Goose Creek text was obliterated in 1994 by chisel-wielding vandals. Their mindless destruction demonstrated the vulnerability of unprotected sites to willful cretins, while pointing up the awful fragility of our past.

Despite official skeptics still unable to prove the inscriptions were hoaxed, it is not difficult to imagine a monk having come all the way from Ireland sitting in his primitive shelter, a thousand years before Columbus, not knowing what the future could possibly have in store for him. Perhaps during some lonely Christmas, he began to think of home and loved ones left behind, realizing that he would probably never see either again. He sings a joyous carol to recover from the depression that has come over him. His melancholy dispelled, he writes a little message, lest he forget his purpose for being here. For the next fifteen hundred years, the brief inscription existed as testimony to the triumph of his faith.

## EUROPEANS IN WEST VIRGINIA

Robert L. Pyle taught classes in archaeology at the Smithsonian Institution (Department of Energy), Carnegie Mellon University, Waynesburg College, and other higher educational institutions throughout West Virginia, Ohio, Maryland, and Pennsylvania. But nothing in his academic career prepared him for the discovery of a lifetime, when evidence for a European presence in America was clearly dated to 1,200 years ago.

An 8th Century Irishman
Visited West Virginia
by Robert L. Pyle

The March, 1983 issue of *Wonderful West Virginia Magazine* published an article about a possible transatlantic quest undertaken by St. Brendan from Ireland to West Virginia nearly 1,000 years before the official discovery of the New World. Mainstream scholars scoffed at the suggestion of any pre-Columbian voyages to North America, but were nonetheless forced to re-consider their skepticism in the light of suggestive human skeletal remains found in a Wyoming County, West Virginia rock shelter. It seems the bones were recovered very near a site already controversial for its non-Indian, pre-modern inscription.

The skeleton had the *brachycephalic* skull of an adult male. *Brachycephalic*, or "round headed," cranial forms imply possible European origins. More certain was the skull's pre-Columbian provenance. Just how old it was could not be determined, however, until DNA and radio-carbon testing could be brought into play to determine its specific age and racial origins. Funding was finally made available as recently as 2001, thanks to a private supporter intrigued enough by the find to subject it to laboratory testing. Mitochondrial DNA was extracted from the roots of the skull's teeth and compared to previously cataloged DNA sequences from ethnic groups around the world. Although no association was found among North American groups, the closest DNA matches were indeed European, complimenting the skull's *brachiocephalic* type. Radio-carbon dating established its age at 1,292 +/-40 years Before Present, or circa 710 A.D. (+/- 40 years).

The West Virginia find thus established positive identification of the earliest date for a European on the North American continent. For the first time, physical evidence suggests with at least some degree of certainty that a man from the Old World visited our continent in pre-Columbian times.

Two decades before the skull's startling testing results were known, I was intrigued by additional petroglyphs found in the mountains of southern West Virginia. At first glance, the "rock letters" resembled archaic runes, those written symbols and characters used by the Norse during the European Dark Ages. They were certainly unlike other Native American rock art with which I was familiar. Particularly intriguing were the petroglyph sites in Wyoming County, where the skeleton was found, and in Manchester, Kentucky. Closer examination revealed that the markings belonged to an ancient alphabet known as Ogam, used in the British Isles, especially Ireland, Scotland, and Wales, more than 1,000 years ago. Resemblances were so comparable to this old script, the West Virginia and Kentucky specimens could be identified with a specific variation of Ogam, referred to as "stem type," familiar in early Christian Ireland.

Their recognition suggested a possible connection to stories of St. Brendan, the sixth century cleric who supposedly set out with a crew of fellow monks across the North Atlantic. In support of a conjectured relationship, the West Virginia and Kentucky petroglyphs were examined by university-trained scholars in Keltic linguistics. Dr. William Grant, from Edinburgh University, Scotland, and Dr. John Grant, of Oakland, Maryland, confirmed that the Wyoming County petroglyphs were indeed authentic archaic Ogam.

In 1998, and again during 2000, I was in Ireland to compare European Ogam scripts with their possible American counterparts. Dr. William Grant was kind enough at the time to invite my participation in research investigating the earliest known Irish Ogam panel. It is located in the remote and rugged mountains of southern Ireland. There I learned that Ogam is commonly found on the corner edges of tombstones, not on rock formations. To my surprise, the Irish Ogam panel, although larger (8 feet high and 20 long) and more complex than its North American versions, comprised many characters virtually identical to the West Virginia and Kentucky petroglyphs.

Wyoming County's eighth century European skull and its proximity to contemporary Irish script combine to make a strong case for the arrival of Old World visitors to West Virginia in the pre-Columbian past.

# KNIGHTS TEMPLAR

For nearly 200 years, the Templars controlled a massive fleet that carried commerce and warfare across the Mediterranean Sea and along the Atlantic coasts of Europe. With their proscription by a French king and an Italian pope, the Templars sought refuge in Scotland. But many of their ships vanished. Could at least some of them have sailed as far as North America? According to Michael Kaulback, a Fitchburg, Massachusetts library technician and historian, in the January/February, 1999 *Ancient American*, the faded image of a 14th-century knight on a New England rock-face may be the answer.

 ## KNIGHTS TEMPLARS IN THE NEW WORLD BY MICHAEL KAULBACK

Shortly after World War II, a local amateur archaeologist made some photographs of a peculiar, weathered engraving on the side of a boulder near the town of Westford, Massachusetts. Published in *The Ruins of Greater Ireland and New England*, author W.B. Goodwin speculated that the faint outline depicted a broken Norse sword of the 11th century. Afraid the faded image might be ruined by vandals, Goodwin never revealed its exact location. But his book continued to attract the attention of other investigators determined to find the site, even after Goodwin's death.

Among them was Frank Glynn, who, after much difficulty, discovered it covered under a mat of moss. He was able to determine that the image had been created by a series of punch-holes made with a hammer. The portrayed sword was identified by British antiquarians as a large "hand-and-a-half wheel pommel blade" of the 13th or 14th century. Careful cleaning revealed what appeared to be the memorial effigy of a helmeted knight-at-arms, complete with sword and shield. It was this shield, or the arms it bore, that identified the depicted knight as James Gunn from Caithness, Scotland. At its bottom was a galley; a star and crescent appeared at top-right, a configuration traced to Gunn.

In life, he had been an associate of Henry Sinclair and was known to have followed him on his sometimes extensive sea voyages. Earl William St. Clair (Sinclair), the last Earl of Orkney, was the Grand Master of Craft-masons in 1439. He was also the Grand Prior of the Scottish Knights Templar and fought along side Robert the Bruce at the battle of Bannockburn with a large contingent of fellow knights. Their victory made Robert a king. Some Masonic scholars believe that "the Bruce" formed their Royal Order of Scotland to reward the Knights Templar for their invaluable services. He knew it was money and military training from the Templar Knights that made the difference at Bannockburn.

The Templars were originally known as "The Knights of the Poor Fellow Soldiers of Christ" and had long before comprised a military-monastic fighting order founded in the Holy Land during 1118 by just nine officers. Provided with living quarters in Crusader King Baudoin II's palace near the remains of Solomon's Temple, they were henceforward known as "Knights of the Temple," or the "Knights Templar." Eleven years later, four of them traveled back to France, where they met with a churchman, Saint Bernard, who introduced them at the Council of Troyes to the Pope. The papal blessing they received from him likewise assured their official recognition from the chief political authority of the time.

Thereafter, the knights grew very rich and influential, particularly excelling in the precarious art of high finance.

As part of their modern legacy, today's banking system was created by Templar economists. Consequently, as their wealth naturally attracted numerous supporters, it likewise created for them many enemies. In 1307, King Philip (known as "the Fair" of France), abetted by the Pope, set out to destroy the Templars in order to seize their vast wealth. In a large-scale military raid, he had all the Templars in France arrested on Friday the 13th of October, from which that unlucky day persists in modern superstition. Although Philip seized their lands and burned thousands of knights at the stake, the Templar fleet, made up of several treasure-ships loaded with centuries of accumulated riches, sailed away from his grasp. The entire armada vanished without a trace. The Pope then issued an international order to seize the knights, but his demand was not obeyed in England and Scotland, where the Order found refuge, and continues to this day. At the 1314 Battle of Bannockburn, a large force of Templars was alleged to have fought under a flag known as the Beauseant. Their participation in this engagement is the last known reference to Templars in battle.

The Westford Stone may be connected somehow through these events in Templar history to an ancient stone tower in Newport, Rhode Island. Its architecture displays northern European influences from the High Middle Ages, and employed a unit of measurement remembered as the "Scottish Ell." Known in England until Shakespeare's time, *ells* were based on Norse fathoms, hence the understandable misidentification by modern Viking enthusiasts who regard the Newport Tower as the work of Northmen. It really more resembles Templar and even 14th-century Scottish counterparts, and is similar to round churches built in the Holy land; examples being the Church of the Holy Sepulcher and the Dome of the Rock in Jerusalem. Interestingly, it was mentioned in documents of London's public record house, dating back to 1632, seven years before Rhode Island was founded.

Another structure on the other side of the Atlantic Ocean also suggests a Templar presence in late pre-Columbian America. Rosslyn Castle, near Midlothian, was begun by Sinclair in 1446. Yet, a surviving carving of maize or Indian Corn and another of an aloe cactus (neither known in Scotland until after the return of Columbus from the New World 46 years later) may still be seen there. The sculpted representations of these foreign plants is believed to have been ordered by William Sinclair to commemorate the voyage of his ancestor, Prince Henry, to "a new country."

In 1365, during a stop-over in Venice during a crusade for the King of Cyprus, Prince Henry was introduced to the Zeno family, Italy's outstanding navigators and cartographers. Nicolo Zeno, it so happened, had been shipwrecked on Fair Isle between Orkney and the Shetland Isles, so Prince Henry put him to working on his fleet of 13 ships. Brother Antonio was eventually sent for, and through these two extraordinary navigators, the Prince became well-versed in the leading maritime theories of the day, one of which involved speculation about a rich, unknown land on the other side of the Atlantic Ocean. In May, 1398, an expedition was financed and mounted by Henry Sinclair.

Outfitting a fleet of 12 Viking-style long-ships, they supposedly made their way west across the Atlantic ocean making landfall in Nova Scotia. Their arrival appeared to have been confirmed by the discovery earlier this century of a cannon of the same kind displayed at the Naval Museum in Venice and typical of the ordinance aboard Zeno's ships. The Nova Scotia cannon is presently housed in the fortress of Louisberg, on Cape Breton Island. Such artillery was obsolete by the end of the 14th century, so the American find dates to the period of Prince Henry's expedition. The Scottish Templars probably wintered in Nova Scotia with the Mic-Mac Indians. In the spring, they traveled down through what would become Massachusetts and into what we now know as Newport, Rhode Island.

Perhaps somewhere around Westford one of the party died and was buried. To mark the site an effigy was etched into a rock outcropping. The image is weather-beaten, badly faded, yet barely perceptible. It was first documented in 1883, when a Reverend Edwin Hodgeman described the rock and included the following comment: "Rude outlines of the human face have been traced upon it, and the figure is said to be the work of Indians."

Why did Henry Sinclair set off with 12 ships and more than 300 men, a rather large force for an exploitative mission, across the sea? The Prince may have been looking for a place to start a colony far away from the suppression that still raged in Europe. His coat of arms was in the shape of a sea-beast or dragon, topped by an engraved a cross above a coronet. This was the symbol of the keepers of the Holy Rood, a reliquary allegedly containing a large portion of the true cross that had long since vanished. Such symbolism may be, at least partially, suggested in the Westford effigy. It could memorialize a unknown man—one of the Knights Templar—who arrived and died in New England some 70 years before the birth of Christopher Columbus.

## LAMPS FROM PREHISTORIC TIMES

Skeptics attempting to debunk any possibility of Old World influences in pre-Columbian America are largely unaware of hard evidence in the form of common, household artifacts found in Ohio and Wisconsin. In his article for the December, 2004 issue of *Ancient American*, publisher Wayne May told how ancient European oil-lamps are throwing new light on the prehistory of our country.

## MEDITERRANEAN LAMPS: ANOMALIES OF THE MIDWEST
### BY WAYNE MAY

There are thousands of objects that crowd the museums of antiquities packed away in the various storerooms and cities across Europe and Asia, but scarcely any are smaller than the terra-cotta lamps used by the ancients. However, from their artistic shape and the innumerable subjects treated on them by way of ornamentation, they are extremely interesting clay objects. The Egyptians and Greeks manufactured lamps very early, yet there is evidence to show that they were not familiar in general among the many other cultures until about 300 to 250 B.C. Pliny says that a lack of oil until about this time prevented their use.

Before its introduction, candles (*candelae*) made of wax and tallow; torches; bits of pine wood or a sort of cornucopia filled with flax, or tow, and covered with resin, oil, pitch, or wax, were used for illuminating purposes. The candelabra commonly mentioned in literature was a support originally intended for candles, and then afterwards for lamps. These were made of wood, bronze, or precious metals, and have been found in large numbers throughout the Mediterranean area. In form, these lamps were usually large, boat-shaped receptacles containing oil, with one or more beaks or nozzles, and were divided into four parts: the reservoir; a circular top, or discus, with rim, sometimes ornamented; the nozzle with a hole for the wick; and the handle, a part not always found in excavations.

In the discus was a small, round hole through which oil was poured. This hole, in the case of bronze lamps, was often covered with a stopper, but terra-cotta versions were not always so equipped. As many as three nozzles have been found on a single lamp. Lamps for carrying were commonly provided with a ring handle, and those without a handle were intended to be stood on a candelabrum or other support. Others were provided with chains of bronze and hung from the arms of candelabra, from a hook, or from the ceiling. The oil used was vegetable, usually olive, though mineral oils are also mentioned in the ancient texts. Wicks were made of tarrow from the pith of various kinds of reeds or rushes. The lamps themselves were fashioned from gold, silver, bronze, or bronze sometimes encrusted with gold, glass, lead, clay alabaster, amber, stone, and clay.

*The ancient Old World oil lamp found in Wisconsin.*

A Near Eastern oil lamp was recovered near Southpoint, Ohio, last fall (2004). John Hudnall found it in his front yard while digging to replace a sewer line at his Lawrence County home. The lamp, estimated at more than 1,000 years old, presents a real dilemma for area archaeologists. Hudnall showed his find to Charles West, owner of the Indian Relic Museum in New Richmond.

After examining the artifact, West said, "It's beautiful. The only problem is, it's not Indian." Hudnall later sought help from Bob Price of the Lawrence County Historical Society, who found similar lamps described in an illustrated encyclopedia of the Bible. West's next contact was the Institute of Archaeology at Andrews University, in Berrien Springs, Michigan. Assistant Director David Merling, said the lamp could have been made between 400 and 800 A.D., somewhere in the Near East or eastern Mediterranean. He went on to say that the lamp was of common origins, but could not pinpoint a specific country. Merling translated an inscription on the lamp to read, "The light of Christ shines for all." An article in the *Portsmouth Daily Times* did not specify the Near Eastern language from which the translation had been made. Hudnall said he would probably lend the artifact to the Huntington Museum of Art in West Virginia for exhibition, then place it permanently with Michigan's Andrews University for study and preservation.

The Hudnall discovery was not the only one of its kind made in the American Midwest. Wisconsinite Robert Freed tells of a similar find that came to light in the western part of his state. "I contacted the individual who sold me the lamp," Freed said. He asked to remain anonymous; his concern was for the privacy of his family who still farm in the area where the artifact was found, although I did get a little more information from him. "The lamp was found during 1969 in Crawford County, Wisconsin, Freeman Township, on a hillside field overlooking the Mississippi River. The plow got hung up on a root, and when they went to clear the plow, the artifact was found face down in the furrow. He (the former owner of the object) told me his brother also found a ten-inch copper spear-point; it had a hole in one side for a place of attachment. There were two barbs on the top, flat base; no socket. Anyway, he had the lamp, spear, and other Indian artifacts in his collection for 35 years."

Exactly one year prior to our introduction, another artifact collector bought his whole collection except for the lamp. Destiny somehow allowed him to hang on to the lamp, and again destiny struck when I was fortunate enough to purchase the lamp from him. "I have attended Indian artifact shows seeking help as to its origin or just to identify what it was. The insinuation of fake or hoax was a common response. But I knew the fellow I purchased it from, and he did not make this thing. It is genuine. Both the artifact hunter and I were under the impression it was an engraved smoking pipe. How excited I was to contact you," Freed told me, "and learn of its true identity. Especially, the area it was discovered is the concentrated area of southwest central Wisconsin, where a large settlement of Hopewell (300 B.C. to 400 A.D.) have left their mark. Could this be a Hopewell artifact? In any case, it is a most remarkable piece of history found here in Wisconsin." It is indeed!

# ROMAN TREASURE UNEARTHED

Dozens of ancient Old World coins have been picked up throughout the Americas since the first English colonists arrived in the 1600s. But few have been so competently authenticated as a cache found with the help of a modern metal-detector on the banks of the Wisconsin River. The story was told by their chief investigator, Dr. James P. Scherz, Professor Emeritus from the University of Wisconsin, in Madison. During the last decades of the 20th century, he was a leading archaeo-astronomer, who discovered the hitherto unsuspected celestial orientations of numerous ancient earthworks across the Upper Midwest. With his article in *Ancient American*'s September/October, 1994 issue, however, Dr. Scherz turned his attention to establishing a Roman impact on our Continent, more than 1,700 hundred years ago.

## WISCONSIN'S ROMAN COINS
## BY DR. JAMES P. SCHERZ

One spring evening in 1994, the phone rang as I was almost out the door to attend our monthly meeting of the Ancient Earthwork's Society held in a classroom at the Engineering Hall of the University of Wisconsin, in Madison, where I work. On the line was Fred Rydholm, a retired schoolteacher in Marquette, Michigan, where he is a renowned expert in the region's ancient copper mines that were operating at a time when Pharaonic Egypt was young. "There's a guy from near Wisconsin Rapids who claims to have found some strange, old coins," he said." Will you check them out?"

*One of the Roman coins found by Fred Kingman while searching the banks of the Wisconsin River with a metal-detector in 1993.*

Long-distance traders, the Kushanas controlled a powerful dynasty along the Silk Roads, uniting various Asian peoples nearly 2,000 years ago. Their commercial network disintegrated concurrently with the collapse of the western part of the Roman World, beginning about 300 A.D. The Kushana Empire was serviced by a people who lived on the coast of the Indian Ocean, the Satavahanas, who sailed in large, sea-going ships represented on their coins, before they too went into decline around 230 A.D., a few generations before the Kushanas. The Satavahana were subservient to their Kushana overlords, but they engaged in separate warfare with another people, the Saka, also known as the Sahkya or Sac. The Kushana themselves were a branch of a larger tribe, the Yueh-ches.

These unfamiliar names belonging to various peoples in control of far-flung trade between China and Rome were repeated along the river networks of North America. Near the Wisconsin River were the Sauk or Saka, and the Yuchi resided between the Mississippi and Ohio Rivers, in what is now southern Illinois. Old memories of visitors from the other side of the world, remembered as the "Keshenas," are preserved in the verbal traditions of the Hopi Indians. Interestingly, "Keshena" is a place-name associated with an Indian reservation in Wisconsin.

A prominent elder amongst the American Yuchi (now in Oklahoma) told of his people, who possessed cows and chickens before the Spanish arrived, "coming to this land in boats." The Sauk, once in Wisconsin and now also on a reservation in Oklahoma, have stories of their ancestors visiting China by way of Alaska.

Considerations such as these perked my interest in the coins Rydholm spoke of, particularly when he mentioned their possible Kushana identity. I told him I needed to see clear photographs of them before undertaking any research. When copies arrived at my office a few days later, I was far from disappointed, although naturally cautious. In any case, I had the photos made into slides as part of a lecture Mr. Fred Kingman was scheduled to make before the Ancient Earthworks Society, in May, about his unusual finds. He told us that the coins had been found the previous fall while searching the banks of the Wisconsin River for antique trinkets with a metal detector. At the time of their discovery in a group, his device registered a "halo," a signal from the surrounding soil attributed to corrosion migrating into the ground over a very long time. The coins were originally found grouped together, as though they had been collected into a bag of perishable material that disintegrated over the years since they were buried.

Although the slides presented enlarged views of them, more impressive were the 10 coins themselves which Mr. Kingman allowed audience members to handle. Most of us were favorably impressed with the realistic art work and the uniformly tiny size of the pieces. Facial features of male profiles they depicted were extremely fine, quite distinctive, and well executed. Interestingly, many of these portraits wore rayed headdresses, as though symbolizing the Sun, reminiscent of similar head decorations occurring among the so-called "Redhorn" wall-paintings in southwestern Wisconsin, at the Gottschall Rock Shelter.

The Kingman coins appeared to have been made by the "die" method, wherein a piece of hot, soft metal was placed on a lower die, then struck with another die from the top, thereby creating an impression on both the top and bottom of the piece. Metal is consequently pushed out near the edges. The dies that produced the Wisconsin coins were obviously created with an extreme amount of artistic and die-making skill. Apparently, no two were made by the same set of dies. Therefore, 20 different dies had been required for their production. Most of the coins appeared to be copper. At least one was a yellow alloy and deeply corroded. A faded inscription could be discerned around the edges of some pieces. Its translation, if possible, could determine the coins identity. It was speculated that they had been minted somewhere in the Old World—perhaps Greece or Rome—a very long time ago.

Not one of us had difficulty. A professor representing the Humanities and Social Sciences faculty on campus, responded to a request from one of our members that someone from the History or Anthropology Departments be present to also hear Fred Kingman's story. For convenience, I refer to this learned gentleman "Professor William."

While we were taking turns scrutinizing the coins, he suddenly blurted out, "They are fake!" I was flabbergasted that a professional colleague, prior to the analysis of basic data, could come to such a hasty and confident conclusion. Worse, I was quite embarrassed for the sake of Fred Kingman and his wife, who, logically assumed, would have done the faking.

"What are the things that led you to this abrupt conclusion?" I asked him. He hesitated, then declared the portraits were facing the wrong way. And the writing had to be read from the inside of the piece, when it should be read from the outside, or vice-versa. Perhaps he was right, although Mr. and Mrs. Kingman, genuinely shocked and hurt by Professor William's implied accusation, were obviously honest people no less interested in finding out the truth about their discovery. If they had not faked the coins, a most unlikely alternative, then maybe the pieces were modern reproductions, perhaps commemorative medallions from a circus or promotional scheme of some kind dating back to the late 19th century, but not before.

No one at our AES meeting, including the skeptical professor, was expert in numismatics, so I initiated my own quest through the research stacks of the University library. In the following weeks, I consulted some 1,300 volumes on Roman Imperial history and numismatics, all the while searching for additional clues that would link the Wisconsin coins with Old World parallels. I learned that coins produced during the reign of Caesar Augustus portrayed his face pointing both left and right, and inscriptions read from either the inside out or the outside in—thereby negating Professor William's contention that the Kingman coins were fake, because the depicted profiles faced the wrong direction and the letters read the wrong way. Even so, I found no matches between them and anything comparable from the world of Augustus, 2,000 years ago.

Moreover, the Wisconsin pieces featured representations of men with decidedly un-Roman, up-turned noses. They reminded me instead of facial features from members of my own family, with deep roots in Germany. The human profiles on the coins struck me, therefore, as less Latin than Teutonic. A numismatic text I found did, in fact, reproduce a Roman Era coin depicting a man with an up-turned nose, his head (similar to those appearing on the Kingman coins) surmounted by a rayed crown. The coin was "of unknown origin," from Bactria, an ancient, Greek-speaking king-dom in the northeastern part of modern Afghanistan, although the "sun-ray" type of cap portrayed was commonly worn along the Danube River Valley during Classical Times. I was troubled, how-ever, by the Greek letters found on the Bactrian examples, because they were wholly unlike those on the Kingman coins, which com-pared more favorably with Latin.

I went on to learn from my library research that the ruler's name, as it appeared on Roman coins, was often preceded by IMP, the same "imperial" designation on one of the Kingman coins, which read, IMPTETRICUS, or "Emperor Tetricus." Excitedly, I checked several listings of every Roman emperor from first to last. But according to these indexes, no such person ever existed. Hoping "Tetricus" might have been a royal nickname of some kind, I took up the laborious investigation of a German-language tome that reproduced the com-plete inscriptions of every Roman Era coin in the possession of the Hamburg Art Museum, which owns one of the largest collections of its kind in the world. While painstakingly examining every numismatic inscription, I found what I was looking for. There, emblazoned on number 1503, the words IMP C TETRICUS P F AUG stood out in bold relief. He was not, after all, a Roman emperor, as I assumed, but the ruler of Gallien, a kingdom along Germany's Rhine River from 270 to 273 A.D.

The elation of discovery faded somewhat, however, when I found what might be part of another title, IMP C CLAUDIUS, on the same Wisconsin coin. The famous Emperor Claudius was in power from 41 to 54 A.D., two centuries *before* Tetricus. It would be unlikely that coins separated by this period of time were carried together, unless in the hands of a coin collector. And I knew that the famous Claudius was not normally shown wearing a sun-symbol headdress, with a beard or sporting a Germanic, up-turned nose. Hoping to find some resolution of these disparities, I resumed my research in the huge German book until I came to a photograph of coin number 1511 with the inscription, IMP CLAUDIUS AUG. This was not the same Claudius of the first century, but a much later emperor, Claudius II, who sat on the throne from 268 to 270 A.D., immediately prior to Tetricus. Both rulers had reigned for a very short period, suggesting troubled times. As later analysis would show, they were very troubled times indeed.

The Emperor Gallienus had been assassinated, and Marcus Aurelius Valerius Claudius chosen by the mutinous army as his successor. The murder created a deep split between the military leaders, who were appalled at the violent death of their Emperor, and the Senate, whose members so reviled Gallienus, they began executing his friends and family. As Roman society was being deeply divided, a serious rebellion in Germany, where Gallienus had been killed, grew yet more dangerous. As the well-known modern historian, Michael Grant, has written, "these Germans had broken through the Brenner Pass and penetrated as far as Lake Benacus (in northern Italy)". Claudius II inflicted a stunning defeat on them, however, capturing or killing half the invaders.

Although he saved Rome, a pretender to the throne had set up a secessionist empire in the west, in Gaul, today's France. Even so, Claudius II went on to win important victories that preserved civilization against constant outside attack by barbarian hordes. These political and military crises were compounded by massive inflation back home and sectarian strife stirred up by religious fanatics. In the midst of external pressure and internal chaos, Christian in-roads against traditional spirituality were contributing to the social confusion. As the ordained protector of Roman values, Claudius II affirmed his allegiance to the imperial cult of Sol, going so far as to have himself portrayed on his coins wearing the rayed-crown of the sun-god. Elements of the old mystery schools of high learning, as well as the philosophies, were incorporated. Aimed at uniting the various religious factions in a popularized belief-system, his sponsorship generated a surge of new adherents, and sporting such solar headgear became fashionable among contemporary monarchs in many parts of the Empire.

But the troublesome, victorious reign of Claudius II was cut short after only two years in power, when he died of a plague in Germany while on campaign. Before his untimely death, he had set up a form of local government to work out differences between the Romans and the Germanic tribes west of the Rhine. This local-based government was called the "Gallic Empire." Its leaders ruled from the city of Trier, home of Tetricus. Taking advantage of the disorientation and uncertainty following the death of Claudius II, Tetricus, a former Roman senator, set himself up as the head of the Gallic Empire to crate a breakaway Gallo-Roman state.

Former political contacts saved his life when the short-lived rebellion was put down, and he brought in chains to Rome. After this public humiliation, he was allowed to retire "in affluence and honorable repose," according to the author of the Hamburg coin book, instead of being executed, as was otherwise the penalty for treason, probably because Tetricus purchased his life with an immense donation to the imperial sun-cult. In the same year he was captured and released, 273 A.D., Rome's Temple of the Sun received no less than seven tons of gold.

The "Gallic Empire" he left behind did not fare as well. Beset by famine, it was ruthlessly dismantled by the Roman legions, its population enslaved or dispersed. But the natives were not with means of escape. Grant writes of the large navies used by the Germans to evacuate as many displaced persons as possible using the mighty Rhine River to find new lives far from trouble.

These historical events seemed to be reflected in the Kingman coins, which were apparently minted at a time of mass-flight from Europe. Could some Roman-era Germans have ventured as far as America? Or were the coins carried here by contemporary Kushana merchants, who, by either accident or design, arrived in North America, where their name was indelibly imprinted in the folk memory of its indigenous people? However they came to rest near the Wisconsin River, the coins found by Fred Kingman are authentically Old World in origin. As such, they are 10 more pieces in the puzzle of our country's mysterious prehistory.

## ROMAN INFLUENCE IN AMERICA

The Kingman Coins are not the only material evidence for ancient Romans in the New World. According to an article in the December, 2000 issue of *Ancient American*, artifacts of an entirely different kind, in a state far removed from the Upper Middle West, were unearthed under the kind of controlled circumstances insisted upon by critics of possible Old World influences during pre-Columbian times. Despite their excavation by professionally trained teams of certified archaeologists working for a state university, the metallic objects were condemned as fraudulent by cultural isolationists, and their enormous potential to revise Americans' understanding of their past was lost.

 ### ROMAN RELICS FOUND IN ARIZONA BY EARL KOENIG

On the morning of 13 September 1924, Charles E. Manier was working in a lime kiln gravel pit off the Silverbell Road, almost 7 miles east of Tucson, Arizona. Unexpectedly, his shovel revealed a metallic shape. Pulling the heavy object free, he noticed at once that it comprised two parts stuck together. He pried them apart and was surprised to see both were lead plates covered with long inscriptions of some kind; one plate was shaped in the form of a crucifix weighing 90 pounds.

That afternoon, Manier did the right thing by taking the strange items to Dr. Frank H. Fowler, at the University of Arizona. The congenial Professor of Classical Literature was fluent in Latin and translated both inscribed plates without difficulty. When he learned where Manier, an uneducated but honest man, found them, he organized an archaeological dig for the next day. Under scientifically controlled conditions, a professional team of excavators began to unearth more buried objects almost at once. They found another inscribed object, this one a foot-long plate.

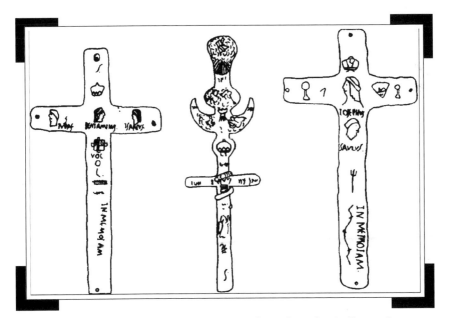

*Three inscribed crosses excavated from the Silverbell gravel pit in 1924.*

Digs continued throughout the year, each time bringing to light more materials. These began to include additional crucifixes, swords, lances, large spatulas, batons, arrow-heads, spear-points, and ceremonial standards, all manufactured in lead. They were encrusted with a hard, crustal coating of caliche that had formed between the reaction of chemical salts and water in the desert soil matrix. Such a process is very gradual, and caliche deposits on the Silverbell finds undoubtedly required several centuries, at least, to accumulate.

Over the next several months, more than 30 such objects were taken from the lime kiln. On 28 November, Thomas W. Brent, who owned the property on which these discoveries were being made, found a second crucifix, this one at 25 pounds. Two days later, Manier brought up another one, likewise inscribed, weighing 10 pounds. On 5 December, hired diggers made the Silverbell Road site's most important find, when they uncovered a 25-pound crucifix emblazoned with the single longest inscription found on all the items.

By year's end, five crosses and nine plates had been found within a radius of 6 feet. The latter objects were manufactured in halves riveted together, their inscribed surfaces coated with an artificial waxy substance chemists were unable to positively identify, "but were unanimous in their opinion that it had served its purpose of preservative with utmost efficiency" (*Tucson Citizen*, 1 February 1925). Their analysis revealed that the crosses and plates were made of a cast led and antimony alloy with traces of copper, tin, silver, and even gold. These ores had been crushed and smelted, then cast and shaped by hammering and smoothing. Workmanship was poor, but understandably so, given their manufacture in the Arizona desert, where natural materials for fine tools would have been scarce.

Dr. Fowler, Charles T. Vorhies (also of the University of Arizona), A.E. Douglas (Directory of the Steward Observatory), Dean Byron Cummings (Director of the Arizona State Museum), and the Museum's Assistant Director, Karl Ruppert, were present when the heavily inscribed crucifix had been excavated under their professional supervision. Later, Dean Cummings verified that all the objects had been removed directly from the gravel pit at the lime kiln under scientifically controlled conditions. A personage no less than the Dean of the College of Mines and Engineering at the University of Arizona, Dr. Gordon M. Butler, personally excavated two halves of a leaden spear-shaft from the lime kiln (*Arizona Star*, February 17, 1928).

"Even if we accept the hypothesis that the soil was washed down by the rains," he declared, "it is ridiculous to contend that the objects were buried there within recent years. There is no evidence of burial or of recent disturbance. To have 'planted' the soil in place would have necessitated moving tons of it at a time." Dr. Alexander A. Stoyanow (Professor of Geology), Dr. T.T. Waterman (Associate Professor of Anthropology), and no less than 10 other professional colleagues concurred with Dr. Butler's assessment of the spear parts' genuineness. He was soon joined by other leading academic figures of the day, including Phoenix archaeologist, Dr. O.A. Turney; Tucson science writer, Clifton J. Sarle, Ph.D.; and Wade H. Ellis, of Washington, D.C.'s National Archaeological Society. The experts were unanimous in their conclusion that the Silverbell Road materials were authentic artifacts belonging to overseas visitors from Europe at least six centuries before Columbus arrived in America.

Translation of the combined Latin text told a surprising story: "*In Memoriam Romani Actius:* In memory of Romans Actius and Theodore, Consuls of great cities. We are carried forward on the sea (to) Calalus, an unknown land (and) a people ruling wildly (Indians?). Toltezus (and) Silvanus are won over. Theodorus brings his forces from the city, Rhoda. And more than 700 are captured. No gold. They are (or shall be) banished from the city. Theodorus, a man of the greatest valor, rules during 14 years. Iacobus rules during (after Theodorus) six years. God helping it is not to be feared. In the name of Israel, Iacobus born again (in) the city. With God's help, Iacobus rules with mighty hand after the manner of his ancestors, and sings to his Lord. May his fame live forever!

"Benjamin was king of the people. He came from Seine to Rome, the bravest of the Gauls. He came to the assistance of the people, to lay the foundation of the city. He built a wall around the city to resist the enemy. Benjamin, mighty in strength. He filled the multitude with religion. He was slain by the Thebans. I heard this from my father five years after, behind the mountain, in memory of his father, Joseph. 880 *Anno Domini*.

"Israel-III was banished, for he had liberated the Toltezus. He was the first to break the custom. The Earth trembled, fear overwhelmed the hearts of mortals in the third year after he had fled. They betook themselves into the city, and kept themselves within its walls. Thou shalt not burn a dead body in the city. Before the city extended a plain. Hills encompassed the city. It is 100 years since Iacobus was king. Iacobus was busy in the front line. He attended to everything, fought much in person, and often struck down the enemy.

"Israel (Israel-III?) gave his attention to the appointment of priests. Life has been granted to us, a people of extensive sway...to serve the king. It is uncertain how long life will continue. There are many things which may be said. While the war was raging, three thousand men were slain. The leaders without their chiefs were taken. Nothing but peace was sought. God ordains all things."

Some of the text seems to have been "signed" with the initials, O.L., although marked differences in the grammatical construction of the various inscriptions indicate that more than one person composed them. "Albion, Iacobus" appeared on the left branch of a crucifix; on the right, "Seine, Israel" perhaps signifying the leaders of Jewish communities in Britain and France, respectively, from which they came to North America. Though the majority of the plates and crosses were inscribed with Latin, some Hebrew was also included.

Dr. Cyclone Covey (Professor of History, Wake Forest University, North Carolina), whose expertise concerning Western European

Mid- to Late Classical Period is formidable, focused on the name Calalus mentioned in the Silverbell inscription. As the author, David Hatcher Childress, explains, "Various Jews had sailed from the Portuguese port of Porto Cale, and founded a city in Florida, naming it Cale. This city is now modern-day Ocala, in north-central Florida." Covey believes that other Jews escaped Rome, and also left Porto Cale, Portugal, for the New World. The Latin form of Porto Cale was Calalus, which became a Jewish-Roman outpost, in 775 A.D. "The city, situated where modern Tucson lies today, was then named Rhoda. One of the leaders, or captain of one of the ships, Covey believes, was born on the island of Rhodes" (pp. 293, 294).

A complete interpretation of all the Silverbell scripts is difficult, because they are themselves incomplete. Moreover, the message of the fragmented text itself is confused. What are we to make of it? The written language is primarily Latin, and Romans (Actius, Theodore, and Silvanus) appear in the beginning as "Consuls of Great Cities," presumably, built in North America after their arrival from overseas—all of which compliments the Roman-style sword blades found in the gravel pit. Moreover, the Romans were great and busy workers in led, the metal used to cast the Arizona artifacts. Some investigators speculate the "Toltezus" cited in the tablets were the Mexican Toltecs. But the text does not confirm their identity, and even suggests, at least once, that "Toltezus" is the name of a man, apparently a military commander of approximate rank to the Roman, Silvanus.

A "Benjamin" is mentioned as having come from Gaul, but his is an incongruous Jewish name one would not expect to encounter in a time and an area of Europe were Jews were not found. "Seine" appears at least twice in the inscriptions, but it implies (through its association with Albion, or "Britain") a place-name, not the famous river in France. The various peoples cited in the Silverbell tablets: Roman Christians, Gauls, Britons, and Jews, comprise an unlikely lot, because European history tells of their mutual animosity. They would hardly seem to have made common cause in some joint venture across the sea to America. But given the time when they supposedly arrived in Arizona, just such an undertaking could have indeed taken place.

The author (or, more likely authors) of the inscribed plates once ("O.L.") wrote in the year 880 A.D. that "it is a hundred years since Iacobus was king." Because Iacobus ruled for six years and was preceded by Theodorus, who ruled for 14, we may deduce that these strangers arrived in Arizona during the mid-700s, making Dr. Covey's date for their founding of the port city, Calalus, about a quarter-century too late. But chronologies developed from the artifacts' internal evidence are unsure. Theodorus and his followers would then appear to have landed in Florida, before moving on to the American south west, sometime after 700 A.D. If so, their transatlantic voyage and resettlement in North America coincided with a period of widespread chaos in Europe.

The armies of Islam swept as far as the Alps, badly shaking the already shaky Byzantine Empire, the debilitated inheritor of Imperial Rome. The Dark Ages, which had already descended upon Europe, were getting darker. And a mixed bag of Christians, Jews, and Keltic pagans were being herded together by a common enemy that threatened them all with conversion by the sword, the Moslem invaders. Faced with trying to survive in a collapsing civilization, they opted for the great dangers and terrible uncertainties of crossing the broad sea to a land perhaps known to them only in oral traditions. But they successfully landed in Florida and built a port there. Then, at least some of them fought their way against native peoples across North America into what is now Arizona.

Their Roman leaders became "consuls of great cities," perhaps a reference to Tuzigoot, Chaco Canyon, Hovenweep, or other monumental ceremonial centers associated with the prehistoric Anasazi and Hohokam in the American south west. Indeed, the brickwork at many of these sites (particularly Wupatki) suggests Roman masonry. But Roman leadership under men such as Actius, Silvanus, and Theodorus began to die out. By default, the Jews replaced them, beginning with Iacobus and Israel-III. At the time their final inscriptions were being made, however, the power of these disparate foreigners appears to have been in steep decline, probably under the hostile pressures of outnumbering native tribes: "It is uncertain how long life will continue. While the war was raging, 3,000 men were slain." The anonymous scribe wrote resignedly, "God ordains all things."

Soon after, the evidence suggests, he and his people were forced out of existence, leaving behind a memorial to their adventure in the led plates found outside Tucson, about 1,000 years later. Incessant battling with numberless tribes of native enemies mentioned in the texts likewise coincides with the onset of the Mississippian Culture. This major transition to a far-flung ceremonial society, although concentrated in the Mississippi Valley, was generated by new peoples pushing up from the south, who dislodged native populations all across North America above the Rio Grande.

Complimenting these historical parallels with the ancient Arizona text, the scientifically controlled circumstances of excavations at the Silverbell site were beyond question. Many professional observers were in attendance. On occasion, they personally excavated some of the led inscriptions themselves, as did Dr. Butler. Describing the inscribed plates 70 years after they were discovered, archaeologist Dr. Gunnar Thompson pointed out that "the texts include numerous quotes from well-known Mediterranean manuscripts, such as Vergil's *Georgics*. Some phrases used in the texts, such as *Dei gratia* (By the grace of God) were common mottos in Medieval Europe." He mentioned Professor Covey "explains that the semi-literate script on the tablets is similar to inscriptions found in ancient Jewish catacombs" (p.181).

Authenticity of the Silverbell artifacts was confirmed by their original discoverer's and present research conducted in both eras by university professionals. Why, then, have so few Americans even heard of the 1924 discovery? And how is it that no U.S. history textbook published since then so much as mentions it?

Certified, university-trained experts who established the lead plates' pre-Columbian identity agreed that their importance went far beyond local significance, with dramatic consequences for American and even world history. Seeking broader recognition for the artifacts, Dean Cummings brought them to Washington, D.C.'s prestigious Smithsonian Institution. But their appearance at the nation's capital immediately called down the ire of archaeology's Eastern Establishment, whose leading figures tolerated no proposition suggesting overseas contacts from the Old World before Columbus arrived. F.W. Hidge at New York's Museum of the American Indian, Heye Foundation, dismissed the Arizona relics as transparent fakes. He was seconded by Bashford Dean, Curator of Arms and Armor at New York's Metropolitan Museum of Art, who said they ranked among the poorest of forgeries. The *New York Times* blasted the Silverbell inscriptions as obvious frauds, in which the led plate text had been taken entirely from three Latin language books: *Rouf's Standard Dictionary of Facts, Harkness Latin Grammar,* and *Latin Grammar of Allen and Greenough.* But names such as Toltexau, Iacobu, or Calalus featured in the Arizona inscriptions do not appear in these standard Latin grammar textbooks of the 19th or early 20th centuries. Not withstanding this fundamental objection, the Eastern press blew up the Arizona discovery into a heated, nation-wide controversy many scholars were afraid might expand into a scandal. Dean Cummings's presentation describing the excavated plates at a meeting of the American Association for the Advancement of Science in Kansas City was met with a stony silence.

Reported the *Arizona Wildcat,* "The attitude of the scientists indicated that they did not consider the artifacts of particular moment." The meeting, representing contemporary American scientific thought, ignored Cummings to award its $1,000 prize to a

Professor Dayton Miller (Cleveland, Ohio), for his paper, which "invalidated some of the major principles of the Einstein Theory."

The AAAS attendees who snubbed Dean Cummings, as with virtually all his critics, never visited the lime kiln in person. Many refused to even look at photographs of its excavated objects, condemning them out of hand.

Soon after the Kansas City rebuff, The *New York Times* fairly exploded with vindictive glee, when it headlined that one Leandro Ruiz, a Mexican immigrant describing himself as "a retired cattleman," was quoted as saying that the Arizona plates were probably forged 40 years before by another Mexican, Timotio Odohui, a sculptor, who lived near the Silverbell Road site. Odohui was allegedly well-versed in Classical literature and executed numerous art objects, mostly in stone, but some (such as a model horse) in lead. No one ever saw him making led crosses or inscribed plates, however, and whatever reasons he may have had for fabricating a hoax were unknown.

Odohui disappeared before the turn of the century, when he might have gone back to Mexico. Other than Ruiz's testimony, no information could be connected to a "Timotio Odohui," who may or may not have even existed. Nonetheless, on this incredibly flimsy, entirely circumstantial, hearsay evidence from a dubious source, the Arizona discovery was loudly condemned as a Mexican forgery.

Unconvinced by the Odohui theory, Dr. E. C. Getsinger, in a front-page story for *The California Jewish Review*, wrote that the inscribed plates were fakes planted at the lime kiln during the previous century by the founder of Mormonism in an attempt to lend historical credibility to his creed. "I believe these Lost-Tribes-of-Israel crosses were planted," Getsinger insisted, "awaiting the time for Joseph Smith to have a 'revelation' concerning them." This despite Dr. Butler's conclusion that geological circumstances did not permit planting the Arizona finds within the previous 500 years.

E.S. Blair, a New York attorney, never saw the Silverbell Road artifacts. But that did not prevent him from receiving lavish newspaper publicity when he declared that they were "fakes planted by some practical joker, or perhaps for a more sinister purpose. Such a result would tend to put a lasting stigma on Tucson, on the University of which we all can be proud, and on the scientists involved. Can it be possible that the learned geologists, archaeologists, and classicists who have vouched for this discovery have been imposed upon?" With this well-publicized outburst from a lawyer, who implied some "sinister purpose" behind the Silverbell Road finds, any scientists who had earlier championed the discovery now felt seriously threatened.

So did Tucson politicians, who cut the University of Arizona's financial support for all further excavations or research of the questionable site. Eventually, even Arizona newspapers joined its nationwide condemnation long after all the principle players had distanced themselves from it. The public campaign to discredit the artifacts found outside of Tucson was stopped only by the economic crash of 1929. But the damage to their credibility through paltry evidence and weak (though vociferous) counter-arguments had been done. Writing about the led artifacts in 1968, E.B. Sayles (a professional archaeologist and curator of the Arizona State Museum) observed, "Had I known about them when the controversy raged, my sympathy would have been with the *Star* (*The Arizona Star* newspaper, whose editor stood up for the object's authenticity) and those who worked to determine their origin and meaning, rather than with those who set out to condemn them before they could be investigated."

At the height of the acrimonious campaign, the *Star* wrote, "Wherever the relics are placed in history, their worth cannot be deprecated by hasty decisions."

Contrary to the accusations of their severe critics, no one ever profited from the discovery, nor implicated in a hoax of any kind. Conveniently forgotten in all the preposterous theories to explain away the artifacts as the work of mysterious Mexican sculptors or even Joseph Smith were the geologists' original test results. They demonstrated that caliche crustal deposits on these objects had taken many centuries to develop, very possibly a thousand years, thereby corresponding to the date of the plates' final inscription, 880 A.D.

Chemical analysis further showed that the objects were made of lead with traces of copper, tin, silver, and gold, hardly the minerals one expects to find in a hoax, especially one from which no one ever profited. But not even the presence of dozens of certified professors in the company of their university-trained staff members at archaeological digs conducted under scientifically controlled conditions were sufficient to silence academic skeptics in absentia, who had long before convinced themselves that such objects must be fraudulent, to the exclusion of all other considerations. Tragically for America, that prejudice still dominates official archaeology. The deniers scoffed that inscriptions on the lead plates were simple Latin phrases obviously "cribbed" from popular language textbooks. Yet, is it possible that (not one, but all) leading language scholars at a major American university, with departments specializing in the Classics, could not have come to the same determination made by out-of-state lawyers and journalists?

Brow-beaten into submission by a hostile press, University of Arizona authorities washed their hands of the whole affair and returned the objects to their original discoverers, Charles Manier and Thomas Brent. Sixty years later, they were again showcased by the University as part of its "Special Collections," less as material proof of Old World visitors to pre-Columbian America, than evidence of a 20th-century hoax. Despite Academia's persistent opposition to their ancient authenticity, the inscribed plates and weapons taken from a gravel pit outside Tucson are elements of one of the most shameful episodes in American archaeology. They wait for a more open-minded time, when impartial scholars will have an opportunity to examine the artifacts for their real identity and significance.

# MINOAN CIVILIZATION

The Minoans built a sophisticated civilization on the Aegean island of Crete, from whence they culturally and economically dominated the Eastern Mediterranean World beginning in the early to second millennium B.C. until the 16th century B.C. Power lay primarily in their expertise as shipwrights and skill as long-distance sailors. Unconventional investigators have long suspected that commercial ambitions may have lured these redoubtable sea-farers across the Atlantic Ocean in search of rich trade goods. But physical evidence of their arrival in America seemed lacking, until a tiny object accidentally found in New England seemed to prove that the Minoans had found their way to our shores after all. The report of its discovery was an *Ancient American* "exclusive" in the January/February, 2002 issue.

 ## MAINE MINOANS
## BY FRANK JOSEPH AND WAYNE MAY

In 1975, Michael Rose was digging a house foundation on the banks of the Penobscot River, near Old Town, 10 miles north of Bangor, Maine. At about a dozen feet down, his shovel unearthed a curious, little metallic object. It was a flat rectangle approximately 1inch long by three-quarter-inch wide and thin as a dime. The obverse shows what appears to be a woman standing in a doorway. She wears a flounced shirt and a high, pointed cap, with a large necklace hanging to her midriff. Her right hand is extended beyond or in front of the doorway, and in her left she cradles either a snake or a fan with serpentine handle. The reverse displays the punch mark that created the female image on the opposite side. The object may be made of a silver-nickel alloy.

Writes Mr. Rose in his correspondence with *Ancient American,* "It was far enough in the ground that we thought it had to be real old, so I just put it away, and recently decided to try and find out what the heck it really is. Beyond that, I'm lost."

Mr. Rose's tiny discovery may be the best evidence yet found on behalf of visitors from Minoan Crete to North America, not centuries before Columbus, but millennia. The Minoans derived their name from an early king, Minos, who later became part of the Greek mythic world, reigning as one of the three judges of the Underworld. The Minoans transformed the eastern Mediterranean island of Crete into one of mankind's most brilliant centers of early civilization. Long before, beginning sometime in the mid-third millennium B.C., their unique society evolved gradually from relatively primitive Cycladic Cultures that flourished in the Aegean.

By 1700 B.C., Minoan Civilization was fully developed, with two great cities, Knossos and Phaistos, dominating the northern and southern coasts, respectively. The Minoans were a literate people, with three written languages: a hieroglyphic syllabary, together with Linear-A and Linear-B. Only the latter, later script, an early form of Greek, has been translated. Minoan religion was filled with the imagery of bulls and serpent-bearing women, symbols of male and female energies. The national emblem was a labrys, or double-headed axe, usually made of copper, in the export-import business of which the Minoans were skilled. As such, they were renowned sea-farers, proficient in the design production and navigation of sea-going vessels that plied Minoan trade from Pharaonic Egypt to Britain's Stonehenge, when that megalithic astronomical computer was still functioning.

For at least three centuries, Ancient Crete was an opulent maritime state, whose sophisticated people used technological innovations from movable type to flush toilets. Their ladies were great lovers of fashion (archaeologists refer to the painted representation of a Minoan beauty at Knossos as "La Parisien"), and everyone thronged to enjoy spectator sports, particularly bull-jumping. Fabulous palaces, with huge courts and fabulously adorned walls, were open to the Aegean sunlight. The Minoans were more mercantile than military, as evidenced by the lack of any defensive walls on the island. Their peacefulness led to their eventual downfall, however, when the Bronze Age kings of war-like Mycenae, Homer's "Heroic" Greeks, rose to power on the Peloponnesus. By the 13th century B.C., all vestiges of Minoan influence had vanished, subsumed in a foreign cultural domination. The small object dug up by Michael Rose a quarter-century ago on the banks of the Penobscot River speaks eloquently of the lost people of King Minos. They invented, as mentioned, a kind of movable type, not for printing newspapers or books, but for astrological purposes. The famous Phaistos Disk is the only complete survivor of many such items used by the Minoans to calculate the positions of certain stellar phenomena, particularly the predicted appearances of certain constellations, such as the Pleiades or the Eagle. The Disk was a simple tablet, into which embossed metal images of the desired stars or constellations were pressed when the clay was soft, before the Disk was baked hard.

*The image on a small metal type unearthed by Michael Rose in Maine (right) belongs to the Earth-goddess worshiped in Minoan Crete, 4,000 years ago.*

The Maine artifact is just such a piece of movable type, matching its Cretan correspondent in size. Moreover, Mr. Rose's find is embossed; its features are prominent enough to distinctly impress themselves into soft clay. The Minoan snake-goddess, invariably portrayed as a woman wearing a flounced skirt, is identically portrayed on the Old Town object. It must have been dropped and lost more than 3,000 years ago by a Minoan visitor who owned his equivalent of the Phaistos Disk, which, researchers believe, was a very common commercial good, probably manufactured in the hundreds (at least) for use by the general public.

But what could have possibly inspired him to brave a treacherous transatlantic crossing so long ago? The answer is simple: copper. The Minoan economy was based on the import-export of the metal. Their own society was thoroughly out-fitted in bronze (manufactured by combining high-grade copper with tin and zinc), from tools to sacred items. At Crete's Iraklion Museum, the salvaged wreck of a Minoan vessel bearing several tons of copper ox-hide ingots is on display. Outside of Cyprus, supplies of high-grade copper in Europe were scarce. Source for the world's highest grade copper is in Michigan's Upper Peninsula. Here, a prodigious mining enterprise was undertaken by unknown miners, who removed a minimum of half-a-billion pounds of copper from 3,000 to 1200 B.C.

This huge operation represents one of the greatest archaeological mysteries, because the ancient copper vanished from North America, just as the Near Eastern and European Bronze Age blossomed. The Minoans, with their able seamanship and sea-going ships (to say nothing of their commercial appetite for copper), were obviously part of Bronze Age efforts to grow rich on Upper Michigan's mineral supplies. Copper was the equivalent of atomic fusion during pre-Classical times, and enterprising copper barons would have gone to any lengths to obtain it for their multi-national clientele.

These considerations are underscored by Mr. Rose's discovery of the piece of ancient movable type near Old Town, just 35 miles from the Atlantic Ocean, on the banks of the Penobscot. In Minoan times, it was a more extensive river than at present, and connected directly with the

Saint Lawrence, which could carry a ship directly to the ancient copper mines of Upper Michigan. But the Maine find is by no means the first discovery of its kind. Representations of the Minoan labyrinth, or ritual maze, have been found as far away as New Mexico and Arizona.

An inscription in Linear-A, dating to 1500 B.C., was found by a trapper, Bernardo Ramos, in Brazil. Another Brazilian find was made in the Amazon Valley by the 1920s Fawcett Expedition, which recovered the Cretan statuette of a human figure holding a tablet covered with Minoan hieroglyphs. Particularly intriguing are Minoan ox-hyde ingots of mined copper used as currency by various Native America tribes as late as the 16th century A.D. These complimentary finds support the authenticity of the Old Town artifact. Even so, it stands on its own as clear evidence of a Minoan arrival in Maine more than 30 centuries ago.

# Conclusion

The great variety of artifacts described in the preceding pages combine to form an impressive body of evidence on behalf of over-seas' visitors to our country centuries, even millennia before the generally accepted, official history of America supposedly began, in 1492. These challenging objects are not without support from complimentary, oral traditions preserved over countless generations by native peoples from the Arctic Circle to the Andes. Together, they comprise the lost, neglected, despised, and occasionally suppressed account of our human origins on this continent.

But the evidence presented in this volume represents barely the tip of the diffusionist iceberg. Much has already been found, and much more is being found to radically revise a consensus-reality engineered by the academic powers-that-be for a public over-awed by scholastic authority. A ground-swell of contrary evidence, generated by rapid advances in research technology, is growing and must inevitably overwhelm the antiquated paradigms still espoused as incontrovertible doctrine by those best served by such narrow-minded dogma. *Ancient America* is the herald of that forth-coming change in perspective, based on the unsuspected depth of our country's profoundly rich antiquity.

# Bibliography

## Chapter 1: Bucking the Archaeological Establishment

### America's First Civilization: Older Than Believed Possible

Chan, Pina. *The Olmec, Mother Culture of Mesoamerica*. New York: Rizzoli Books, 1989.

Cooper, Gordon. *A Leap of Faith*. New York: MacMillan Co. Inc., 2000.

Gruener, J. *The Olmec Riddle, An Inquiry into the Origin of Pre-columbian Civilization*. Rancho Sante Fe, Calif.: Vengreen Publications, 1987.

Sitchin, Zechariah. *The Lost Realms*. New York: Bear & Co., 1997.

### Kennewick Man: Still Politically Incorrect After Nine Thousand Years

Marks, Jonathan. *What it Means to be 98% Chimpanzee: Apes, People, and Their Genes*. Los Angeles, Calif.: University of California Press, 2002.

Quinone, Peter and Carol Lever. "Kennewick Man: May He Rest in Peace?," *Ancient American* Volume 6, Issue 37 (February, 2001).

*The Real Eve.* Directed by Andrew Piddington. Hollywood, Calif.: Lions Gate Home Entertainment, 2002.

Wells, Spencer. *The Journey of Man: A Genetic Odyssey.* New York: Random House Paperbacks, 2003.

## The Michigan Tablets: An Archaeological Scandal

(Fr. Charles Sheedy to Milton R. Hunter, pers. comm.)

(Henrietta Mertz and Fr. Charles Sheedy, pers. comm.)

(James Bird, Paul Roundy, and Milton R. Hunter, pers.comm.)

(Milton R. Hunter and Fr. Charles Sheedy, pers. comm.)

Baldwin, John. *Ancient America.* New York: Longstreet Publishers, 1998.

Carter, Leonard D. and Paul R. Cheeseman. "Historical Background of the Soper-Savage Collection of Inscriptions and Drawings," Salt Lake City, Utah: BYU, 1977, p. 2.

Mertz, Henrietta. *The Mystic Symbol.* Green Bay, Wisc.: Ancient American Press, 1994.

Powell, John Wesley. "First Annual Report." Bureau of Ethnology. Washington D.C., 1880, p. 74.

Russell, John. *Prehistoric Discoveries in Wayne County.* Lucedale, Miss.: Corner Press, 1911.

Talmage, James E. "Flow of Twaddle begs Question," *Deseret Evening News,* November 5, 1911.

## Humans in America One-Quarter of a Million Years Ago

Boule, M. H. Vallois. *Fossil Men.* New York: The Dryden Press, Inc., 1957.

Cremo, Michael A., "The Controversy over 'The Mysterious Origins of Man.'" New Zealand: *Nexus Magazine,* May,1998.

Cremo, Michael and Richard Thompson. *Forbidden Archaeology.* Berkeley, Calif.: Bhaktivedanta Institute, 1993.

De Carrero, Jose. *Liberdad Humanas de las Pueblas.* Mexico City: Estrella, 1996.

Gabel, Creighton. *Man Before History.* Upper Saddle River, N.J.: Prentice Hall, Inc., 1964.

Leaky, L.S.B. *The Evolution of Man.* New York: Harper & Row, 1960.

Traxler, Benjamin. *Human Evolution in the Americas.* London: Presidium Press, Ltd., 1989.

## No More Clovis Moses

Cremo, Michael A. "The Controversy over 'The Mysterious Origins of Man,'" *Nexus Magazine,* May,1998.

Doutre, Mark. *Ancient Celtic New Zealand.* Wellington, Australia: Dé Danann, 1999.

Sunfellow, David. "The Great Pyramid and The Sphinx." *www.nhne.com/specialreports/pyramid.html,* November 25, 1994.

# Chapter 2: Ancient Technology

## Super Science From Pharaonic Egypt to Pre-Spanish Peru

Childress, David Hatcher. *Lost Cities and Ancient Mysteries of South America.* Kempton, Ill.: Adventures Unlimited Press, 1986.

Hodges, Henry. *Technology in the Ancient World.* London: Marlboro Books, 1970.

Kirbus, Frederico. *Enigmas, Miserios y Secretos de America.* Rio de Janeiro, Argentina: Rio de Janeiro Press, 1978.

Moseley, Michael E. *The Incas and their Ancestors.* London: Thames and Hudson, 1994.

Wilkins, Harold T. *Mysteries of Ancient South America.* Kempton, Ill.: Adventures Unlimited Press, 2000. Reprint of the 1947 original.

## The Bell and Hammer: Two "Impossible" Finds

Corliss, William R. Archaeological Anomalies: Small Artifacts. Md.: The Sourcebook Project, 2003.

Steiger, Brad. *Atlantis Rising.* New York: Dell Publishing, 1971.

Thompson, Dr. Gunnar. *American Discovery, the Real Story.* Seattle, Wash.: Argonauts Misty Isles Press, 1994.

## Did Ancient Americans Know About the Bermuda Triangle?

Alexander, William. *North American Mythology.* New York: Harcourt Brace, 1935.

Berlitz, Charles. *Mysteries of the Bermuda Triangle.* New York: Harcourt Brace, 1979.

Marriot, Alice and Carol K. Rachlin. *American Indian Mythology.* New York: New American Library, 1968.

Munck, Carl. *The Code-2000.* Seattle, Wash.: L.L. Productions, 2000.

## The Aztec "Vessel of Time"

Burland, C.A. and Werner Forman. *Feathered Serpent and Smoking Mirror, the Gods and Cultures of Ancient Mexico.* New York: G.P. Putnam's Sons, 1975.

————.*The Gods of Mexico.* New York: G.P. Putnam's Sons, 1967.

Carrasco, David and Eduardo Matos. *Moctezuma's Mexico. Visions of the Aztec World.* Boulder, Colo.: University Press of Colorado, 1992.

Jimenez, Dr. Randall C. and Richard B. Graeber. *The Aztec Calendar Hand book.* Saratoga, Calif.: Historical Science Publishing, 1993.

Shearer, Tony. *Beneath the Moon and Under the Sun. A Poetic Re-appraisal of the Sacred Calendar and the Prophesies of Ancient Mexico.* Santa Fe, New Mexico: Sun Books, 1975.

Tompkins, Peter. *Mysteries of the Mexican Pyramids.* New York: Harper & Row, 1976.


## Germany's Bronze Age Disc: A Transatlantic Device?

Bailey, J. *Sailing to Paradise.* New York: Simon & Schuster, 1994.

Bernal, I. *The Olmec World.* Berkley, Calif.: University of California Press, 1969.

Casson, L. *Ships and Seafaring in Ancient Times.* London: British Museum Press, 1993.

Fell, B. *America B.C.* New York: Pocket Books, Simon & Schuster, 1994.

Ferryn, P. "Five Thousand Years Before Our Era: The Red Men of the North Atlantic," *NEARA Journal,* Vol. XXXI, No. 2, 1997.

Heyerdahl, T. *The Ra Expeditions.* London: George Allen & Unwin, 1971.

Jairazbhoy, R.A. *Ancient Egyptians and Chinese in America.* Princeton, N.J.: Rowman & Littlefield, 1974.

Jonge, R.M. and G.F. Uzereef. *De Stenen Spreken.* Utrecht/Antwerpen: Kosmas Z&K, 1996.

———— and J.S. Wakefield. *How the Sun-God Reached America, A Guide to Megalithic Sites.* Scottsdale, Ariz.: MCS Inc., 2002.

Joseph, Frank. *The Destruction of Atlantis, Compelling Evidence of the Sudden Fall of the Legendary Civilization.* Rochester, Vt.: Bear & Co., 2002.

Lambert, J.D. *America's Stonehenge, An Interpretive Guide.* Kingston, N.H.: Sunrise Publications, 1996.

Owen, Weldon. *Old World Civilizations, the Rise of Cities and States*. Sydney, Australia: McMahons Point, 1995.

——————. *People of the Stone Age: Hunter-Gatherers and Early Farmers*. Sydney, Australia: McMahons Point, 1995.

Stuart, G.E. "New Light on the Olmec." *National Geographic*, Nov. 1997

Thompson, G. *American Discovery*. Seattle, Wash.: Argonauts Misty Isles Press, 1994.

Wachsmann, S. *Seagoing Ships and Seamanship in the Bronze Age*. New York: Dover Pub, 1973.

## Chapter 3: Lost Races
### Was Atlantis in Cuba?

Collins, Andrew. *Gateway to Atlantis*. London: Headline Publishers, 2000.

Heimer, Paul. *Caribbean Mythology*. London: Thackery &Sons, Ltd., 1961.

*Plato's Dialogues*. Krajewski, W. (trans.) New York, NY:Hanshoffer Publishers, 1942.

### America's Oldest Cemetery: The Copper Miners' Graveyard

Corliss, William R. *Ancient Man: A Handbook of Puzzling Artifacts*. Md.: The Sourcebook Project, 1980.

McCarthy, Silvia. *Ancient Copper Miners of the Upper Midwest*. Detroit: University of Michigan Press, 1952.

Olsen, Brad. *Sacred Places, North America*. San Francisco, Calif.: Consortium of Collective Consciousness, 2003.

Scherz, James P. "Ancient Trade Routes in America's Copper Country." *Ancient American*, 1755:35 (October 2000): 32.

### The Caucasian Mummy People of Alaska

Bandi, Hans Georg. *Eskimo Prehistory*. Fairbanks, Alaska: University of Alaska Press, 1969.

Clark, Ella E. *Indian Legends of the Pacific Northwest*. Berkeley, Calif.: University of California Press, 1953.

LaGuna, Dr. Fredericka de. *Archaeology of the Cook Inlet*. Little Rock, Arkansas: Harbor Press, 1969.

Noorbergen, Rene. *Secrets of Lost Races*. New York: Barnes and Noble Publishers, 1977.


### Who Were the "Western Whites"?

Goodman, Dr. Jeffrey. *American Genesis*. New York: Doubleday, 1979.

Mallan, Chicki. *Catalina Island Handbook, A Guide to California's Channel Islands*. San Francisco, Calif.: Moon Publications, Inc., 1992.

McCall, Lynne and Rosalind Perry. *California's Chumash Indians*. San Francisco, Calif.: EZ Nature Books, 1990.

Spence, Lewis. *The Problem of Lemuria*. New York: Mayflower Press, 1933, page 22.


### Giant Bears Terrorized Ancient America

Richards, R., W. Turnbull, and E.J. Neiburger. "Giant short-faced bear (Arctodus simus yukonensis) remains from Fulton County, northern Indiana," *Fieldiana*, series #30, 1995.

Tompkins, C. *The Lewis and Clark Trail*. New York: Harper & Rowe, 1965.


### The Vanished Builders of Bronze Age Michigan

Davies, Norman. *Europe: A History*. New York: Oxford University Press, 1996, 78.

DuTemple, Octave J. "Prehistory's Greatest Mystery: Copper Mines of Ancient Michigan." *Ancient American* (October 2000).

Fitting, James E. *The Archaeology of Michigan: A Guide to the Prehistory of the Great Lakes*. 2d ed., Bloomfield Hills, Mich.: Cranbrook Institute of Science, 1975.

Hinsdale, W. B. *Primitive Man in Michigan*. Ann Arbor, Mich.: University Museum, University of Michigan, 1925.

Hubbard, Bela. *Memorials of a Half-Century in Michigan and the Great Lakes Region*. New York: G.P.

Joseph, Frank. *The Lost Pyramids of Rock Lake: Wisconsin's Sunken Civilization*. Lakeville, Minn.: Galde Press, 1992.

Martin, John Bartlow. *Call It North America*. New York: Alfred A. Knopf, 1944.

Martin, Susan P. *Wonderful Power: The Sign of Ancient Copper Working in the Lake Superior Basin*. Detroit: Wayne State University Press, 1999.

Phelps, Louise. *Early Narratives of the Northwest*. New York: Charles Scribner's Sons, 1917.

Quimby, George Irving. *Indian Life in the Upper Great Lakes, 1000 B.C. to A.D. 1800*. Chicago: The University of Chicago Press, 1960, 50-51.

Rydholm, Fred. "Historical and Geological Record of the Copper Country," *Ancient American* (October, 2000).

Scherz, James P. "The Stone Face at Mummy Mountain," *Ancient American* (April 2000).

Scherz, James. "Mummy Mountain," *Ancient American*, 5:35 (October 2000).

Short, John T. *The North Americans*. New York: Harper and Brothers, 1880, 515.

Shute, Nancy. "Where We Come From: Recent Advances in Genetics Are Starting to Illuminate the Wanderings of Early Humans," *U.S. News and World Report*, 29 January 2001.

Sodders, Betty. *Michigan Prehistory Mysteries*. Au Train, Mich.: Avery Color Studios, 1991.

Stengal, Marc K. "The Diffusionists Have Landed," *The Atlantic Monthly*, January 2000.

Trento, Salvatore and Michael Salvatore. *The Search for Lost America: The Mystery of the Stone Ruins*. Chicago: Contemporary Books, 1978, page 176

# Chapter 4: Pre-Columbian Visitors From the Pacific
## Searching for a Maya Pyramid in Java

Bellwood, Peter. *Man's Conquest of the Pacific*. London: William Collins, 1978.

Childress, David Hatcher. *Lost Cities of North and Central America*. Kempton, Ill.: Adventures Unlimited Press, 1992.

Kearsley, Graeme R. *Mayan Genesis, South Asian Myths, Migrations and Iconography in Mesoamerica*. London: Yelsraek Publishing, 2001.

## Ancient Chinese Gold in California

Childress, David Hatcher. *Lost Cities of China, Central Asia and India.* Kempton, Ill.: Adventures Unlimited Press, 1985.

Christie, Anthony. *Chinese Mythology.* New York: Peter Bedrick Books, 1977.

MacKenzie, Donald A. *Myths of China and Japan.* New York: Gramercy Books, 1994.


## Washington State's Mystery Beast

Davis, Frederick H. *Myths and Legends of Japan.* Singapore: Graham Brash Publishing Company, 1989.

Jett, Stephen C. "The Jomon of Neolithic Japan: Early Ocean-Goers," *Pre-Columbiana,* volume 1, numbers 2 and 3, (June/December, 1999).


## Seeds of Paradise

Ashraf, Jaweed. "Maize In India: Introduction or Indigenous?," *Annals, NAGI,* Vol. XIV, No. 2. (December, 1994).

Babcock, William H. *Legendary Islands of The Atlantic, A Study in Medieval Geography; Research Series No. 8.* New York: The American Geographical Society, 1922.

Burtt-Davey, Joseph. *Maize.* New York: Longmans, Green & Co., 1914.

Hobhouse, Henry. *Seeds of Change: Five Plants that Transformed the World.* London: Sedgwick & Jacks, 1985.

Johannessen, Carl L. and Anne Z. Parker. "Maize Ears Sculptured in 12th and 13th Century A.S. India as Indicators of Pre-Columbian Diffusion," *Economic Botany,* Vol. 42 (2), 1989, pp. 164-180.

Markham, Clements R. Ed., *The Natural & Moral History of The Indies.* London: Hakluyt Society, 1880.

Riley, Carrol. et al., *Man Across The Sea,* Austin: University of Texas Press, 1971.

Thompson, Dr. Gunnar. *Nu Sun:Asian-American Voyages, 500 B.C.* Seattle, Wash.: Argonauts,1989.

————. *American Discovery, The Real Story.* Seattle, Wash.: Argonauts,1994.

————. *The Friar's Map of Ancient America.* Seattle, Wash.: Argonauts,1996.

## Chapter 5: The Vikings Have Landed

### The Newport Tower: Colonial Mill or Viking Lighthouse?

Chapman, Paul. *The Norse Discovery of America*. Ga.: One Candle Press, 1981.

Grandvick, Eleanor. *Vikings in the West*. Chicago: Archaeological Institute of America, 1982.

Holand, Hjalmer R. *America: 1355 to 1364*. New York: Duell, Sean, & Pierce, Inc., 1946.

### The Viking Cat that Discovered America

Collin, Sally. "Maine Coon Cats: Their Viking Blood is not to be Denied." *The Cat Fancier Digest*, vol. 5, nr. 3,. (October/November, 2001).

Hastings, Sammy. "Why prefer being a Maine Coon." *Cat Lovers Magazine*, vol. 12, nr. 7. (February, 2002).

Heyerdahl, Dr. Thor. *Early Man and the Ocean*. New York: Doubleday, 1978.

Thompson, Dr. Gunnar. *American Discovery, the Real Story*. Seattle, Wash: Argonauts Misty Isles Press, 1994.

Woodhouser, Henry. *Feline Evolution*. Fla.: Animal Ark Press, 2002.

### The Kensington and Heavener Runestone Hoaxes

Anderson, Harry. *Fraudulent Science*. Chicago: Dempsey Press, 1983.

Goldstein, Irving. *Conspiracies in Archaeology*. New York: Woodward Jones, Inc., 1977.

Heiland, Maxwell. "I Faked the Kensington Runestone!" *The Skeptical Observer*, vol. 1, nr. 2, (winter quarter, 1993).

Rudinsky, Irving. "The Heavener Runestone and Other Archaeological Tricks," *Oklahoma History Magazine*, vol. 9, nr.1. (March, 1990).

### Minnesota's Runestone Is Authenticated

Enterline, James R. *Viking America*. New York: Doubleday, 1972.

Golding, Morton J. *The Mystery of the Vikings in America*. Penn: Lippincott, 1973.

Ingstad, Helge. *Westward to Vinland*. New York: St. Martin's Press, 1969.

Leutner, Margaret. *The Kensington Runestone*. N. Dak.: Kanzler Press, 2000.

Wahlgren, Erik. *The Vikings and America*. London: Thames & Hudson, 1986.

### Oklahoma's Giant Runestone

Anderson, Col. W. R. *Viking Explorers and the Columbus Fraud*. Chicago: Wells Street Publishers, 1961.

Farley, Gloria. *In Plain Sight*. Georgia: ISACPress, 1994.

Stromsted, Astri A. *Ancient Pioneers: Early Connections Between Scandinavia And The New World*. New York: Erik Friis, 1974.

Van Osten, Harald. *Evidence of Vikings in North America*. Iowa: McCready Press, 1979.

## Chapter 6: East Meets West in Ancient America
### They Came for the Cocaine

Balabanova, S. and F. Parsche. "First report of drugs in Egyptian Mummies." *Naturwissenschaften* 79:358, 1992.

Boucher, D.H. "Cocaine and the coca plant." *Bioscience* 41:72-76, 1991.

Bryan, C.P. *The Papyrus*. New York: Appleton, 1981.

Kennedy, J. *Coca exotica: the illustrated story of cocaine*. Teaneck, N.J.: Fairleigh Dickenson University Press, 1985.

Lewis, W.H. *Medical Botany*. New York: Wiley & Sons, 1977.

### Point: No Egyptians in Ancient America

Attenborough, David. *The First Eden*. New York: Little Brown & Co., 1987.

Casson, Lionel. *Ships and Seafaring in Ancient Times*. Austin, Tex.: University of Texas, 1994.

Davis, Nigel. *The Aztec Empire*. Norman, Okla.: University of Oklahoma Press, 1987.

Drews, Robert. *The End of the Bronze Age*. Princeton, N.J.: Princeton University Press, 1993.

Hayes, William C. *The Scepter of Egypt*. London: Harry N. Abrahms, 1957.

Heyerdahl, Dr. Thor. *The Ra Expeditions*. New York: Doubleday, 1971.

Keating, Richard. *Peruvian Prehistory*. Cambridge, Mass.: Cambridge University Press, 1988.

Lurio, Eric. *A Fractured History of the Discovery of America*. New York: Doubleday, 1990.

Mosley, Michael. *The Incas & Their Ancestors*. London: Thames & Hudson, 1992.

Rice, Michael. *Egypt's Making*. New York: Routlege Press, 1991.

Shele, Linda and David Freidel. *A Forest of Kings, the Untold Story of the Ancient Maya*. New York: William, Morrow & Co., 1990.

Thompson, Dr. Gunnar. *American Discovery, The Real Story*. Seattle, Wash: Argonauts,1994.

## Counterpoint: Egypt's Role in Ancient America

Bierhorst, John. *The Mythology of South America*. New York: William Morrow and Company, Inc., 1982.

Boylan, Patrick. *Thoth, the Hermes of Egypt*. Chicago: Ares, 1979.

Brooks, John. *The South American Handbook*. Bath: Trade &Travel Publications, 1975.

Childress, David Hatcher. *Lost Cities and Ancient Mysteries of South America*. Kempton, Ill.: Adventures Unlimited Press, 1986.

Motet, Pierre. *Lives of the Pharaohs*. New York: World Publishing Company, 1968.

Petrie, W.M. Flinders. *A History of Egypt Vols. I, II and III*. New York: Charles Scribner's Sons, 1905.

Thomson, Dr. Gunnar. *American Discovery, The Real Story*. Seattle, Wash.: Argonauts,1994.

Zorate, Augustin de. *The Discovery and Conquest of Peru*. Lima Treasury Publishers, 1968.

## Chicago's Great Stone Face

Hollstein, Alfred. "Carthaginian Seamanship," *Ancient World Magazine*, vol. 1, nr.1, June, 1980.

MacKenzie, John. *The Waubansee Stone*. Chicago: Regnery Press, 1960.

Mercer, Robert. *The Phoenicians*. New York: Daily Books, 1978.

Nuttall, Zelia. *The Fundamental Principles of Old and New World Civilizations*. Boston, Mass.: Peabody, Harvard University, 1900.

# Chapter 7: Out of Africa

## Ancient Americans: Red or Black?

*The Art of Terra-Cotta Pottery in Pre-Columbian Central and South America*. New York: Crown Publishers, 1965.

Ben-Jochannan, Yosef. *Black Man of the Nile*. Md.: Black Classic Press, 1970.

De Angleis, Pedro Martir. *Decadas del Neuevo Mundo*. Buenas Aires, Argentina: Editorial Bajel, 1944.

Leslie, Jill and Peter T. Furst. *Pre-Columbian Art of Mexico*. New York: Abbeville Press, 1980.

Morris, Ann A. *The Temple of the Warriors at Chichen Itza*. Carnegie Institution of Washington, 1931.

Thompson, J. Erik. *Maya History and Religion*. Norman, Okla.: University of Oklahoma Press, 1970.

Van Sertima, Ivan. *They Came Before Columbus*. New York: Random House, 1976.

Von Wuethenau, Alexander. *Unexpected Faces in Ancient America*. New York: Crown Publishers, 1975.

————.*Unexpected Faces in Ancient America*. New York: Crown Publishers, 1975.

## The Great Stone Heads Speak

Bernal, Ignacio. *The Olmec World*. Berkeley, Calif.: University of California Press, 1969.

Bradley, Michael. *The Black Discovery of America*. Toronto: Personal Library, 1981.

Coe, Michael and Richard Diehl. *The Land of the Olmec*. Austin, Tex.: University of Texas Press, 1980.

Van Sertima, Ivan. *They Came Before Columbus*. New York: Random House, 1976.

# Chapter 8: Pre-Columbian Europeans on Our Shores

## Was King Arthur Murdered in America?

Deacon, Richard. *Madock and the Discovery of America*. New York: Brazilier, 1966.

## The Lost Ancient Irish Inscription of Kentucky

Fell, Dr. Barry. *The Epigraphic Society's Occasional Papers*: ESOP , Vol. 16, 1987.

## An 8th-Century Irishman Visited West Virginia

Ashe, Geoffrey. *Land to the West: St. Brendan's Voyage to America*. New York: Viking Press, 1962.

Boorstein, Daniel. *The Discoverers*. New York: Random House, 1983.

Fingerhut, Eugene. *Who First Discovered America?* San Francisco, Calif.: Regina Books, 1984.

McGlone, William R. and Phillip M. Leonard. *Ancient Celtic America*. San Francisco, Calif.: Panorama West Books, 1986.

## Knights Templars in the New World

Davis, Nigel. *Voyagers To The New World*. Santa Fe, N.Mex.: University of New Mexico Press, 1979.

Pohl, Frederick. *Prince Henry Sinclair*. New York: Clarkson N. Potter, 1974.

Withey, Lynne. *Voyages of Discovery*. New York: William & Morrow, 1987.

## Mediterranean Lamps: Anomalies of the Midwest

Bailey, James. *The God-Kings and the Titans*. New York: St. Martin's Press, 1973.

Bancroft, Hubert H. *American Antiquities*. New York: Bancroft & Co., 1883.

Emery, W.B. *Archaic Egypt*. London: Penguin Books, 1971.

Fell, Barry. *America B.C.* New York: Simon & Schuster, 1989.

## Wisconsin's Roman Coins

Chattopadhyay, A. *The Age of the Kushanas, Numismatic Study*. Calcutta, India: Punthi Pustak, 1967.

Gardner, Percy Litt. D., *Coins of Greek and Scythic Kings of Bactria and India*. Chicago: Argonaut Inc., 1966.

Grant, Michael. *The Roman Emperors*. New York: Barnes &Noble, 1997.

Millar, Fergus. *The Roman Empire and its Neighbours*. 2nd Edition, London: Gerald Duckworth and Co., 1981.

Mukherjee, B.N. *The Rise and Fall of the Kushana Empire*. Calcutta, India: Firma KLM, 1988.

Postel, Rainer. *Katalog Der Antiken Munzen in Der Hamburger Kunsthalle*, Hamburg, Germany: Hans Christiens Verlag, 1976.

Sarma, I.K. *Coinage of the Satavahana Empire*. Delhi, India:Agam Kala Prakashan, 1980.

*The Student's Gibbon, A History of the Decline and Fall of the Roman Empire*, Part 1, London: A. H. G. Greenbridge, 1899.

## Roman Relics Found in Arizona

*American Discovery, The Real Story*, by Gunnar Thompson, Ph.D., WA: Argonauts Misty Isles Press, 1994.

*The Arizona Daily Star*, February 17, 1928, "Leaden Spear-Shaft Found in Location of Famed Artifacts." *The Arizona Daily Star*, December 13, 1925, "Roman Relics Found Here Baffle Science."

*California Jewish Review*, January 18, 1925, "Arizona Discoveries of Ancient Hebrew Culture Branded As Fake," by Dr. E.C. Getsinger, p.1.Childress, David Hatcher. *Lost Cities of North & Central America*. Chicago, Ill.: Adventures Unlimited Press, 1992.

Covey, Dr. Cyclone. *Calalus*. New York: Vantage Press, 1975.

*Daily Northwestern*, IL: Evanston, January 6, 1926, "Astronomer Will Speak on Arizona Discoveries Tomorrow."

E.B. "Ted" Sayles with Joan Asby Henley, *Fantasies of Gold, Legends of Treasures and How They Grew*, Chapter X, "Lead Crosses", Tucson: The University of Arizona Press, 1968.

*New York Times*, January 19, 1925, "Say Mexican Made Arizona Artifacts."

*Tucson Citizen*, February 1, 1925, "Inscribed Plate Found Near City May Tell Untold Story of an Early Race Here."

*Tucson Citizen*, December 14, 1925, "Leaden Relics Genuine, States U. of A. Archaeologist, Who Replies to Doubting Thomases."

*Tucson Citizen*, December 15, 1925, "Relic Texts Are Cribbed From Dictionary Glossary Charged."

## Maine Minoans

Daniel, Glyn, editor, *The Illustrated Encyclopedia of Archaeology*, New York:Thomas Y. Crowell Co., 1977.

Evans, Arthur J. *The Palace of Minos*. Vols. 1, 2 & 3. London: Macmillan, 1935.

Imel, Martha Ann and Dorothy Myers. *Goddesses in World Mythology*. Oxford University Press, 1993.

Thompson, Dr. Gunnar. *American Discovery, The Real Story*. Seattle, Wash.: Argonauts,1994.

Wyse, Elizabeth. editor, *Past Worlds, The Times Atlas of Archaeology*. New York: Crescent Books, 1998.

# Index

# About the Author

**Frank Joseph** is the editor-in-chief of *Ancient American*, a popular science magazine describing overseas' voyagers to our Continent hundreds and even thousands of years before Columbus. Since its first issue in 1993, he has traveled from Canada to Peru in search of evidence for the arrival of prehistoric mariners on our shores. He has also published a dozen books about ancient civilizations, including *The Atlantis Encyclopedia*, released by The Career Press. Frank Joseph lives with his wife, Laura, and 4-year-old son, Sammy, in Colfax, Wisconsin.

20234501R00163

Made in the USA
San Bernardino, CA
01 April 2015